T0306341

WHAT PEOPLE ARE SAYING ABOUT

FAMILY PLANTING

This is a story that has been told before, of course, because moving to the country is a great fantasy and dream for many. But rarely has it been told with this kind of honesty and psychological insight. There's a great deal to learn here, no matter where you live.
Bill McKibben, author of *Eaarth: Making a Life on a Tough New Planet*

With endless reports of environmental and financial disaster, Family Planting *offers a rare ray of hope. Kimerer LaMothe artfully weaves together philosophical vision and social criticism to create a work that opens new ways of seeing and being. This book is a pleasure to read and will leave you with questions we have been avoiding far too long.*
Mark C. Taylor, Columbia University, author of *Field Notes* and *After God*

Sensuous and intriguing. LaMothe's narrative of her family's experiences alone is worth the read. It is so deliciously written, you could make a meal out of it.
Shannon Hayes, author of *Radical Homemakers* and *Long Way on a Little.*

Family Planting *is a book about LOVE, and the dynamic, yearning, moving, painful, sublime truth of being human. LaMothe uses her own life in connection with the roots and branches of her own family tree as a laboratory for conscious living. Beautifully written and True.*
Susan L. Franklin, Psy.D.

LaMothe has done it again and delivered yet another profound and exuberantly told book that interweaves her experiences of living on a farm with insights into relationships with parents, partners, and progeny. She offers a rich, deep, and accessible philosophy that is a joy to read and an inspiration to live by.
Colby Devitt, Author

Family Planting

A Farm-Fed Philosophy of Human Relations

Family Planting

A Farm-Fed Philosophy of Human Relations

Kimerer L. LaMothe

BOOKS

Winchester, UK
Washington, USA

First published by O-Books, 2011
O-Books is an imprint of John Hunt Publishing Ltd., Laurel House, Station Approach, Alresford, Hants, SO24 9JH, UK
office1@o-books.net
www.o-books.com

For distributor details and how to order please visit the 'Ordering' section on our website.

ISBN: 978 1 84694 410 9

A CIP catalogue record for this book is available from the British Library.

Design: Stuart Davies

Printed in the UK by CPI Antony Rowe
Printed in the USA by Offset Paperback Mfrs, Inc

CONTENTS

Also by Kimerer L. LaMothe

What a Body Knows: Finding Wisdom in Desire

Nietzsche's Dancers: Isadora Duncan, Martha Graham, and the Revaluation of Christian Values

Between Dancing and Writing: The Practice of Religious Studies

For more information about Kimerer and her work, please visit:

www.vitalartsmedia.com

Acknowledgments

A book has a life of its own. It beats and breathes and pushes its way into this world through the person it chooses, setting in motion a host of repercussions that vibrate through that person's relationships. So it has been with this book. This book wanted to be born, and as it came, it changed everything. The process of writing down what was happening after our move to the farm with my parents, partner, and progeny deepened my experiences of it all. Reflecting upon our relationships focused my attention to the challenges, refined my sense of what was possible, and helped me appreciate the larger significance of what we were and are creating.

Much of what appears in this book is pieced together from extensive journals I kept during our first three years of living here. The narrative frame of the book spans the eight-month period (July 2008 – February 2009) in which I did most of the stitching.

In this work, I have enjoyed a wide web of support from people who appear in its pages and others who don't. Colby Devitt, reading an early draft, responded with buoying encouragement and pointed questions. Susan Franklin, Melissa Schulz, Tony Stiker, Kathleen Skerrett, Gay Lynch, Sharron Rose, and Courtney Bickel Lambert provided helpful words along the way. I am ever grateful to Mary Pipher, Ellen Langer, Diana Eck, Mark C. Taylor, and Bill McKibben for the time they each spent with the manuscript. The footnotes in the text chart the relationship of this work to authors in philosophy, psychology, and related disciplines whose work has influenced me. The tireless O-Books team smoothly guided the publication process from start to finish. That the book exists is a testament to all of these individuals, though the fault of none.

Above all, I am steeped in boundless gratitude for the

parents, partner, and progeny who inspired me to write this book. Every day I discover more of what my parents, Cynthia and Jack LaMothe, have already given me. My debt to them is incalculable. I am overwhelmed by the beauty and passion of my children, Jordan, Jessica, Kyra, Kai, and Leif. Every day their lives impel me to live my own with more understanding and more compassion. I am in awe at the mystery that my partner, the consummate musician, ever-present muse, and expert editor, Geoffrey Gee, chooses to spend his life with me. Every day I learn more from our practice of total presence about what love can be. *Thank you.*

Prologue

A Farm Family

We need the tonic of wildness... We need to witness our own limits transgressed.
—Henry David Thoreau[1]

July 1, 2005. We are alone in the wilderness, or so it seems. It is 5 p.m. on a Friday afternoon. My partner, Geoff, myself, and our three children have been moving since this morning, in hot pursuit of a long-held dream of rural living that is now coming true: we are buying a farm in upstate New York.

We left Boston at 6 a.m. with our rental truck and trailer, drove for four hours, signed closing papers, returned to our newly purchased 1840s homestead, and began unpacking our belongings. We are not finished. The sun is still beating hot.

We bought the house "as is," and it is as I remember it from my sole visit forty-five days earlier. Tangled weeds cling to peeling house and barns. The driveway buckles unevenly, crumbling around the edges. The barnyard is a jungle. Inside offers little relief. Not one room is habitable. Bugs rule. Mouse and rat poop is piled in every corner. A dead bird graces the hallway floor. The windows are painted tightly shut. There are no screens. Doors and cabinets shed layers of coloring. Plaster dangles from a bedroom ceiling. There is no telephone service, no heat, and no running water, no toilets, baths, sinks, or showers, except for the cold tap in the kitchen sink. I have spent the afternoon with that faucet gushing, finding hope for humanity in its cooling, cleansing flow. Minutes ago, the river slowed to a stream then a trickle. Now there is nothing. Not one drop.

So much for being close to nature.

I have rarely felt so alone. How can we stay here? There is no one to call. No neighbor across the road. No family close by. Sure, Geoff and I have each other, but I am nine months pregnant and our children are nine, seven, and three. Each body extends the surfaces of my vulnerability. Geoff is working mightily to unload the basics we brought with us from the truck. The rest is in storage until we are ready for it. We aren't. The truck is due back soon. When?

I decide to leave Geoff and the kids and drive into the local village. I will find out when the telephone company plans to connect our service and when the rental place closes. Yards from our house, as I begin to breathe through the fear and uncertainty, an idea ripples into view: *Harold*. Harold is the farmer whose family owned our farm for generations before selling four years ago to the absentee investor landlord who sold it to us. Harold lives a half mile down the road.

I stop in front of his house, get out of the car, and yell "Hello" at the older man walking towards me across the yard.

"I'm no longer the justice," he calls back. I must look distressed.

"I don't need the justice, I need you!" I reply.

Minutes later, I am sitting comfortably in his living room, ear pressed to the receiver, staring down at a polished golden oak floor, grateful to be in this clean, neat place. Harold drives his truck down to our place to help Geoff with the well. The telephone company isn't coming until Tuesday—in four days. The rental place, in the closest city, forty minutes away, is open until 8 p.m. Less than three hours to go.

I drive back to the house. By now Harold has led Geoff up the hill, about 100 yards from the house, where they are poking their heads into a cock-eyed wooden shed: our well house. Harold confirms that the pump isn't working. He shows us how he used to hit it with a screwdriver. No juice. We thank him and continue unloading. The kids, ablaze with some unknown fire, play in the yard.

The last box is in Geoff's arms. The time is 7:10. Geoff closes the truck and climbs into our Honda Civic to drive it off the attached trailer. The car won't start. The battery is dead. Small drops start to drizzle. As the sky falls, we jump-start the car under an umbrella. About to leave, we realize that there are no locks on the farmhouse doors, and no way to secure our belongings. There are no keys to the house. We grab my laptop and leave the rest, hoping.

Motoring our caravan along farm field roads, barely visible in the drenching downpour, we get lost. Finally in town, we get stuck in a Burger King parking lot while asking for directions. We arrive at the rental shop half an hour after it closed. Roused by our desperate knocking, the attendant responds. He kindly takes the truck and trailer. We are suddenly light, exceedingly grateful, and on our way again, looking for a place to stay, with a pool. We find one alongside a state thruway.

We will spend our first night in rural paradise at a highway hotel.

After a 9:30 dinner in the hotel restaurant, the kids beg to go swimming. How can we refuse? Rarely had their cooperation been as important as it was that day. They had enabled us to do what we needed to do to make a home for them. They want water too.

We leave the pool at 11 p.m. and drop into bed, damp, reeking of chlorine, and wondering. What will tomorrow hold?

Close to Nature

Back in college, when I was wrestling to make sense of my vague but persistent thirst for closer proximity to the natural world, Henry David Thoreau helped me name it. I read *Walden* as a freshman, not missing the irony. I had grown up a mile through the woods from the idyllic body of water where Thoreau lived for two years, simply and deliberately, tuned to the rhythms of the natural world. While living there, however, I had rarely visited the pond. It was for tourists and city swimmers; our family went to the country club. Even so, something from the place must have seeped through my pores. Far from home, I discovered the inspiration I had left behind.

A few months ago I picked up *Walden* again. After so many years I was astonished to realize how much our mission in leaving Boston for the woods and fields of upstate New York aligned with Thoreau's own "experiment in living."[2] While I had forgotten his words, I recognized their uncanny echo in my own questions and concerns.

Thoreau was seeking a closer relationship to the natural world, not only as a refuge from the noise of social life, but also as a fund of patterns and symbols that would help him to understand and live his life fully awake, with love. We were too. He was dogged by a nagging suspicion that urban ladder life fosters ways of thinking and feeling and acting that are not healthy. We were too. He was seeking a set of experiences that would help him establish a critical perspective on contemporary culture. We

were too. He was motivated by a desire to free his thinking from ruts of convention and common sense. I was too. I moved here to dance and write in a place where I could not ignore the spinning of the earth, the cycling of the moon, the shedding of time. Like Thoreau, I wanted to align my art more deliberately with the forces that sustain the best in human being.[3] I am firmly convinced that without such connection there is no consciousness, no accountability.

Nevertheless, in pursuit of his goals, Thoreau went to the woods by himself. He built his own cabin, furnished it sparsely with furniture he made, and fueled it with wood he cut. He carried his water from the pond. He walked, thought, wrote, and planted beans. I, on the other hand, moved with my family of five, becoming six and then seven, to an abandoned farmhouse nestled next to a road, in dire need of new systems, windows, and walls. We hired a contractor for the larger repairs and set up our computers in order to stay connected with city-sources of income. Could there be any similarity?

I saw it. Thoreau, alone in nature, had discovered what I too was discovering with family on the farm: how inextricably webbed we humans are in a matrix of relationships that extends in space and time far beyond our singular selves. He wrote to share his experience of the "infinite extent of our relations."[4] I do too.

Even though Thoreau went to the pond to live there by himself, in his writing, he rarely is. The "I" he retains—confined, as he claims it is, by the "narrowness" of his "experience"—is a hub of interactions with writers and orators, poets and saints, fishers and farmers, past and present, as well as with birds and animals, plants and pond, all of whom animate his thoughts, enabling him to perceive and conceive as he does.[5] Thoreau's writing *enacts* this radical interdependence of all living and nonliving things, including his own self. He writes as a poet and philosopher who is self-consciously participating in a "poem of

creation" that is "uninterrupted."[6] He calls his readers to find in nature the *sensory experiences* that will help them understand themselves as relational creatures, fellow participants in this poem of creation. I do too.

Thoreau, however, ended his experiment. Having discovered and affirmed his relational self, he returned to Concord where he dwelled in closer proximity with other humans, compiled his field notes, and wrote his book. What he did not write was a sequel that would share with his readers how he lived as an infinitely webbed creature in actual relationships with the concrete humans without whom he could not and would not be who he was.

Our experiment continues. I want to know: what difference does it make to our *human* relationships to think and feel and act as a participant in an ongoing "poem of creation"?

Reinventing Family

Our farm is a ninety-six acre swath of grass and trees, with a sparkling stream, two placid beaver-enhanced ponds, and a slew of tumble-down buildings. It is located in a county that remains an agricultural holdout amidst spreading suburban sprawl. Rolling hills surf blue sky. Shorn patches of pasture turn with the seasons, stark white to glowing green to stubby blond and crackling grey. Cows and horses, goats and alpacas lift their heads from grazing to contemplate passers-by. Tractors and milk trucks rumble by several times a day. People work hard.

From our first day, despite the drought, we were thrilled to be careening toward our dream of nature-enabled art. Yet days after landing, as we fixed the well pump, restored our water supply, connected with the telephone grid, and began resurrecting the homestead, our sense of mission began to unsettle and soften. *Why are we here?*

This piece of earth, whose beauty had beckoned us so undeniably, was now calling us to participate in the activities that

had cultivated its fields, cleared its vistas, and opened its panoramic views. We found ourselves *wanting to farm*. We were not interested in raising crops for cash or equipping ourselves with tractors, pesticides, and chemical fertilizers to boost field production. We were, like Thoreau, rather critical of industrial farming practices driven by the desire to increase short-term yields.[7] Our desire was to nurture the ongoing health and fertility of our soil and so of our selves. We wanted to bring our farmyard back to life as it had been in its haying days, when our barns were standing straight and tall, red and white, home to creatures great and small; when the fields were fenced, grazed, and manure-enriched; when paths led from place to place, as tracks of effort and appreciation.

The problem was that we weren't farmers. Geoff and I moved to make art: *culture* not *agri*culture. What would we do? Applying our city skills, we started to read books about the history of farming in the United States, the rise and fall of the family farm, the details of gardening and animal care, and the experiences of modern homesteaders who often traced their lineage to Thoreau. We read homesteading classics by Scott and Helen Nearing and Wendell Berry, as well accounts of contemporary agricultural practices by Scott Chasky, Michael Pollan, and Barbara Kingsolver.[8] We talked.

Meanwhile, I walked the land, day in and out, calling to it as it called to me. I felt alternately pulled and torn, unable to get traction towards a vision that seemed to fade as rapidly as I approached. How were we going to connect with this place? How were we to connect with our work now that we were here? What was I going to write? Or dance?

Unlike Geoff and me, the children knew what they wanted. They wanted cows and crops, flowers and fences.

Winter flipped into spring. We began to help our kids unfold their visions. Pushed by them to learn *how* to farm, we started to appreciate *why* it was necessary for us, as artists, to do so.

Farming is more than a matter of growing plants and tending animals. It is more than a matter of mastering the economics, politics, or biological chemistry of food production. Farming describes the range of activities that humans undertake in order to create a mutually enabling relationship with nature—one that will provide them with the nourishment they need to survive now and forever. Whether neuroscientist, actor, or accountant, every human alive (with the exception of a few remaining hunter-gatherers) is absolutely dependent every day upon the actions of farming in order to exist at all. Farming is that basic to humanity. It is so obvious, but we forget.

Our biggest revelation, however, came on the heels of this one. We realized that the work of farming is not just about creating a mutually enabling relationship with the natural world. Farming is also about creating relationships among the people who do it and depend upon it. Farming is about growing *humans* who can and will and want to create a mutually enabling relationship with the natural world; *and* it is about growing humans who can and will and want to create mutually enabling relationships *with one another* as the condition that will enable their success.[9] Historically speaking, across many times and places, especially in the United States, farming makes *family*. The work of farming creates the tightly coordinated team of people grown on the farm, by the farm, to run the farm, generation after generation.

Answers to my questions began to take shape: in order to connect with our art in this place, Geoff and I would have to cultivate the connections with our children and one another that would sustain each one of our family in living the rural life we all wanted. We would reinvent the farm family. Our desire to live in closer connection with the natural world was providing us with the opportunity—by making it necessary—to learn *what love can be*.

What we were learning took us beyond what we had read in the homesteading and environmental literature; for the challenge

we humans face in developing an ecological consciousness involves more than learning to interact in life-enabling ways with plants, animals, rocks, and streams. We must also find ways to move in our relationships with other humans that support us in becoming people who can and do live that proximity with the natural world. The two go hand in hand. One enables the other.

If we are to connect with this planet in mutually life-enabling ways, we must learn to love one another. If we are to connect with one another in mutually life-enabling ways, we must open ourselves to the sensory experiences our movement through nature provides.

As Thoreau insists, it is not enough to *know* in intellectual terms that we are richly connected with the natural world; we must also *sense* and *practice* that connectivity in the relationships that matter most. *We are nature too.*

Impulse to Connect

As a family on the farm, the relationships that mattered most appeared in sharp relief as a threefold matrix, common to every human—parents, partners, and progeny.[10] It was what we had. It was who we were. It was in trouble. I was further from my parents than I had ever been for longer than six months. I was in closer contact with my partner than we had ever been in our fifteen years together. I was more dependent on my children for helping me take care of them than I had ever been, and in each case, past patterns of interacting were failing. At every turn I was emotionally wrenched. I felt as if I was disappointing my now-distant parents. I felt irritated by my now-proximate partner. I was constantly worried whether my children were getting what they needed to thrive. Something had to shift. If I wanted this experiment in living close to nature to work, I would have to recreate the shapes of these primary relationships. Without the support of these persons, it would be impossible for me to do the nature-tuned writing and dancing I wanted to do.

I read books in psychology, philosophy, theology, ecopsychology, and neuroscience. I danced. I walked. I worked hard on my relationships. I wrote. I came to the conviction that enlivens this book: *we humans are nothing more or less than an impulse to connect*. As bodies born helpless, we become who we are by virtue of the relationships we cultivate with those who enable us to thrive. Yet we are not individuals who attach to one another; nor are we static sites where relationships intersect. In our most fundamental bodily selves, we are the *movement of connecting*—the movement of creating patterns of sensing and responding that guide us in relating with whomever and whatever will sustain us in our bodily becoming, whether person, place, or planet. We are these patterns of sensing and responding—the kinetic images—that we are creating in every moment of our lives.[11]

Of the many implications this conviction carries, *Family Planting* elaborates one: a vision of what love can be. In this book, I share what we have discovered: *to love is to open to another as a cause of our being*. Love, in this sense, is what human beings are born to do; love is the action, the condition, and the context that enables our best becoming. At the same time, we are not born knowing how. Where an impulse to connect provides us with the motivation and direction to learn how to love, the bodily challenges of our primary relationships offer us the opportunity.

Moving to the farm, I committed myself to an experiment in living whose logic Thoreau would recognize as expanding the work he began. How do we live deliberately in our relationships with those primary persons whose living enables ours? How do we learn to *connect* with caregivers, partners, and progeny in ways that honor the earth? How do we open to affirm human, animal, plant, and pond as causes of our being? What can love be?

I am convinced that the day in, day out work of learning to love those who care for us before we are able, those we choose to

accompany us along our journey, and those who are given to us to tend is some of the most exciting, path-breaking philosophy there is to be done in pursuit of a healthier planet.[12] *It's why I'm here.*

What appears in the chapters to come is a loose chronicle of the first three years of an adventure that is ongoing, unfinished, and still producing beyond our wildest dreams. The "narrow I" that circumscribes my writing is propped open by a co-creating partner and our five sense-extending children, as well as by a raft of authors and artists who have engaged my attention.[13] Where chapter 1 introduces a framework for understanding the bodily challenges of our primary relationships and how they entwine, subsequent chapters tell our story in three overlapping waves. I work through relationships with my parents, with Geoff, and with our children, to fund an earth-friendly philosophy of human relations.

The perspective on love that emerges expresses a hands-on, intellectual, and spiritual engagement with one matrix of entwined lives. It is a philosophy that is local and living, embodied and enacted. Its content and form render it ripe for an age in which people are looking to connect with the earth, with one another, and with their own spiritual, sensory selves in ways that demonstrate care and respect. In promoting the primacy of relationship, it offers a view of human being that poses a radical challenge to enlightenment notions of persons as individual agents. In all these ways, *Family Planting* maps a shift in consciousness that is desperately needed to support us in creating mutually life-enabling patterns of interacting with the earth in us and around us. Whether we live on a farm or in a skyscraper, alone or with crowds, the work is the same.

Life on the farm is teaching our family what we humans need to know: we are not who we *think* we are. We are not rational minds or salvation-seeking souls sitting awkwardly in earthly vessels.

We are our bodily selves, ever moving and connecting with the people, places, and elements we need to thrive. We are relations before we are subjects; we are movement before we stand still. We are earth, air, fire, and water; carrot, apple, egg, and milk; infant, child, partner, and parent. We are *nothing more or less than an impulse to connect, born to live in love as the condition that enables us to become who we are.*

1

Moving Matters

> [N]o generation has learned to love from another, no generation is able to begin at any other point than at the beginning.
> —Søren Kierkegaard[1]

July 2008. It is one of those days; a gorgeous blast of life alive. Bird songs pull me out of a dream-clotted sleep. As eyelid images fade, a clear sky appears, and a squared blue ray peeks through the skylight. Then I see gold, streaming through, streaming down, lighting the round green of birch tree leaves and the tousled greens of the hillside. How could a scene be so peaceful and so full of life?

I creep downstairs, careful not to wake anyone else. This time

is mine, 6 a.m., perfect. Sneaking around the kitchen, munching on a banana, I see Precious, our Jersey heifer, out the window, up the hill, munching on grass. She lifts her long back leg and scratches behind her ear. Amazing feats cows do with those pegs. We had her bred a couple of weeks ago and I wonder. Is she a mama? Does she know? We won't for a while yet. We have to wait to see if she starts bellowing for a bull again. If she doesn't, we'll know.

Farming. As we are learning, it's all about generations, one to the next, parents, partners, and progeny. The farm survives based on its members' ability to reproduce themselves. For this reason, it places great stock in its females—the breeders. Most of the males—the beefcakes—are expendable, that is, edible. The few males kept to mature, at least in the case of bulls, are reduced to test tubes of seed. Left on their own, males are troublemakers, for they compete with humans over the means and methods of reproduction. The females are the valuable ones. They have the power to give life in the form of milk, eggs, or more young, including the meaty males.

Perhaps it is not surprising that many anthropologists credit women as the first farmers, inventors of animal husbandry and crop management. Women have direct experience of how fertility cycles. They know where the power pools. It is also not surprising that the males of our species soon stepped in to protect—and control—the fruits of female laboring. Farming makes family. But what kind of family? "Husbandry," Thoreau laments, "was once a sacred art," an act of worshipping the goddess of fertility and her human counterparts.[2] Might it be again?

Morning mocha mix in hand, I head off to my study. Steps from the door, I hear the unmistakable sound of small feet padding above me across our bedroom floor. The door to our room opens and a plaintive cry tumbles down the stairs. "I want mama!" Speaking of generations.

I walk to the bottom of the stairs and scoop up small Kai, snuggling his compact two-ness to my chest. As we walk into the kitchen, he is still wailing, "I want mama!"

"You have me." I reply gently. "I'm right here." He's still not sure, half awake and so half asleep. Hungry too. I fix him some orange juice, a bowl of cereal, and take another look at the clock. I recalibrate. OK, I'll be working by 6:30.

What are you enabling, little one? It's my mama mantra, tested over time. I know. My children, even when pulling against the current of my desire, are always enabling me somehow to come to a thought or experience or action that I need to unfold who I am. What is it now?

As Kai quietly crunches, I decide to process milk. I pull out the large stainless steel pot we keep in the refrigerator. Milk goes there after Jordan, now twelve, pulls and squeezes it from our cow Daisy's udder. Half a day later, the first skin of cream has risen. I skim it with a large spoon, lifting its thick velvet folds of gold. It hangs together, a slick sheet, and slides off my spoon into a glass jar. Tonight we will make ice cream.

Soon, pearly white liquid shines through the remaining threads of cream. I pour the milk into two pans, one for yogurt and one for cottage cheese. I will cook today too, later, after I write, before making ice cream. The rest of the milk goes into glass bottles we bought online from an Amish family business. I wash my first bucket of the day and glance up at the pasture. Daisy and Precious are both there now, swatting each other's flies in the sunshine.

I turn to Kai. He asks for more "seewe-al." Maybe then he will be happy and play, and I will get to work. Still, I don't resent his intrusion on my time. Not yet. After all, he is the one who helped me grasp what it is I want to write about this morning: the *impulse to connect* that animates our bodily selves. It was watching Kai, Geoff and my fourth child, and his sheer *will* to *connect* with the piano, the walls, the chairs, the kitchen faucet,

the dryer, his siblings, and doing so with trucks, balls, body parts, and various sharp implements that set me on a path to articulating what I was learning about human being from our life on the farm.

We humans are nothing more or less than an impulse to connect.

Washing another bucket, I think back to that moment of discovery. I was in the midst of writing my first farm book, *What a Body Knows*, eager to help readers find and trust and move with the wisdom in desire.[3] What is needed, I was arguing, is an *experience shift*: we need to cultivate a sense of our bodily selves as *movement*, and specifically, as *the movement that is making us*. We are not bodies that move; we are movement that takes shape in the patterns of sensation and response that bodies are. This idea lies at the heart of the philosophy of bodily becoming that I am living and thinking—a philosophy that privileges this self-creating movement as the source and telos of human being.

As soon as the idea of an impulse to connect took shape in my mind, however, I knew I would have to write another book. My philosophy of bodily becoming was evolving, with small Kai as its catalyst. Saying that we humans are the movement that is making us does not go far enough. Left intact is a privilege granted in western culture to an autonomous individual self, presumed to exist over and against his or her relationships. However, if the movement that is making us is *an impulse to connect*, then we are *not* individuals first. We are able to think and feel and act as individuals—as if we are individuals—only because of the relationships with other persons, places, and elements that are always already supporting us in doing so.[4]

So too, if we are the relationships we participate in creating, then we unfold our potential as individuals only by *learning to create the relationships* that will support this becoming. There is no possible separation between the two. We can't be individuals outside of relationships. We can't be in relationships without unfolding our individual capacity to create them. In short, if we

humans are bodies whose movement is making us, then we will find our freedom *in* relationships, *through* relationships, and *because* of our relationships, as we learn to *open* to the others in our lives as *enabling* our ability to think and feel and move at all. That's love.[5]

Kai is finally finished scooping and swallowing his cereal. He follows me into my study. I lie down on my stomach on the rug, pull out my notebook, and begin to write. Kai climbs on top of me. His warm length spans my back. For a while, he lies quietly then begins to wiggle. Suddenly, he is gone. Whatever connection was needed, he has received.

Another idea has formed, "Kyra," replacing "Mama." He is off in search of his older sister, longing to connect with her. I hear their morning greetings. Soon he is laughing. She is making him laugh, as she loves to do. She laughs too. I smile. He has found his freedom, and me mine.

Now alone, my thoughts swim and dive as so many of Thoreau's fish. What is it about being on the farm that has yielded this lived sense of being an impulse to connect? Is it simply the changed realities of family life? I think about Thoreau. For him, the natural world provided experiences of livingness that quickened his sense of his own creativity, his own movement. The same has been happening to me. It is not just that I am here with my partner, at a distance from my parents, in closer proximity to my children. The experience of living here, surrounded by such complex, ever-evolving beauty, cows, hens, horses, and hayfields, is quickening my senses. I see and hear and taste and smell and move *differently* because of time I have spent exploring this land. With senses so awakened, it has become impossible to ignore the tremors of dissatisfaction in my primary relationships that signal the presence of issues to address. At the same time, with senses so awakened, I find, at my fingertips, resources I did not have before for helping me move in relation to these others in ways that will not reproduce the pain.

It is the message this book enacts: when we bring our senses to life, by connecting with the earth in us and around us, we awaken in ourselves the resources we need to seize the challenges posed by parents, partners, and progeny as opportunities to unfold our capacity to love. We find new ways to move that foster mutually life-enabling relationships with human and non-human others.

Why is this *sensory* education so important? It is because the challenges of these relationships are rooted in the *bodily changes* that occur as these relationships succeed. With caregivers, for example, in so far as the relationship succeeds, we grow from wholly dependent infant to independent adult. With partners, we evolve from a clothed and protected single to a bared and vulnerable mate. With children, we morph from an isolated adult to a shared flesh extending across generations. In each case, in order to negotiate this bodily transformation in a way that allows the relationship to continue, we must create new patterns of relating with the other. In so far as the transformation involved is *bodily*, the task of navigating it demands a similar skill: we must learn to welcome sensations of displeasure arising in and because of the relationship as essential information that is guiding us to move in ways that *we want and need* to move in order to become who *we* have the potential to be. And this skill is what time in the natural world, attuned to the movement of our bodily selves, can help us develop.

Could it be true?

My task for the morning is to explain why, laying out a template for the chapters to come. I have my work cut out for me.

Geoff is awake now. Through the wall, I hear him shepherding the kids through their chores. Always adventures befall. It may be a stray kick from a cow, a dead rat in front of the chicken coop door, a snake in the hay or, from time to time, an overturned bucket of milk. Every day it is different, and the kids' interest hasn't waned.

Today a cow foot lands in the bucket. The pail doesn't tip. Not a drop of milk is lost. Nevertheless, there remains the unavoidable fact that a dirty hoof plunged in and out leaving all kinds of particles in its wake. Jordan, Jessica (ten), and Kyra (five) debate what to do. *Was it true? Did it really happen?* After a bit of mourning, the kids reluctantly agree to dump the morning's catch.

I yank my attention back to the page.

What are you enabling, my little ones?

Distance from Parents

The hardest part of moving was telling my parents. Did I think it would be easy? We were living close by—a mere fifteen minutes—and had been for over ten years. When Geoff and I met, married, and made their grandkids, my parents were there. They were there when we bought our first house, and forged our careers. We saw them several times a month at least, often on Sunday afternoons, when they would invite the kids over to their house. My parents cherished their grandchildren time.

Our first conversation about the farm was good. My parents were surprised, but supportive. As the dream became real, however, other feelings percolated through. My mother's disappointment was understandable: "You are taking the grandchildren away!" The one in my belly included.

As the sting of my mother's displeasure shot beneath my skin, everything in me reared up in defensive response. I breathed deeply, and tried to imagine her words sliding down my back, like drips on a resilient duck.

"Yes, I know. I am sorry. Come visit! Stay for a while! You will have more quality time with the kids than ever before!" Still, it hurt. I hurt. I wanted her approval. I wanted their approval. I wanted them to see how good this move was for me—how daring, how bold, how aligned with my deepest dreams for my family and for myself.

All I could hear in my mother's words and my father's silence was one more example of a long-standing dynamic that has ever eroded my sense of self-worth. I was convinced that all they wanted was for me to be smaller than I am—to fit into a life that would make them happy. They *say* they love me and they *think* they love me, but they don't love *me,* or so I feared. The distance between what they give me and what I want from them has seemed an unbridgeable chasm. The distance between their house and the farm made that chasm real.

Of course, my responses to my parents are far from unique. How many people do you know who can comfortably affirm that they received everything they wanted from their caregivers—all the love and attention and encouragement and guidance and support they could ever want? Can you name any?[6]

I know very few, though my father happens to be one of them. "He was the darling of his mother's eye," my mother recounts wistfully. She did not receive the love, self-confidence, or emotional support she wanted and needed from her own mother. She wanted more. In her eyes, my dad's mom had given it.

Is it surprising that so many people want more?

Think about what being a human baby entails. Think about the *bodily changes* that occur as a person matures. When born we are helpless, unable to secure for our bodily selves the food, warmth, and protection we desperately need. All we can do is *move* in response to sensations of pleasure and pain. As we move, we grow. We create patterns of sensing and responding that connect our moving selves with what is being given: we suck, swallow, and smile. We curl and cry, stretch and relax. These patterns guide our subsequent movements towards what we have learned gives pleasure and away from what does not. Then, as our bodily selves move to connect with what nourishes, our needs evolve. Desires proliferate; we learn what more there is to want. In so far as our caregivers have been minimal providers, we tend to want that more from them.

Nevertheless, our caregivers are not always there when we need them, and not always available when they are. They do not always have what we want, or are not able or willing to give it to us. It is inevitable, at some point or another, regardless of their intention, that our caregivers will not give us what we want from them. In their unyielding resistance to us, we feel it: *the sting of an impossible desire.* This sensation settles into our flesh and flashes pain. We recoil in response. A pattern of sensing and responding forms: *I want what I cannot have. I cannot have what I want.*

Because we are bodies born both helpless and moving, it is inevitable that we will feel this pain *and* that we will do all we can to make the pain go away. Pain registers in us as a need to move, to change positions, so as not to feel that pain. In our effort to craft responses that will protect us, we draw on the basic bodily movement patterns we have mastered. We angrily push our caregivers away. *I don't need them. I'll do it my Self.* We spit out their disapproval or disappointment. *They don't love me.* We turn against ourselves in blame. *I must deserve it. It is my fault.* We extend and retract, twist and arch, push and pull, take in and expel, mimicking in our emotional lives the increasing mobility of our bodily selves. We seek to establish our independence from our caregivers as a way to stop feeling hurt.

Making these movements makes us. An ego forms—a scab on the wound of our impossible desire. As challenges arise, we cling to this burgeoning sense of ourselves as an autonomous individual, believing that it will protect our vulnerable bodily self from further stings of impossible desire. We live in fear. We set out to conquer nature, beginning with our own.

This dynamic feeds a frontier mentality: individual first. Recommendations pass from therapist to client, talk show host to audience, friend to friend. *Establish your independence from your caregivers. Build boundaries. Give yourself what you want.* We take it for granted that it is up to us to fill the cavernous, ravenous gap

cracked open in our bodily, sensory selves by our experiences with caregivers. Disappointment simmers, untouched and alone.[7]

I had tried for years to follow this advice. I failed. I tried to break from my parents and assert my emotional independence. I tried to reinforce the walls of a self against intrusion with soothing mantras, ducking and distancing behind them. I tried to find satisfaction by controlling my own bodily desires in advance of their criticism. I tried to accept my parents as they were. Nothing worked. I couldn't not care what they think about me or my life. To cauterize my relation to my parents in the name of some individual self would mean silencing parts of my bodily being that were, at least once, *open* to them as source and cause of my happiness and well-being. So I remained, well into adulthood, far too vulnerable and defensive, a brittle shell still smarting over undelivered desirables, poised to crack.[8]

Moving to the farm, it was clear: I wanted to feel more love in relation to my parents, not less. But how? How could I stay open to my parents when I sensed their resistance to my best judgment and their disappointment in my most cherished action? How could I move in myself and in relation to them so as to heal this pain? What could love be? I had to find out.

Proximity to a Partner

Geoff and my decision to transplant ourselves from a pleasant suburban street to an overgrown farm in rural New York was easy. Soon after meeting, we had begun imagining ourselves together in the country, doing our art, ever more intimate with each other, our kids, and the natural world. When Jessica was six weeks old, we began a yearly pilgrimage to Vermont, driving through town and country, real estate brochures in hand, in pursuit of what seemed like a nearly impossible desire. We were game. We had each other. For Geoff and me, moving to the farm was a dream come true.

So why weren't we happy? The dreams we dream never play out as we imagine. Geoff and I soon found that it was difficult to be with each other day in and out. We were exposed as never before to each other's bodies—to our respective rhythms of hope and frustration, wakefulness and exhaustion, clarity and fuzziness, excitement and irritation, desire and satiation. We were so bare in a situation that itself involved more chaos, more mess, and more uncertainty than anything either of us had ever tackled before. We were no longer able to escape into dreams of the life we wanted to live. This was supposedly it!

Our love needed to grow strong enough to realize the dream it had been bold enough to dream. But how?

Often, the self-protecting moves we make in relation to our caregivers end up limiting our ability to open to others as well. We cling to the saving notion of ourselves as individuals and claim that we don't need anyone else. We insulate ourselves from the tremors of our own desires and the feared sting of impossible desire. Our hurt and resentment are too fierce. We may shy away from intimacy or seek it subversively, wanting to connect without taking the risk of exposing ourselves again.

Nevertheless, if we have been loved enough to feel the sting of impossible desire, it is inevitable that some person, at some time, will stir in us a memory of an ancient connection, once longed for and enjoyed. We may not always have received the love we wanted, but we received enough to know that we want more of it. We want someone to help us continue the work our caregivers began along the trajectories of unmet desire that our caregivers helped us discover. We want a partner in our journey.

When we meet a potential someone who fires our impulse to connect, the brand of impossible desire throbs in us with a hope we hardly dare to hope. *Maybe I can have what I want after all.* We pursue the relationship in search of ourselves.

Yet just as conflict is inevitable in relation to caregivers, it also is in relation to partners. The reasons are similar. As partners

move to connect in ways that give pleasure, their bodies change. With partners, we show and tell, share and reveal, touch and are touched. New landscapes of pleasure open within us. Places once frozen in frustration warm and release. We move. We heal. Our sense of ourselves evolves and it is inevitable: we want *more* of this freedom, more of this love. We want more of the sensory experience of living in the world that opens within us when we are open to one another. We want to be the self who can abide always in the love that flows when we are.

As our desire to connect ever more deeply grows, however, fear creeps in too. We have been here before, vulnerable to another, needing someone else to give us what we want. We fear our nakedness and the sting of impossible desire. We fear that in asking for what we want, we will drive our partner away or be driven away ourselves. We fear that we will lose our partners or lose ourselves in them. So we do with our partners what we learned to do with our caregivers: we cling to our hard-won illusions of independence. *I don't need anything.* We say no to ourselves, convinced that our partners, like our caregivers, cannot possibly love us as much as we want or need. *I can't ask for that.* Our desire for more registers in subterranean forms: a cramp of irritation, a surge of jealousy, a whiff of boredom, a wave of dissatisfaction.

Cultural wisdom here aligns with the advice given to adult children in relating to their caregivers. *Build boundaries. Soothe yourself. Sacrifice and compromise are inevitable for getting along. Master your bodily nature. Passion inevitably wanes. Accept it.*[9]

I tried. I tried to take time to myself, to nurse my wounds and unravel the sources of my discomfort. I practiced asserting my independence while buttressing myself against the waves of Geoff's anxiety, depression, and desire. I tried to be the individual self I thought I had to be to feel happy and safe—a self in control.

It didn't work. Day by day, hour to hour, the façade of self-containment was impossible to sustain. Our proximity was brittle

and I wanted more from our relationship—more intimacy, more presence, more love. I wanted to be able to stretch out in the comfort of my own skin with Geoff, as open in my senses as when I walk the land. I wanted to surf the waves of our collective energy, open and free, all the time. It is why we moved in the first place. How could I learn?

How could I stay open to my partner when we were arguing over how to install the dishwasher? What moves could I make when his ongoing depression that he didn't have a job was depressing me? Where could I put the irritation I felt when a day passed and I hadn't been able to engage in any form of bodily movement? How could I find ways to move in this new farm-fed proximity that would express love? I had to find out.

Interdependence with Progeny

When we began making plans to move, I was worried. I thought my kids would be upset about leaving the city. Our suburban house was the only home they knew. It was where they had crawled, toddled, and made their first snow forts and dirt pits. They would be leaving friends and playgrounds, school and neighborhood parties. Was it selfish of Geoff and me to consider uprooting them from their happy lives and transplanting them to a place where the quality of the schools and neighborhood were unknown? Would they resist? How could they even conceive of a new place to live?

Soon, however, they corrected my way of thinking. The kids had their own dreams. Imagination is their specialty, and they apply it generously. When Geoff and I began to flesh out our hopes and plans for the future farm, the kids were right with us. Jordan wanted space to roam and trees to climb. Jessica wanted horses and stables and riding rings. Kyra wanted whatever Jordan and Jessica wanted and lots of it. It seemed miraculous. Our kids' dreams, as different as they were from ours, aligned with ours, complemented ours and even, as we soon learned,

were enabling ours. At the same time, as our lives on the farm entwined ever more thickly, I found that each child was more able than ever to squeeze some invisible button known only to him or her that ejected me from my sense of well-being into the mental space of a raving lunatic.

Was it a coincidence?

No. Just as our relationships with caregivers and partners are fraught with promise and peril, so too are our relationships to those for whom we are responsible caregivers. The reasons are similar. As partners allow their openness to one another to transform their bodily selves, their mutual impulse to connect inevitably wants to conceive. It wants to bring into existence new movements that further extend and entwine partners' bodies in space and time—plans and projects, dreams of a home or life together, and in some cases, children. And this extension, as with any increase in bodily exposure, heightens our vulnerability to the sting of impossible desire.

How so? With biological parents and children, this extended vulnerability is easy to conceive. Kids' bodies are their parents' bodies. Every cell and limb, every neuron and organ expresses the genetic meeting of the parents' twenty-one chromosomes. Biological children literally extend their parents' bodies, giving their parents' genetic potential a new life.

Even so, parents have little idea of what they give through their genes. Not only does each partner pass on a package of traits that he or she did not realize in his or her own life, the interaction between the partners' genetic material allows novel possibilities to find expression. Each child is wholly unique because that child is a singular moment netted in a web of relations extending back into infinity. As a result, even though kids contain nothing genetically that their parents have not given to them, they can twine their threads in ways that contrast sharply with their parents' weave. Even biological children have different paths to follow, different abilities to unfold, and

different requirements for health and well-being than those whose bodies they extend.

Moreover, genes are only one measure of bodily interdependence. As important are the *memes* that caregivers share with their children—the non-biological units of culture embodied in gesture, language, attitude, values, actions, and the whole host of interaction patterns that children and caregivers create between themselves. Children learn by watching. Consciously or not, they mimic the movements that they see and hear and feel. They try out the movements, experimenting with gesture and tone, word and deed. As a result, they adopt bodily patterns of sensation and response for their own use that rehearse what they have absorbed from the persons responsible for them. This dynamic is so strong, as Daniel Siegel affirms, that even adopted parents are "biological": early experiences shape our neurological development.[10] Caregivers, then, biological or not, create beyond themselves in ways they can neither fully imagine nor control.

As in our relationships with parents and partners, then, conflict is inevitable as a result of the bodily changes that the success of this bond begets. In so far as our children thrive, they constantly want more from us, as we want more for them and from them. We not only want everything for them that we have ever wanted for ourselves—including freedom from the sting of impossible desire—we want from them the knowledge that we are succeeding in saving them from the sting of impossible desire. We are thus prone, as nowhere else, to experience our progeny as wielding the definitive word on our deepest fears: *do we want what we cannot have? Will we not have what we most want?*

At first it seemed as if the red button encounters with my children were unrelated, unique to a child, a time, and a place. However, as I began to work on my relationships with my own parents and with Geoff, I began to notice the similarities. Suddenly the truth was glaring in my face. What unhinged me

every time was a shock of recognition: I saw in a child of mine a pattern of sensing and responding that I detested in myself. I saw him or her suffering from the sting of impossible desire. They were feeling it, and because their bodies are my body, I felt it too. Jordan turns on himself in a self-harming fury. Jessica loses all presence to earth-shuddering sobs. Kyra crumples into a ball. Kai screams from head to toe that he is not getting what he wants. In response, I know I should feel compassion, but I rail against the injustice of living my own hell twice. I don't want my children to know that despair of not getting what they want. Even more to the point, I don't want to be the one responsible for them not getting what they want. Their experiences of impossible desire trigger my own. I am suddenly awash in the non-negotiable certainty that I will never be the mother I want to be, or the writer, dancer, partner, or child. I hate myself for wanting, and for failing.

One day, as I lurked locked behind my stormy glare, it occurred to me: "This is my problem. It is not my children's fault. If I want to help my children find helpful ways to respond to their inevitable sensations of impossible desire, then I must first find those movements in myself. And I must do so in relation to them. I have to, because I want so much to connect with them." My own impulse to connect refused to settle for anything less.

An insight is not the answer. The hardest work remained. At least I knew what it was. Rather than upbraid my children to toughen their sense of self against their desires; rather than stoking their illusions of individual autonomy and control, or suppressing my own rage, the task was to open as widely as possible to the sensations of impossible desire that my children were igniting in me, and so opened, to draw on my farm-fed sensory awareness to find in those fears an impulse to move *closer towards my children*. The fact that they were triggering fear in me was providing me with an occasion to learn from them how to find more freedom in myself in relation to my own caregivers

and to Geoff. With their enabling push, I was on my way to discovering a well of gratitude towards my parents and a practice of total presence with Geoff. My kids were teaching me more than I had known about how to love.

Life on the farm, and the fact of our family's heightened interdependence, shifted my experience of parenting into a new register. It was increasingly apparent that the cultural common sense urging caregivers to sacrifice their own dreams for the children's sake or provide the discipline needed to enforce a child's sense of bounded individuality was missing something crucial—*the impulse to connect.* Missing was any awareness that caregivers and children *want* to connect with one another, and that they are impelled by their inevitable bodily entanglement to cultivate this connection between them as a condition of their mutual health and well-being.[11] Every relationship between child and caregiver poses a question that only they can answer: what can love be?

Also missing was the sense that this vital link between caregivers and kids not only has the potential to be mutually beneficial, but has this potential because of the ways that our children's *movements,* in all senses of the word, reflect back to us images of what our movements in thinking, feeling, and acting, are creating. Our children's presence in our lives calls us with penetrating honesty to acknowledge the sensory footprints of the choices we are making, and ask ourselves whether or not the world we are creating is a world in which we want to live.

The truth is that Geoff and I learn as much or more from our children than we are supposed to be teaching them. Our relationship with them is far more complex than can be mapped with lines of tolerance and respect. It isn't just that our children need us in order to become who they are. *We need them to be and become who we are.* It is our impulse to connect with them that helps us become the singular selves we are, as we discover and unfold our capacity to love, for their sake.

How can I negotiate the extended surfaces of vulnerability that my kids are? How can I move in relation to them when they are smarting from the sting of impossible desire? How can I create the world in which I want my children to live, beginning with our relationship? I was determined to find out. Life on the farm was making it both possible and necessary.

I pause from my writing and look out the window. I have plowed my patch, tracing the distinguishing features of our relations with caregivers, partners, and progeny in terms of distance, proximity, and interdependence. I have a clear sense of the bodily challenges each relationship entails and the skills required to navigate them successfully. The stories I have to tell of how and why sense-awakening movement matters in helping us learn to love can now take root and flourish in chapters to come.

It is raining. The golden hum of the morning has morphed into watery sheets. Geoff and the kids are unfazed. Regular chores done, they are planting corn in the furrows tilled yesterday by our new walk-behind tractor. The tractor was a compromise. Geoff would like a real tractor. Jordan would prefer a team of oxen. Jessica and Kyra want draft horses. While none of these options are currently within reach, we need some way to get vegetables into the ground for the season. We are already late. Our wild and wooly farmyard is out of control. So we got what we could get. It is working. Oblivious to the rain, the kids are arranging the thirty-two eighteen-inch corn sprouts into six rows.

Thirty-two plants, I counted. Yesterday, when Geoff and the kids came home from the garden store, they proudly carried a full flat, fifty plants in total. We put the tray under a backyard birch tree while we tilled the soil. Minutes later, when we turned around, Kai was crouching beside the plants, his favorite scissors in hand. He had decided it was time to "cut" the corn—right down to the roots—of eighteen plants.

I reminded myself through a fog of frustration that Kai just wants to connect—with us, with the growing green, with the earth, with the work at hand. He wants corn—from one of our remaining thirty-two plants. He wants to be a part of the farm family too.

I sigh and smile. The corn will grow. So will Kai. I close my notebook.

The kids are finished with their work too. They tumble into the kitchen, shedding wet shirts, shorts, and shoes, as they chatter over their hopes for the harvest. I can hear the laundry pile growing. Kai is asking when the corn will be ready.

"Can we have some tomowow?"

2

Healthy as a Horse

> If we are to hope to correct our abuses of each other and of other races and of our land... We are going to have to rebuild the substance and integrity of private life in this country.
> —Wendell Berry[1]

August 2008. I don't want to go. I am tired, having just slogged through a round of errands, from home to hardware store to library to supermarket and back. The kitchen is in shambles again. An instant without my attention and it is strewn with stray cups, plates, crumbs, pencils, paper scraps, and toys. I would rather stay in the house, cleaning and sorting, doing my own thing. Dinner is around the corner. Besides, I have not fully

recovered. The miscarriage took more from me than the growing bean. It has been nearly a month and I still feel empty, weak. Nevertheless, Marvin needs to be ridden—every day—and now is the moment. Jordan is ready.

This horse is demanding. It is my kids who ride; it was their idea. They were the ones who begged for a horse. Yet somehow the responsibility for making sure Marvin gets what he needs is falling on me. I find myself prodding the kids to do what they say they want to do most and doing so for Marvin's sake. Shouldn't it be the other way around? Shouldn't I be prodding Marvin to care for my kids? I don socks and lace up my sneakers. *I'm coming.*

A horse? It was bound to happen. After all, it was Jessica's desire for one that propelled her to the computer on that April day in 2005 when she Googled "Vermont farms" and found this "Vermont-border farm." The question has always been when.

Four months ago, news of a horse appeared, arriving in an email message from the owner of the barn where the kids take weekly riding lessons. The message described a seventeen-year-old Quarter horse, not too expensive, well-trained, but out of work and needing a family to take over his care. We squeezed in a time to take a look at La Star Bonanza, otherwise known as Marvin.

Was it love at first sight? Pretty close. While the kids swarmed around him, he stood calm and still. Despite their buzzing, he did not swat. For all I know about horses, and that is next to nothing, he seemed to appreciate the attention, a gentle, alert soul. The owner put Marvin through his paces, showing Jordan and Jessica how. We took a video of Marvin to show the experts at our riding barn. We got the big OK. We looked the gift horse in the mouth and he passed the test. There was simply no reason to say no.[2]

I gather sunglasses and hat and yank myself out the door. Jordan is on Marvin's back just outside. We walk on together, north along the road, to warm up our legs before cutting west up

onto our land, and south again across the shoulder of our hill. Already Marvin needs a nudge, which is why I am along. Ever since he has been on the farm, he has wanted company in order to go forward. He prefers to have someone walking in front of him, testing the path, assuring him that all will be well. I do and we move on.

Horses, as Marvin is teaching us, need a purpose, even more than humans. They need to know what they are doing and why. Otherwise, they would much rather be tugging grass at the roots. Marvin responds well and follows me up the path. At the corner, he takes the lead.

Momentarily freed, my eyes drift sideways, pulled softly. I am snapped into the presence of this place and suddenly aghast at its beauty. *Today*. The grass is overrun with wild flowers. Gentle Queen Anne's Lace float in the breeze, arches askew one to the next. Below the bobbing white, dusky blue chicory flowers pepper the green. Perky perpendiculars of milkweed stalks punctuate the flow, stopping traffic. A truck hurtles by on the road below.

Walking along the graceful hill, my thighs begin to burn with the effort. It is that sense-opening, wake-up kind of burn, where muscles yell out to the places you have been spending and storing fuel—usually hands and brain—and demand their share. It is a searing-into-presence, a plunge into a cold pool. The sensation will ease in a moment. I breathe, coaxing the transition along. I press belly button to spine, and sink my exhaling breath down into the bowl of my pelvic cradle where it rolls and crashes out through my legs. In inner emptiness I begin again, drawing earth energy up through the straw of my bodily self. "Heaven is under our feet as well as over our heads," wrote Thoreau.[3]

Marvin plows on through clusters of clover and purple-petal-shedding oregano, up the angled face of the hill. The path is faint. I haven't been this way in a while. My breathing is starting to feel more supple and loose. It is good to be back.

Since trucking Marvin to our riding barn for a test drive, the learning curve has been steeper than this pitch. Our advisors were smart; they gave us only one piece of information at a time. We could see just far enough to know where to step next. Soon, however, we were going straight up a bewildering slope and there was no turning back. There never is.

We make it up to the meadow. I am breathing hard now, more easily winded at this juncture than I would like to be. Emerald splendor spills open before me, beside me, below me, catching my breath. The rolling field rises then falls then rises again against a backdrop of distant forests sporting fluffy white mushroom caps.

Breathing out, I release myself into the healing force of this place. Something very green seeps in through my pores. The land is calling to me.

Come back to yourself! Come back to me!

I am seized with gladness at having left that kitchen mess behind.

Incalculable Debt

As I turn the corner of the hedgerow and move down the slope into the first meadow, I pass through the quiet place, the most protected place of our land, and suddenly my emptied mind explodes. I am flooded by the memory of a conversation with my mother that happened in this field. I gasp with the grip of its pain.[4]

My mother was here for a short visit to see the kids' music concert, and we were managing to fit in a walk up the hill before she left. She was asking me about summer plans.

"Will you come spend some time with us at Kimball Lake?" she asks.

I pause. Kimball Lake is a fixture in our lives. Something significant always happens there, and Geoff and I haven't missed a year in the last ten. Still, there are issues to consider. Someone needs to stay at home to take care of the cows. Geoff wants quiet time to do some recordings of song birds for his software project. I could leave Geoff here and take all

the kids to the Lake, but if I do, I will need some help. I need to work too.

"I don't know. I would like to come, but I have to work. Would you be willing to take care of the kids for a few hours in the mornings while I do?"

Mom is silent. Her exasperation breaks through. "Can't you just spend a few days with your parents?"

I am stunned, confused. I assumed that she would respond gladly to the request. Doesn't she want to spend time with the kids? I don't want to burden her. It is her vacation too. I just want her to know that if she wants us there, she can have us there—if she is willing to help.

I respond carefully. "No," I try to explain. "I can't. I mean my work is who I am, Mom. It is what makes me happy, and I want to be able to do it. I have to be able to do it. I can't be there with you if I can't be who I am!"

"You are so difficult!" she fumes. My heart plummets.

I was so upset. I didn't understand why it was so hard for her to understand me. Soon we were spiraling into a familiar pit. I accused her, as I have before, of not *seeing* me, not supporting me in my work, not encouraging me for being who I am, and not loving me in the way I need and want to be loved. She told me, as she has before, that she has a right to share her feelings, that she has always done her best in parenting me, and that what she had to offer just wasn't enough.

I curled in, protecting my brittle edges, and vowed not to go to the lake, knowing that I would. How could I not go? How could I go? Hurt her or hurt me? Why must I choose?

The ache was acute. The last thing I ever want to do is to make my mother feel hurt or inadequate because of me. Her pain is my pain. Yet what I wanted from her was so simple, so easy, so UN-difficult, and she wouldn't give it. To me, her resistance has always felt like a lack of love. I can't seem to experience it any other way. I convince myself that she is bent on robbing me of the small amount of pleasure I need to thrive.

As we walked down the hill, I scanned my sensory self for a way out. I told her that she had a right to her feelings and to sharing them. I insisted that I have a right to respond. She heard me and told me that she would help out with the kids. Even so, the dynamic between us simmered, unhealed and unresolved, ready to erupt again.

My head is down, my eyes glazed, my legs churning. I begin to notice that although I am surrounded by incredible beauty I am seeing nothing but the ragged linings of my thoughts. My eyes spring up from the ground and rest on the horizon of great-growing green. I am walking. I let go and let my movement pull me out of myself through my senses into a wider world. I see where I am. The views from this spot arc out in three directions. A mountain wall guards my back, its shoulders reach around me. I love this cradle. Life inside me rises up to meet its embrace, pressing against the winded weakness that clings to my cells, and pushing it away.

Senses humming, I think again about that conversation with my mother and others like it. Is it really true that my mom and dad have not loved me enough? Sure, I *feel* as if they haven't, but is it true? Even in this case, my mom wanted me with her and my dad at the lake, on vacation, enjoying the water, the sun, and the nearby mountains. Isn't that love? Isn't that enough?

Desire wells. *I want more.* I want her to want *me*. I want her to understand who I am. Is that so wrong?

A fiery pain blazes along the well-worn paths my mind is treading. I feel it—the gut-wrenching sting of impossible desire. *I can't have what I want.* The sting branches instantly into a tree of corollaries. *I can't have what I want. I won't get what I want. I will never have what I need.* I vibrate with the pain, convinced, in this moment, that *the universe exists to take my pleasure away*. The feelings sear through my walk-softened self, but I don't stop. I keep moving, breathing, pushing ahead, stretching and thinning the sensory knots.

The hill dips. I am going slightly downhill now. The walking is easier. The scalding subsides, and in its wake, new thoughts begin to unfold within me, pulled into view by the movements I am making.

What if my parents have loved me, and loved me *enough*?

I reject the idea. Then after a moment, I return to it and turn it over. What counts as *enough*? I can't deny it. My parents did take care of me for years when I was unable to take care of myself. They gave me my life; they fed that life, clothed it, warmed it, hugged it, and enabled it to grow. It's rather obvious: if it weren't for them, I would not exist. Period. Isn't that enough?

As I near the bottom of the meadow, my thought bends. There is another view to see here. My parents loved me enough not only to nourish my life; they also loved me enough to awaken in me a *desire for more* of *what* they were offering. They loved me enough to awaken in me a desire for more *than* they were offering too: more love, more life, more connection with them, more connection with what is.

The realization blooms. They loved me *enough* to stir in me a desire for more of what they helped me learn was worth wanting from my experience with them.

This is good! So what is the matter? Why do I hurt?

It's the sting. It's the sting that haunts me. Why?

I reach the bottom of the field, brushing up against the briars that mark its limit, pondering this sting. The sting hurts and haunts because of what I think it *means*. It's not just the ping of the sting. It's the meaning it carries with it, and that meaning is one that my parents guided me to give it. For as my desire for more grew (thanks to their good nurturing), I turned to them for the more they made me want (thanks to their good nurturing). And when they resisted my desire, I stayed turned to them to figure out why (thanks to their good nurturing). The litany of reasons I collected from them was long. *You are too complicated.*

You are too defensive. You are too sensitive. You think too much.

I believed every word. I wanted to please. I wanted more love. The sounds of their voices carved patterns of sensation and response into my growing self, and I learned. Whenever the sting of impossible desire threatened, I would respond by blaming my self for wanting more than I should want, for being too selfish, or for not thinking about other people enough. My pain was my fault. It was what I deserved. I was too much and never enough. Never good enough, never worthy enough. This pattern of sensing and responding to my own desire that cropped up in relation to my parents had come to define my relationship with life itself. *I am too much to love.*

The memories ball in my belly as I round out the far corner of the field and begin striding up its western side. The churning of my thighs pulls on the wads. The surge of my sensory self balks. Am I really too much to love? Something alive in me refuses to accept it.

Freed to move by the vivid, living green, another response wells from within.

No, I am not too much to love. *I am just me, wanting more of what is good.* I am just me, reaching for what I need to thrive. I am just me, wanting and needing to connect with what will support me in continuing to become who I am. My parents' explanations stick as barbs in the flesh, yes, but not because they are true. Their explanations pierce my well-being because I know: I love them and they love me.

The revelation jolts me awake to another horizon. A grass-covered hill stretches up before me, reaching to touch the innocent sky. *This sting of impossible desire is not what it appears to be.* It is not an indelible wound in my tender flesh. Nor is it a sign that I am doomed to disappointment. It is not a blot on my being, delimiting the arc of what is possible, nor an obstacle to my pleasure.

No. I feel this sting because *I want more of what is good,* and it is good to want more. It is how I grow. I want to grow! This sting

won't let me settle for less than what I want and need to flourish. When I feel this sting, then, I do not need to respond by blaming myself or anyone else. There are other ways to move.

Plowing upward through the tangled stalks, I am awash with gratitude. This desire for more is a gift—a great gift—perhaps the greatest gift. It is *me*. It is my spirit surging forth in and through my sensory self, wanting life. Because of this impulse to connect with what is, *I am here,* climbing my mountain. *I am.* Loving the land. Loving me.

If I had never wanted more of what my parents were giving, and never felt the sting of impossible desire, I would never have made it here, never have been willing or able to open to Geoff, never had the courage to extend my flesh through the lives of my children and open to this great earth. My parents' love—and its limits—catalyzed in me a desire to continue the work that they began, creating the relationships that would support me in becoming who I am.

Because of that sting I have discovered, at the heart of who I am, an impulse to connect with people and forces other than them.

I owe my parents an incalculable debt. I am ever, forever, infinitely grateful to them for stirring to life in me a desire for more than they could provide.

Jordan, Marvin, and I make it up the face of the meadow and pause at the top. The breeze plays in my hair and around my face. I bob in the rocking wake of my insights. "Only thoughts reached by walking have value," Nietzsche wrote.[5] I tend to agree.

Marvin dips his head to graze. Jordan looks so comfortable up there, a regular cowboy. He sits tall and proud, with a swagger in his seat. Happiness spills through my heart. Jordan enabled this moment of understanding, and this moment is enabling me. Marvin lifts his head, nostrils open to receive; a regal golden-red glow of a creature, shining against green field and blue sky. He is at home here. Me too.

Total Presence

I take the opportunity to look at Marvin closely. In the end we didn't buy him, we rescued him. I won't easily forget the tears that escaped from my eyes as the vet pulled clumps of hair from his back during the pre-purchase exam. It was horse talk, she said, for "I've been ignored." He was suffering from "benign neglect." Horses do that. People too. We had no idea, though the signs once noted were obvious. Besides the lost muscle and hair, his skin was flaky, his legs stiff. Had he felt the sting of impossible desire?

The day the vet came, Marvin was limping visibly. She almost recommended that we send him back to his owner then paused. Other qualities appeared to her, the ones that were drawing us toward him too. Marvin was sane. He was safe, well-trained, what our riding instructor called "broken to death" even. He was intelligent. As he warmed up, his gait improved a bit. He wasn't worth buying, but perhaps he could be rescued.

The vet left us with a laundry list of things to do *now* and *soon.* Now: give antiseptic bath, administer dewormer (worms must be stealing his nutrients), change feed (horses cannot digest the corn base), mount shoes at least on the front, take X-rays to ensure the right shoe fit, and groom, groom, groom. He needs attention, care, and love, love, love.

Soon: add hind shoes (and change again every five weeks), have his teeth filed (yearly), administer more dewormer, deliver vaccinations (yearly). Our eyes grew. There is no such thing as a free horse.

Along the way, I kept pummeling Jessica with questions. I asked: How often do you deworm? She replied: Once a season and twice during the summer. How do you know how much a horse weighs? You multiply length times girth (around the belly) and divide by 230. What is Coggins? A disease. If a horse has it, you have to put him down. I looked at Jessica in wonder. How do you know that? She smiled. I already know. She's been reading

horse books for years.

Meanwhile, back at home, we were trying to ready our barns for the arrival of our new charge. We spent several afternoons cleaning a corner of the heifer barn, putting up new siding, and pouring concrete onto the floor. Then we learned: horses shouldn't stand on concrete.

We abandoned that stall, moved our plans to another barn, and started again. We cleared out old hay and trash. Geoff and I spent a morning of our own work time building two walls. Marvin would have a waterside suite, complete with pond, traveling geese, and homing herons. Dandelion, our newborn calf, would be two stalls down to keep him company. We would care for him and he for us. No more benign neglect. No more sting of impossible desire.

I am behind Marvin now, admiring his gait. Already his newly formed muscles are pulling his legs under his hips, where they should be. A few months ago it was as if his hooves were toeing an imaginary line beneath him. As a result of our care and attention—and walks like this—his body is changing. Marvin is getting stronger, and wanting more. He wants to do more, to give more. I knew that these hills would be good for him.

They are good for me as well. I breathe down into my own gathering strength. The hole left inside by the lost embryo is filling again with hope. *I want more too.* Perhaps I can open again soon.

A wave of joy catches me by surprise. I run down the peninsula of land that juts out into another meadow sea, flinging my arms out from my sides, chin up and breast forward, riding the breeze. I stretch wide from side to side, beyond and over the edges to the left and right. I am flying, falling, catching myself, and moving on, more alive than before. It's as if Thoreau's "tonic of wildness" is streaming through my limbs, waking me up to my bodily self.[6]

My movement is making me.

At the bottom of the hill, I stand, smiling, waiting for Marvin and Jordan. I look down to my left, and my eyes skip across the beaver pond from lily pad to lily pad. There is a spot down there where I go to dance. There is a tree whose long slender trunk makes a perfect partner. There is also the place where Geoff and I had one of our hardest and most illuminating conversations ever. Pain shimmers through me as I remember. He was so upset, so furious with me, with himself, and with life.

It was a busy time, and I was beside myself with a twisted anxiety whose shape I didn't recognize. The obvious object on which the fear feasted was an unpublished manuscript. I was waiting for my agent to gather my materials and send them to the list of editors she had handpicked for the occasion. It was all good news. My emotion was way out of proportion to the facts on the ground. Why?

I couldn't figure it out. All that week I had been holding the anxiety close to my chest, not able to admit to it. I couldn't speak. I felt that if I tried, the sky would thunder down upon me. My silence was keeping Geoff and me apart. I knew I had to share at some point. My desire for him was knotted, and with every move I tried to make, the tangle tightened.

When Saturday dawned spring-warm and spring-green, I had mustered some courage and began to speak. Soon the words were tumbling out.

"I just want so much for this book. I have so many hopes for it. There is so much I want it to do for us. I want this life to work. I want to keep doing what we are doing!"

Hearing my own words redoubled their revelatory force. In that instant I saw through my anxiety to its core: a deep and abiding desire to live in the world of love that opens when Geoff and I are together. Anxiety melted into affirmation. *It is my impulse to connect! It is good!*

I was somewhat dazzled by what the effort to communicate with him was opening in me. I felt grateful. Soft. Geoff was quiet,

listening. Further revelations cascaded through me. I surrendered to the stream.

"I see too, that I fight so hard for my right to this life because I feel like nearly everything in my life until now—everything until you—has conspired to take away my pleasure. At some level I am convinced that the universe exists to deny me what I want. My body is not mine. My sexuality is not mine. The fruits of my work are not mine. I have no right to any of it. Experiences with my parents, in summer camp, with friends, with employers, with work, with boyfriends—it seems that every time I open to receive, what I most want is whisked away."

It was one of those moments: a series of connections clicked their way into my sensory awareness for what seemed like the first time. I felt the sting of impossible desire (*I can't have what I want*) and my response to it (*It's my fault; I want too much*) as a *pattern of sensing and responding to my own desire for more* that I have carried around with me as a protective talisman in every realm of my life. Whenever I want more, I always have a ready-made reason why I cannot, or should not, or simply will not get what I want.

Nevertheless, there is always another part of me that resists this interpretation and, at that moment, I could feel why. It's a dynamic Nietzsche describes. In the attempt to make myself smaller, I was exercising and strengthening the very self I was trying to diminish.[7] Every turn against my self expressed my self. I moved to squelch my desire for more because I wanted more, so the wanting refused to die. Thank heavens. *Wanting is good*!

The feeling of freedom was intoxicating. I knew viscerally how inadequate this pattern of sensing and responding to the sting of impossible desire was and always has been. Not only was it not true (how could it be?), but it didn't work. In fact, it locked me into a place of fear where I was constantly looking for, and thus immersing myself in, the pain of inevitable disappointment. My self-protecting strategies kept breaking open the wound of my own despair.

So much hope was banging about in my heart. I wanted that hope to stay. I didn't want to stop the nourishing flow of my words coming through.

"I am so sure that any desire I have will usher in the pain of disappointment. I'm just convinced. I have learned to fear it, to try to protect myself from it. Yet my fear is just another expression of my wanting. That is it! I cannot stop wanting! I want to want! But I don't want to be disappointed! So whenever the potential for pleasure looms on the horizon, I hunker down, ball my fists, and fight my own fear for what is rightfully mine. Tight and defensive, I cut myself off from my own sensations. I close down, afraid to feel what I might feel. In the process, I lose all access to the very pleasure I am refusing to give up!"

As I wait for Jordan and Marvin to catch up with me, memories of that moment with Geoff run round and round. I feel the ground pressing up against my feet. I consciously sink the memories down. Then I lift my chin and swing the memories around in the blue-lit space, airing out the ache. Jordan and Marvin arrive and we walk on, up around the shoulder of the hill. We are not going down to the pond today.

Geoff and I kept talking. Or at least, I kept talking. Geoff was listening. I talked myself into this place where I felt light, formless, expansive, and very alone.

"I feel like I am in la-la land!" I cry.

Geoff responds. "You are."

I remember how the hope I was feeling slid into desperation. I liked la-la land, but not enough to stay there all by myself. I wanted even more to come to a place where Geoff and I were together in the wonder of my revelations. I was seeing these views because of us. My impulse to connect with him was dredging up this muck and forcing me to face it and share it. Though it felt so good to do so, I was not proud of what I was seeing. I wanted him to affirm that he understood. I wanted him to affirm his desire for someone who could see all this about herself and need to say so. I wanted to know that I wasn't too much.

Suddenly I was afraid again and choking on panic. *Is Geoff going to take away the deep pleasure of these revelations? Is he going to prove them false by refusing to hear them, share them, see and love me through them?* In that moment, it seemed to me that he had the power to dismiss everything I had said as so much nonsense.

"Can we talk some more?" I ask. "I still need something." Silence. I feel him closing. I keep trying, struggling to keep my fears at bay. "Our conversation is helping me a lot! I'm just not quite there yet. Can you say something else, please?"

I was flailing. Soon it was obvious. Geoff couldn't hear me. As I had been speaking, he had tumbled down into a sinking hole of self-loathing doubt. When I had told him that I had not yet gotten enough from him, all he could hear was that he was not enough. He was convinced: he was not giving me enough and he could not give me enough. He felt horrible and was furious at me for making him feel so inadequate.

The grass brushes against my shins, swishing with the rhythm of my quickening gait. I feel again the paradox of that moment. There I was, wanting Geoff to tell me I wasn't too much, and there he was, sure he would disappoint me, suffocating under a blanket of fears that were as toxic for him as my fears of pleasure were for me. Yet he too was fighting mightily against these fears, refusing to accept them as what must be true. That is why he was furious with me.

It was that day, that long-long day, that Geoff and I began to recognize how deeply our ways of interacting with one another had been shaped by patterns of sensing and responding to the sting of impossible desire that we had each mastered in relation to our parents long before meeting one another. Our ways of interacting with one another had reinforced those past patterns, without our realizing it. Over time, we had learned to respond to one another as if the other posed a threat to our ability to get what we most wanted and needed to thrive. It wasn't true. It was deeply ironic. For what we each wanted then and ever since is to

connect with one another, to be connected with one another, and to live in feelings that flow when we are.

My pace slows. I sigh with sadness and relief. Jordan and Marvin and I reach the crease where the land begins its rise to Moon Rock, the highest point on our property. I hum with the yearning I had felt as Geoff spiraled down and away from me, away from us, into his own nightmare, right at that moment when I was trying to escape my own nightmare and move towards him. I tried to reach for him, tossing out line after line of life-saving words. I tried to reassure him that I wasn't too much and that he was enough. The effort pulled other insights into view.

"I am asking you for more because I believe you have it, because I love and want you, because I appreciate you for helping me come to the insights I am having, because I want you with me. I am asking for more because I believe in you and in our love—not because I don't!"

The going was slow, but finally Geoff began to grasp what I was saying. We saw our respective fears as a wall that rises up between us. We saw our respective impulses to connect battering against that wall; we realized that we had grown. We were now at a place in our lives where we were no longer willing or able to tolerate degrees of distance between us that had once been commonplace. For the first time, we both admitted that the pain of being separated emotionally from one another was more acute than our held-over fear of feeling the sting of impossible desire. We were changing; our relationship was changing us. Our bodily selves wanted more—more proximity, more openness to one another, more flexibility in recognizing in each other's words and actions an impulse to connect with us. We named that more: *total presence.*[8]

Total presence. The idea came to us that day, that weekend, that spring. It was the shape of desire that the movements we were making towards one another were making in us. It was an expression of our ever-evolving impulses to connect. We arrived

there together, and felt a huge sense of relief, excitement, and hope. We wanted more, and we knew what.

We wanted, in every moment, to be free from our self-protecting fears and present to what our impulse to connect with one another was creating in us. We wanted to live in the flow of our love—open to one another as causes of our being. We wanted, in every moment, for this openness to be more real than any pain either of us had experienced. We wanted to make it so. We could taste the possibility.

I smile remembering how much of a breakthrough we thought we had made. We had a vision of our relationship that felt unique to us, but no sense of what it would take to realize it. Although we had identified how our parent-inspired patterns of sensing and responding to the sting of impossible desire were holding us apart, we had no clue how to create new patterns, or what they would look like if we could. We would have to learn.

What was clear, however, was that the process of learning to make those moves would involve immersing ourselves in gratitude towards the caregivers who had awakened in each of us a desire for more than those caregivers could give. For even though it was our experiences with our parents that had entrenched patterns of relating to others that were driving us apart, it was also the desire for more that our caregivers had brought to life in us that was impelling us towards one other. Because of that desire for more, Geoff and I were willing to stand face to face and take the risk of being hurt again.

It made sense.

Only by feeling gratitude to our caregivers for awakening in us a desire for more than they could provide can we release the power of our impulse to connect from the patterns of sensation and response it took in relation to them. Only then can we move with that impulse to create a relationship with a partner that continues the good work our caregivers began, along the trajectories of unmet desire they helped us discover.

Letting Live

Jordan and Marvin reach the ridge before me, and pause at the path leading up to Moon Rock. I slip beside them and start up, giving Marvin someone to follow.

"Mom!" Jordan cries out from behind me, distress in his voice. "Can you help?" Jordan is tugging firmly on the reins and pressing with his legs, but Marvin is not listening. Marvin wants to go in the other direction: down, towards home, hay, and the end of his hard work. Jordan is on the verge of tears.

I move instantly to help, but can't stop a smile inside. Jordan doesn't always go where I want him to go either. How many times have I asked him to do something, like pick up his dirty clothes or put his dishes in the dishwasher, and he has not listened to me?

Marvin needs some polite conversation. I grab his reins and point up the hill. "Marvin, there," I say out loud. "That is where we are going, yes, up to Moon Rock. That is where I need you to carry Jordan. Come along. It's a beautiful view. You will love it."

I am not always so patient with Jordan. In fact, one of my greatest parenting challenges is dealing with him when he gets upset. When I ask him to do something that he doesn't want to do, or that he already was planning to do, or that he realizes he should have done, he inevitably turns his anger against himself, exploding in fury at what an "idiot" he is, or how "dumb." As soon as he makes this turn, something inside me ignites in a blast of rage whose force I can barely manage. I am furious with him. I see what he is doing. I see the move he is making. It is the move I make when I turn against myself in response to the sting of impossible desire. He, like me, is trying to resolve the sting by trying to annihilate his desire for more. *I am a bad rider.*

I can't stand it. I don't want him to do what I do. I especially don't want him to do what I do as a way to respond to me! I don't ever want to be the cause of his pain. At the same time, I am livid with him for making me feel like I am! The fact that he is making

this move seems to me to be a screaming accusation of me: *you are an unreasonable ogre.*

It is a slippery slope, steeply pitched. When I turn against myself in anger for being an ogre, while still fighting against what seems like an unjust accusation, it doesn't take much to convince myself that Jordan is taking away my pleasure. He is taking away my pleasure at being a mother by making me feel like I am a bad one. It happens in a flash. Of course, as Jordan feels the intensity of my own turbulence, he blames himself for being such a horrible person even more. Soon we are flailing alongside one another in a riptide of pain and desire.

As I pull Marvin's head around and set him going up the hill, I breathe with the difference of this moment. Seeing Jordan so hamstrung by his own frustration stirs to life a new resolve in me. I really want to be free from patterns of sensation and response that turn me against myself in a vain effort to secure protection from the pain of disappointed desire. I don't want to feel these feelings any more. I don't want to model them, or inadvertently pass them on. I don't want Jordan to experience the pain I have felt in relation to my parents, or even in relation to Geoff.

What do I want? I breathe through the shape of remembered discomfort and find the desire at its core: *I want to let live.* I want to connect with Jordan in ways that encourage him to let his own desire live without blaming his pain or himself or me. I want to act in relation to him in ways that help him welcome the sting of impossible desire as an opportunity to discover and exercise his own impulse to connect, as I am doing too with my parents and Geoff. I want him to learn how to create the relationships he needs to support him in becoming who he has the potential to be, including his relationship with me. I want his health and well-being for my sake, and his.

How can I get what I want? As I push my palms down on thrusting thighs, charging up the steepest part of the slope, the

pieces fall into place. If I am going to succeed, I will have to find my way not only to a place of gratitude towards my parents, but also to a place of total presence with Geoff, where I am living in love, free from the fear of feeling the sting of impossible desire.

The logic dazzles me. Jordan, without knowing it, is serving as a catalyst for my own deep healing. Jordan is pushing me towards gratitude to my parents; for my experience with them has enabled me to discern how I want to connect with him. He is pushing me towards total presence with Geoff, as a practice of opening to embrace my own desire for more. He is pushing me to discover this freedom in myself—the gratitude and openness—so that I am able to let him live in his difference from me as an extension of my flesh. In all these ways, Jordan is enabling me to see how my relationships with parents, partner, and progeny are thoroughly, inextricably entwined; and he can serve as this catalyst for me because my persistent, undying impulse to connect is bending me toward him.

Jordan, I realize, along with all of the others, is teaching me about love. He is not only providing me with the occasion for learning *how* to love, he is providing me with an opportunity to articulate anew what *love* itself can be.

To love is to open to another as a cause of your being.

I turn to Jordan, teaching him what I know I need to hear as I navigate the rapids of our relationship. "It's OK, Jordan. You and Marvin—it's a relationship. It's just a matter of learning to communicate with one another. Just figure it out. Don't take it personally. Marvin is not taking away your pleasure in riding. He is providing you with the opportunity to feel the joy of learning to communicate with him. You are a good rider. Just figure it out. You can."

Jordan listens, Marvin too, passing me along the path. I follow along, a cloud of thoughts whirling like gnats. I know intellectually that it is impossible for anyone *not* to feel the sting of impossible desire. Jordan will feel it just as I did, regardless of my

best and brightest intentions. I cannot prevent it. What I can do, however, is help Jordan learn to feel and respond to that sting differently than I have, so that he can stay open to himself and others, open to love. So too, I can do that for him by learning how to make that move myself. I don't have much time. He is growing up. They all are.

Walking on, I chant what I want in time with the rhythm of my steps. *I want to let live.* I want to let my children live. I want to be free in myself—grateful to my caregivers, present with my partner—so I can let my children live, and maybe even one yet to come.

I want to support my children in letting their desire for more bloom and grow into a strong and vibrant force. I want them to learn to dwell in the suspense of desire, tasting the sweet anticipation of its fulfillment. I want my kids to be able to do the work of creating patterns of sensation and response that express their impulse to connect with whatever is enabling their becoming.

I want my kids as healthy as a horse, or at least as healthy as this one.

We make it to Moon Rock. Here, the view fans out in a circle. It is hard to know where to look. Looking one direction I don't see another. The best picture always seems to hover at the vertical edge of what I can see. I stop trying to look and open to feel the view in the round, with my whole body, steeping myself in its expanse. The spherical setting inspires me. I want to move with the infinite possibilities of this horizon. I want to create and become the patterns of sensation and response that will guide me to think, feel, and act in ways that express love in the moment and for the moment as the most important thing. If I can do it, then my children, my partner, and my parents may learn from me.

The grass up here is long and tangled. Marvin steps through it tentatively, before burying his nose in its nourishing clumps. He is happy to be here after all. Jordan stays on Marvin, taking

in the scene from five feet up. I walk the perimeter of the hilltop, another place where I often dance. I don't feel like dancing now, well maybe a little.

"Which way do you want to go down?" I ask.

"This way." Jordan starts out along the path that leads through the rough fields and back down by the maple woods. I follow along. Bubbles of gratitude rise and pop, releasing ease and well-being.

I move ahead of Marvin now, finding the path that leads down around and back towards the first field we entered. I love this moment of the property. It is not one whose appeal is obvious. At first it seems a mere scraggly transition between hilltop vista and meadow span. The view is split to either side. But if you find the right angle, a sudden sweep of intention appears in the course of the valley as it parts the hills. It is as if to say: there is a reason for this. It took me a while to be able to see it and be present in it.

The flowers are taller here, reaching to grab at wayward limbs. We plow through more slowly, following the occasional deer path. As I look down to find my footing, I feel the sky above me, pulling me up and out of myself. I walk along with the clouds at my back, breathing deeply with each step. The work is easier now. The movement has blast open airways in muscles and cells, and filled my sensory spaces with a buoyant glow.

Just ahead, another favorite glimpse slides into view. Behind a near hill is a far peak peeking through. I can only see a corner of its mound and the shoulder of a neighbor; but somehow, it is all the more inviting in its elusive mien than some of the brasher bumps in the near-ground. The peak seems to recede as you look, dissolving into a blush blue. Yet there it remains, near and far, appearing and disappearing, open to me in its mystery, like love.

As we near home, I feel the glee in my heart, the warm tingling of pleasure in my fingers and toes, arms and legs. I am so glad that I went on this walk! Without Jordan, without Marvin, without Jordan's dreams and Marvin's needs, I would have

shackled my own desires to the tasks at hand, riding on fumes. Without Jessica's willingness to stay home with Kyra and Kai while Jordan and I went out, I would not have made it either. Without the parents who birthed me, the partner who released me, the progeny who prod me, I would not be here, loving all of this.

I feel my freedom. My energy swirls with delight. I am ready to work hard and sing as I do, greeting whatever challenges come my way as opportunities for practicing boundless gratitude, total presence, and the art of letting others live.

Thanks, Marvin.

3

Fair Enough

Could a greater miracle take place than for us to look through each other's eyes for an instant?
—Henry David Thoreau[1]

August 2008. 6 a.m. The beep of Jessica's wristwatch alarm tickles my ear, waking me to the hum of an ever-present generator. Eyes crack to a swath of blue canvas. To one side and the other are sleeping-bagged bodies, swaddled in purple and

green. I remember. We are all here, the whole farm family, in our tent on the grounds of the Washington County Fair. It is the last week of August and it is time to get up. Jordan, Jessica, and Kyra tumble out onto the grass. Their cows are waiting.

Or rather, they are wading—in their own muck. Our three Jerseys are here: two-year-old mother, Daisy; one-year-old heifer, Precious, and Daisy's daughter, the five-month-old definition-of-cuteness, Dandelion. The cows sleep in the stalls of the Youth Barn where they are tied to metal bars that give them just enough room to stand up and lie down. When it is time to do their business, they have nowhere to go, which is why they need so much attention. They wake up covered in it.[2]

6:25 a.m. The kids lead their beasts down the sawdust path to the cow showers—yes, cow showers—carrying buckets, a scrub brush, and some Ivory laundry detergent. The showers occupy a large open-air room with three wide aisles. The scene reminds me of a coin-operated car wash, except that the cows line up side by side rather than front to back. Given the close quarters, it is an acquired skill to wash your cow without washing your neighbor as well. Experienced cow cleaners wear boots.

For their part, the cows don't seem to mind the trip to the spa. Pampered and primped, they return to their stalls ready for display. On a given day, thousands of people will stroll through the barn, chatting and pointing, while the cleansed cows chew away.

6:30 a.m. Back in the tent, Kai rolls over and wakes up. Geoff sleeps. I sort tired belongings into piles, strap Kai into the stroller, and push him over bumpy ground to the barn. Jordan and Jessica are happily feeding and watering their cows, shoveling manure and sweeping the aisles. Kyra is still at the showers. I circle back to see if she needs any help.

Did you know that cows are contagious? I didn't before our move. Back in Boston, our degree of cow interest had been relatively low. We liked milk and cheese. We had a stuffed animal

or two, and the usual farm books, toys, and puzzles. Cows, however, had never ranked as high in the world of play as horses or Harry Potter.

Four months after we moved, however, the ranking shifted. Jordan developed a sudden and unexpected passion for bovine animals. He wanted a Jersey cow to be exact, a smaller breed bred for the high butterfat content of their milk. It was the kind of cow that his grandfather, Peter, had showed in his youth, and one of the cutest. Not your typical black and white spotted Holstein, Jerseys range from dark to deer colored. Their signature large brown eyes are rimmed with black.

"Don't you want a horse?" I had asked.

"Yes," he replied, "and a cow!" For months Jordan would draw cows, play with plastic cows, build farm complexes and tractors with Lego blocks for his cows, make lists of supplies he would need to care for a cow, and read books on how to do so. When not actively pursuing his plans for a cow—or pleading for one with Geoff and me—he would crumple in despair at not already having one. "I can't live without a cow!" He was only ten.

After four months of his consistent prodding, Geoff and I began to sense that this desire for more was too strong to ignore. *What are you enabling, child?*

We signed up with the local Cattle Rustlers 4H, located a couple of Jersey calves for sale, picked one, cleaned out a stall, bought a bucket and lead rope, and had her delivered. There she was, little Daisy Mae, named after Grandpa Peter's prize-winner. Her shaggy self was not much bigger than a large dog. Jordan loved her. As spring hatched, he and Daisy would run together through the fields and then snuggle in the sun for a nap. That summer was our first fair.

Did I mention that cows are contagious? As 2006 passed into 2007, signs of infection spread to Jessica. "Cows are easier to take care of than horses," she argued. "Besides, we already have one!"

Jordan had one. Jessica too wanted to join 4H and show at the fair. Unprompted, she entered an essay contest whose prize was a young Guernsey cow. She did a report for the Science and Art Fair on cows. She insisted that her life depended on having a cow. This time we found one already named: Precious. She was. Our second year at the fair, we had two kids showing two cows.

Was I surprised that several months after that fair, the cow bug bit Kyra? At the time, Daisy was pregnant and Kyra decided, much to Jordan's dismay, that she wanted Daisy's calf. Just six, Kyra also wanted to join 4H and show at the fair. When Daisy obliged with an adorable heifer, Dandelion, Jordan agreed to let Kyra lease his cow's calf. Kyra paid her dues, got her 4H card, and here we are: year three at the fair with three cows. What's next?

I meet Kyra on the path to the showers, coming back with a bucket in one hand and Dandi's lead rope in the other. She is grinning happily. Her calf is clean. I smile back.

6:45 a.m. Milking time. We milk one cow, Daisy. Rather, Jordan milks Daisy. "We" enjoy the results, and have ever since Dandelion's birth in March. Like humans, cows won't make milk until after they give birth. If you want milk, you must find a cow with a calf and become a surrogate child—a cross-breed breast feeder. For a few months after Dandi was born, we shared Daisy's milk with her. When Dandi started on grain and grass, Daisy's milk was ours.

People are generally surprised to hear that cows must give birth to make milk. In western culture, we equate "cow" with "milk" to the point of assuming that cows exist to make milk for us. In some senses, they do. As many in the burgeoning food field now report, standard industrial dairy practices convert cows into milk machines.[3] Commercial businesses tend to dole out care based on how it affects the *quantity* of milk a cow can make. To bump up production, farmers feed out tons of nutrient-dense, corn-filled grain, even though a cow's digestive system is better suited to grass. Before a given cow's milk flow slows, farmers

catch another heat cycle and call the sperm seller, pushing the limits of her reproductive capacity. Meanwhile, cows are often crowded together in tight quarters, anonymous numbers all, and shot with antibiotics to prevent them from catching the diseases they are likely to contract given such unhealthy living conditions. We stuff them, drug them, plug them in, turn them on, and drink up. *Got milk*?

Jordan, however, has decided to resist the mechanizing mindset of modern cow culture. Daisy is no machine and he refuses to pump her with suction cups. She is a friend with a name. He milks by hand. He wants a share of Daisy's milk, but not enough to boost production to a teat-bursting, life-shortening level. He doesn't milk her out completely, preferring to take a gallon or so at each milking and allow her udder some slack. Sitting on an overturned bucket, flexing his forearms, he draws a crowd.

I think back to our first milking on the night of Dandelion's birth. It wasn't so easy. At 2 a.m., in a cold, dark barn, milking was an emergency procedure and a team effort. I held the bucket and pulled on one teat. Jordan pulled on two teats, rotating to the third. Then we switched places. Stress levels were running high. Would Daisy kick the bucket? Would the calf get the early milk, or colostrum, she needed to prime her immune system? She did. Our team milking continued for a month or so until Jordan began to take over. He was so good at it and loved doing it, preferably alone. How had he known that he would?

7:30 a.m. Breakfast time. After the cows come the humans. The kids and I crowd around a picnic table outside the Youth Barn. I open the cooler and pull out cereal and bread, peanut butter and jelly. Ironically enough, we buy a quart of milk.

It is amazing how much effort it takes to eat well here. The Washington County Fair is the agricultural event of the year in a county that lives and breathes farming. Traditionally, it has been a time for farmers isolated by land and work to strut their

strengths, share their wares, and build community. It is a time to celebrate the harvest. Some of that still happens. For the most part, however, the fair has evolved, or devolved, into a full-blown sensory assault.

As I pour milk into the cereal bowls, I see the Ferris wheel at the far end of the fairgrounds, arrested against the morning sky. The amusement rides that hurl, twist, drop, spin, shake, and otherwise throttle you through space are now quiet and still and will be until 11 a.m. So too are the food wagons that line the lanes to the rides. To hitch a ride, you must walk through clouds of spiced grease emanating from row after row of trailers peddling fried you-name-it: potatoes, onions, zucchini, chicken, steak, fish, cheese, dough, and even Oreos served in large tubs or plate-sized dog bowls. Next door you can purchase soda, lemonade, or mix your own fabulous fruit slush in liter cups, complete with fast flowing, wide mouth straws. A good dose is sure to make your ride even more amusing.

I hand the kids their spoons, pour them some milk, and sit down to eat the oatmeal, grape-nuts, and cottage cheese I brought for myself from home. There is hardly anything here that I can or would want to eat. In this hub of agriculture, I can't buy a decent salad or a piece of whole wheat bread. There are a few ribbon-decked examples of prime vegetable specimens in the Domestic Arts building, but they are not for sale. The kind of farming celebrated here is largely based on oil—corn oil, cooking oil, diesel oil, and gasoline. Agricultural incense.

A Giving Impasse

As my eyes roam the empty aisles, my sights fill with memories of earlier in the week. My parents were here at the fair for the second year in a row. I couldn't believe they had liked it the first time, and yet they insisted on coming again.

My parents live in an immaculate home whose groomed gardens exude a welcoming order. They travel in automobile

style to the country club and back, and journey around the world from one well-appointed spot to another. This spot is not well-appointed. In fact, anticipating their visit, I had been wracked by anxiety. I was sure that they were going to hate it, and sure that that hate would be reflected back as disappointment with me. *Why have you taken our grandchildren so far away from the comfortable suburbs to this agricultural wasteland?* It was that old stinging feeling, coloring my world: *I am always too much and never enough.*

Jordan decides he is going to use a coupon he earned by working the previous night in the 4H Food Booth to get some pancakes. He comes back with a pile of white rounds and begins to eat. Minutes later he stops.

"I have a stomach ache," he confesses.

"You don't have to eat them all," I reply.

He pushes the plate away. "It's all right, I'll get over it." He points to a nearby poster. "Mom, did you see that sign? It is telling you to go to the Family Health Center for a chance to win a Nintendo Wii!" He is laughing. Healthy video games. Kind of like jumbo shrimp. Or 4H pancakes.

The kids finish their breakfasts and pop back to the barn. Kai plays in the dirt. I pull out my journal and jot down some thoughts.

My parents. Our relationship is changing. Since moving to the farm, a distance has opened up between us that has, paradoxically enough, allowed me to feel closer to them than ever before.

I think back to the catalyst—other than the move itself—that forced me to make some new moves in my relationship with them. It was seven months after the move, December 2005. My mom's sixty-fifth birthday was approaching and Geoff and I had invited everyone to come celebrate at the farm. Although we were not as far along in house renovations as I had hoped, we knew we could provide a comfortable sleeping surface for everyone, some privacy too. When everyone accepted, I began

happily scheming. It had been part of my vision for this place from the beginning to host such events.

Soon after making the arrangements, I received an email from my dad telling me he had made reservations for out-of-towners at a nearby mansion that had been newly converted into a bed and breakfast. His message explained: big bodies and bad backs need king-sized beds, firm surfaces, private rooms, and a big-screened television for the weekend's football game.

I was devastated. The message knocked the wind from my belly and sails. It was palpably clear: my dad was giving up an opportunity for cozy time with his grandkids for a night in deluxe accommodations. The farm wasn't good enough. I was beyond disappointed.

I wrote back, pleading with him and them to come and stay here, sharing my ideas for hosting everyone comfortably. He stuck to his plan, insisting that he was doing it for me. It would be easier for us. When I said that having everyone at the farm wouldn't be too much for us, he accused me of not thinking about others.

"You are imposing your vision on everyone else," he insisted.

I was stunned into silence. I knew that in his mind he was being generous and thoughtful, as he is. But what he was doing *for me* was *not what I wanted*. The hurt was unbearable. I wanted to call the whole thing off.

That night I couldn't sleep. I crawled out of bed to find solace in the yoga practice I have been doing on and off for over twenty years.[4] I thought it might help me breathe through the knots in my heart. In the wee hours of the morning, I moved through a series of standing postures. The pain began to shift.

I remember the feeling. I was doing the part of the sun salutation where my arms reach high into the sky and then swim in a long half circle to the mat. Hands on the floor in front of my toes, I lifted my eyes to the wall in front of me and let them fall again. I reached one leg back and then the next. I opened to the pain. Words popped into my mind.

It's a giving impasse. I want to give something; my parents do not want to receive it. They want to give me something; I do not want to receive it.

I welcomed the words and responded by breathing again, down my lengthened limbs, releasing this image of a giving impasse into the earth. As I did, I uncapped a deep well of disappointment. It gushed forth.

I am so disappointed with my parents for not wanting what I have to give. I feel how disappointed they are with me for not wanting what they have to give. They are blaming me for being selfish because I don't want what they are offering. I am blaming them for not seeing and understanding me because they don't want what I am offering.

I moved into the triangle pose, reaching for the comfort it regularly provides. As I breathed into the posture, it rearranged my bodily self. Energy flowed easily down my legs into the ground, up through my hips along the length of my back, and out through my arms, all at once. At the center of the crossing currents, my head turned to gaze into the palm of my outstretched hand. Insight dawned.

We are stuck in a cycle of escalating disappointments. I responded again by breathing and releasing further into the posture. More disappointment crashed through me and in its wake, a familiar imprint.

Of course. This giving impasse is triggering the sensation of the sting of impossible desire! I am sure that I can't have what I want. It is releasing my well-worn response to it as well: I am too much and never enough. And simmering beneath the surface of this disappointment is the conviction that I am to blame. It is my fault. Everything is my fault.

My legs threatened to buckle under the weight of the thoughts, but I stood, breathing myself open. As usual, something inside me refused to accept the interpretation that it was all my fault. I paddled through the pain, searching for the alchemical current that would help me transform this ache into some other sensory substance. *What other moves can I make?*

I returned to standing and moved into the triangle on the other side. As I sunk my effort into the earth and dove inside myself, it was as if a veil dissolved. I saw the desire at the core of the pain.

A simple affirmation formed: *I want. I want to give. I want to connect. I want to connect with my parents, and that is why I hurt. I hurt because I want to give. That is it. Period. That is all. It has nothing to do with whether or not I am too much or never enough.*

I inhaled again and welcomed this desire to give that overflows in me and toward them. I chanted: *I want to connect. I want to connect. There is nothing wrong with wanting to connect.*

Seconds later, I moved into the warrior pose, forward knee bent and back leg outstretched, head lifted and arms aloft. My thoughts were flowing, each pulling into view the shape of another.

If what I have to give is not welcome, then that fact is no judgment on the act of giving. I don't need to blame myself for wanting to give. I don't need to blame my parents for not receiving. I don't need to judge myself or the gift as inadequate. Nor do I need to vow never to give again. I don't need to go there. The insight glowed.

I don't need to go there. The weight dropped.

The fact that I am not getting the reception or recognition I want right now is not a sign that I will never get what I want! Giving is good. I am free. All I need to do is remain open to the stream of generosity coursing through me.

As I moved through the postures that night, my despair and disappointment fell away. I could see with clarity the move that I had been making, which was making me so miserable. I had been looking at myself through my parents' eyes and hating what I saw. *Your farm is no mansion.*

The yoga-inspired message from my moving bodily self to my stuck mental self rang clear and true. *When I try to live my life through what I imagine my parents will think, nothing I do is good enough. Everything I do and am is a disappointment. Everything—my life, my kids, my dreams, my self. Shifted I'm shafted.*

I don't need to go there.

I remember how sweet the sense of liberation was. Not only was I seeing an old pattern of sensation and response implode, I was making a new move and I knew it. Instead of responding to the pain by clamping down on my self, I was moving in ways that allowed me to affirm the impulse to connect at the core of that pain. The movements I was making on my mat were allowing me to find in that familiar gut-emptying feeling of not being enough an affirmation of my desire to give. In the process, I was changing. I was creating myself into someone who chooses to participate consciously in the rhythms of her bodily becoming.

As I basked in its glow, the beam of this affirmation opened to include my parents. I knew: I wouldn't have discovered this power in myself to make new movements in relation to my parents if my parents hadn't loved me *enough* to make me want more than they were giving. *They loved me enough.* It was because of the unmet desire for more they had stirred to life in me that I was here in my favorite farmhouse, in the middle of the night, doing the yoga I love, going deep inside my sensory self, and finding sources of freedom and creativity in the shimmering sensory spans of my own bodily movement. *Because of the sting I know this delight.*

In a flash I knew: I could celebrate my mom whether she was staying at my house or not. I could because I wanted to.

I wound up my yoga session, bathed in relief, and crawled back into bed. As I did, the thrill of what Geoff and I are doing at the farm crested into an overwhelming gratitude towards my parents for kindling in me a desire for more than they could give. *I am so grateful!*

I was swimming with joy. Gratitude is what I feel when I am open to my parents as causes of my being. It is what I always want to feel in relation to them. It is a feeling that feels good to feel. It is who I am and want to be—someone who can recreate past pain-perpetuating patterns of sensation and response, learn

new moves, and set herself free. Someone who lives in love.

Kai is done with the dirt. He wants to join his siblings in the barn. I put my notebook away, clean up the rest of the breakfast mess, and follow him over. He finds the sandbox filled with corn and asks me for his bag of trucks.

Sitting on the hay-bale edge of the corn-box, my thoughts continue to hover around my parents. What I have experienced with them in the past couple of years goes against everything I have learned from western culture and its experts about how to grow up. According to most psychological theories of the family, children become adults by separating themselves from their parents, hardening themselves against the sting of impossible desire, and establishing themselves as individual agents. While the umbilical cord will be cut for them, children must sever the emotional, moral, and intellectual cords themselves. Attached to parents, kids learn to make sound decisions; detached from them, they order their lives accordingly.[5]

Are building walls and breaking bonds the only moves for growing children to make? What if attempts to separate from caregivers are futile? What if reigning ideals of individual selfhood are illusions behind which we are hiding from the sting of impossible desire?

What if our task as children is to find the distance from our parents that allows us to appreciate with gratitude our incalculable debt to them for stirring to life in us a desire for more than they can give?

My parents and I are not only related to one another, we want to be. They want to give to me; I want to give to them. In this context, the idea that I must buttress myself against the sting of impossible desire misses the meaning of that sting to my adult self. It is an expression of my impulse to connect. I feel it because the patterns of sensation and response I have created and become in relation to my parents are no longer working, if they ever did. I am too easily spun into a cycle of escalating disappointments.

My parents are too. The sting, then, is calling me to wake up to the power of bodily becoming that enabled me to connect with them in the first place, and create the relationships I need to become who I am, with them and beyond them.

It is a radical, paradoxical idea. No matter how much we love a caregiver or how much a caregiver loves us, we can never avoid the giving impasse: gifts that they want to give us and gifts that we want to give them will not always land as planned. Desires will not be met. Even when there is no conscious or unconscious intention to harm, feelings will be hurt. Disappointment will occur and can escalate quickly. This giving impasse is a primary obstacle to feeling the gratitude that frees us to affirm and move with our own desire for more.

When such mismatches happen, however, rather than retreat behind illusions of independence, we can learn to make moves that affirm the impulse to connect at the heart of the struggle. When we do, we can transform the pain of disappointment into boundless gratitude for the bodily self we have been given. We can open to affirm our caregivers as causes of our being.

That birthday was over two years ago. Yet as I look back, I see the trajectory it set in motion. My relationship to my parents edged into a new register. Insights that arose as specific, tactical responses to unsettling situations began to live in me as visceral possibilities for sensing and responding to a wider range of moments with gratitude. I learned the same lesson over and again, and slowly it began to take hold as the primary response. I refused to be shifted or shafted so easily. I was learning to live in love.

My eyes. My parents' eyes. They taught me to see, and with their care, I grew to see other things too. I am having my own experience of the fair this year. The thought cheers me. The fair is what it is. My parents are who they are, and I am becoming who I am by virtue of how I am learning to connect with them.

Fair enough.

Wanting the Same

8:15 a.m. Back at the barn, the kids are getting ready for the 9 a.m. show. Kyra is first. She dresses in white shirts and pants, emblems of dairy clean. Her hair is brushed and back, face washed, and work boots carefully laced. Her calf too receives a final shine. Dandi's tawny coat, already spotless and shaved to a smooth fuzz, now receives top line treatment. With hairspray and a blow dryer, Jordan and Jessica help Kyra get the hair poking out of Dandelion's spine to stand up straight, enhancing the illusion of her long and flat back. The judges will be looking for this line as evidence that Dandi, when fully grown, will be able to carry calves and milk with ease. The kids then tease Dandelion's tail into a soft fluffy ball, for better decoration of her hind end. Finally, as the moment nears, Kyra dresses Dandi in a show halter made of leather and chains, and hairsprays Dandi's hooves for a ruddy gleam. Look like a cow? She's gorgeous!

9 a.m. Kyra's class begins. She prepares to enter the ring, studiously ignoring the straps of her number harness that keep falling off her shoulders.

"Good luck!" I whisper to her. "What is the most important thing?" I ask.

"To stay calm," she replies.

"Yes! Whatever Dandelion does, just stick with her. Don't get frustrated. Keep telling her what you want to do. She will learn."

Kyra leads Dandi into the show ring. The ring is filled with sawdust under cover of a roof, with open walls and four-row grandstands on each long side. The calves enter at one end and parade clockwise in a circle. The aim is to "show" the animal by having her pause every few steps with her legs positioned in a way that highlights her dairy characteristics. We have not practiced enough. Dandelion is not very good at it, and even though she is only five months old, Dandi is far bigger than Kyra. I watch as Kyra wrestles mightily to keep Dandi's head up and her body in line. Kyra is staying calm. I am very proud of her.

Three weeks ago Kyra was too scared to try to lead Dandi. Now she is holding her own. I am also proud of Dandelion. She is my baby too and she looks good compared to the competition.

Yes, the competition. Is your cow *very dairy*? The judges are looking for a good overall size, deep front, that long and strong top line, a sprung rib cage, straight legs, angular hips (or hooks) and of course a well-attached udder with four symmetrical, easy-to-milk teats. Then there are the more subtle traits that I have picked up from the ruminations of various judges: how smooth is the transition from head to shoulder to leg? How does her walk swing? Does she have style? Even flair? It has taken me three years to begin seeing the differences from one bovine to the next, but I am finally noticing some. Dandelion places second.

I thought that perhaps as a parent I might end up on the sidelines of soccer games or gymnastics tournaments, in the audience for skating lessons or piano recitals. But cow shows?

10:30 a.m. It is Jessica's turn. Her heifer, Precious, is the most rambunctious of the three, and their size difference is the greatest. I am about to release my eighty-pound daughter into the ring with a nine-hundred-pound cow.

Three yards into the ring and Precious hauls her head around in a wide circle and smashes Jessica against the guardrail. The sound reverberates around the ring. I wince. Spectators hush and stare. Jessica pops back up, spine erect, hands gripped tightly on the harness. Her face betrays nothing. It must have hurt. What am I doing letting her in there? Jessica is determined. She wants to be there, I remind myself. Step after step, Precious of the Hurricane Head fights to go left or right but never forward. Jessica hangs on. Several hour-long minutes later, Jessica places last in the class. The judge tells her she deserves a gold medal.

I sit there on the bleachers, swearing to myself. If we do this again—and I mean *if*—we are going to practice and practice and practice!

We take Precious back into the barn. Of course, when not in the ring, Precious trots along merrily behind Jessica. What is that cow thinking?

Jordan's class is not until after lunch. The kids are hungry. I pull out some homemade zucchini muffins and oatmeal chocolate chip cookies. The kids munch while hanging on the bars of the cow stalls. Then Kyra climbs into the stall where Dandelion is lying down and curls up under Dandi's chin. Dandi lifts her head up and around to embrace her small friend, and continues napping.

11:30 a.m. Kai is getting restless. The corn-box at the end of the Youth Barn has lost its allure. He has been scooping and plowing and trucking around the hard kernels, and now wants to see some real tractors. I click him into the stroller and wave to Jordan, Jessica, and Kyra, leaving them in charge of the cows. Kai and I walk.

The fair is starting to wake up. The doors are officially open. Guests are milling about, lining up for food, for rides, for events, for shows, and for the bathroom. I watch from a distance inside myself, as if from behind the scenes of a carnival. I am still trying to make sense of this fair. Is it a fun escape or an unhealthy binge? Is it a celebration of farm life or a testament to its demise? Homegrown or Florida-fed? A time to spend with family and friends or a time to spend ignoring them? What would Wendell Berry think?

I am solo today. Geoff and I take turns going home, doing Marvin chores, cat chores, chicken chores, washing clothes, packing food, getting as much work done as possible, and returning to the fair with dinner and supplies. Today is his turn to be home.

I think back to the delightful yesterday I had at home. It was so calm, so peaceful, so productive, so alone. I didn't want to come back. I pinch myself to remember: being here today enabled that then. A residual calm clings. I will use it to keep writing and

thinking, stealing silent moments between animal shows and stroller walks.

I push Kai across a dirt path and onto a stretch of pavement. The relief from arm-jiggling pebbles is instant. I enjoy this brief bit of smooth sailing. We glide past the sheep barns, the goat barns, the chickens, and the rabbits en route to the tractor display. Next to the ring where the tractor pulls take place are riding rigs of all shapes and sizes, mostly huge. Kai calls to me to stop and look. I pause and let him out of the stroller. He disappears.

"Kai! Where are you?" He peeks out from behind a haybine and grins. To these machines he is a blade of grass.

I wonder how Geoff is doing and when he will come back. Not yet, I know, but he could surprise me! No, give him his day. I am trying hard to stay open and not count on a given time. I remind myself: he can return whenever he wants. Or, whenever he returns will be the right time for me too.

In this regard, it has been quite a week. My greatest challenge has not come from cow showers or food shortages but from the transitions between time with Geoff and time apart. When both at home, we regularly create a nearly seamless integration between work and parenting, self-care and child-care, coupling and careering. It is our way of recreating the farm family, our homestead for the twenty-first century. We find synergies where most authorities in our culture find choices and tradeoffs.

During fair week, however, our base splits. Not only is one of us away from the farm, but we have no easy way of connecting when the other of us is home. There are no payphones on the fairgrounds. We don't have cell phones. By the time the working, house-caring partner returns, both partners are hot, hungry, tired, and on edge from missing one another. I feel further away from Geoff and more alone than when he was in South America earlier in the month.

Kai moves quickly around the back of a corn harvester. He is so fascinated by these clean and quiet machines. Why? He didn't learn that from me.

It has been a disaster, really. Earlier in the week, when Geoff first left for the day, we had agreed, or I thought we had agreed, that he would be back by 8 p.m. I was so good for the whole day, stretching to enjoy this time with the kids. I was being so flexible, so darn flexible. I was counting on that hour between 8 and 9 p.m., after he returned, to grab a moment alone, go for a walk and gather myself. It didn't turn out as I had hoped.

At 8 p.m., the kids and I had started to wait, piled into the stall of the barn. At 8:15 p.m., we decided to wait for five more minutes before going to buy ice cream. By 8:25 p.m., we were still waiting—in line for cones—with someone standing sentinel by the barn door so as not to miss dad. By 8:45 p.m., we were back in the barn, with Kai on my lap finishing his last drips. At 8:50 p.m., the kids decided to go back to the tent to get ready for bed. I was still waiting. I had gone through the happily expecting stage, the I'm-sure-he's-safe stage, the where-is-he-I'm-worried stage, the appreciate-this-time stage, the frustration stage, and was really, really ready. Every cell stretched towards his approaching presence. *Where is he*?

Finally, he arrived. It was 9 p.m. He was flustered. He had left late and was pulled over by the police for a failing headlight. I was quiet. I couldn't speak. I was so glad to see him but that happiness was locked inside the accumulated hour of waiting, and a long day of walking and waiting. He began to defend himself. I tried to explain what I had hoped would happen. I was disappointed, yes, but I wanted to share the desire at the heart of my disappointment—my yearning to be with him. All he could hear was criticism for how he had failed me. It was our old pattern—familiar, worn, and far from comfortable.

I stayed quiet and tried again, looking for a way in. After another half hour round and round he began to hear my disap-

pointment as a desire for him. I began to hear his defensiveness as a desire to be with me. We met when we realized: *we are already together in the same place. What we want is the same. All we want is to connect, to be connected, to feel the power of our connection! It is because of this impulse that we feel twisted and hurt. We want more with each other, for each other, and from each other. This is good! All good.*

Kai comes up to me and pulls on my hand. He is finished with the tractors. I buckle him back into the stroller.

"Let's go down around by the horse ring and then back to the barn," I suggest. Kai agrees. We walk on. I am breathing down into the sandy ground. Breathing out into the warming air; breathing through the thoughts tumbling through me. Even though Geoff and I had wrestled our way back to intimacy that night, traces of trauma remained. The day after Geoff's late return, it was my turn to go home again. I remember how ecstatic I was.

From the moment I hop out of the car, I am running, ever so delighted to be in my beautiful home with its soft slopes and rich smells and the tuned buzz of cicadas. I cruise back and forth between barn and coop, graining and watering Marvin, graining and watering the chickens, feeding the cats and loading laundry. I dive into my writing, make brownies, knead bread, and compile dinner. I know I am pushing it. I am not giving myself time to move into my body. There is a moment when I have a choice to do yoga or finish my book. I choose the book.

I race back to the fair, determined not to be late, determined not to disappoint anyone, determined to prove that it is possible not to disappoint anyone. I arrive right on time with dinner in hand. No one is waiting for me. No one is ready to eat.

I find Geoff. His eyes are glazed. "The kids are participating in the Junior Farmer Olympics. I have no idea when they'll be done." He is glad to see me, but already I feel his gladness as a downward pull. He is one more responsibility for me to carry. I brace myself. I will

be fine if we can just all go somewhere, sit down, and eat. It's not happening.

I try to tell Geoff about my day, listing all the marvelous tasks I accomplished. Instantly I am awash in a sense of profound inadequacy. I am too much; I am not enough. I am sure he is judging me. I plummet rapidly. No one is appreciating what I have done. Despite my herculean efforts, I am a disappointment and I have nothing left to give.

I take a different tack, spinning amusing anecdotes about my search for the proper grammatical uses of a hyphen. My façade starts to crack. I am withering inside, falling, flailing, and Geoff, dazed by the crowd, isn't there to catch me. I know: I have to move. I have to do something to drop me into my bodily self and wake me up to myself; otherwise I am going to combust like a weight-pulling tractor engine.

"I'm going for a walk," I announce abruptly. "I'll take Kai." At least Geoff will have a baby break. I set out from the show ring. I walk hard, jerking the flimsy stroller across dirt and gravel. Kai doesn't seem to mind. I go as far as I can go in one direction behind the amusement rides where the public doesn't go. I see the truck beds beneath their cardboard pop ups, supporting colorful illusions of solidity. Play world as fake world: the Wizard of Oz exposed. Like me. I push Kai to the far end, turn around, and walk clear to the other side of the fair, behind the tent with large lumbering draft animals.

All along, I am breathing, stepping, sinking into myself. What I am feeling? Why am I so wrapped? Breathe down. Open. In. Through. What is going on here?[6]

Pain. The first thing that opens, big and fierce, is my own pain at being disappointed. No one even cares about what I did. Instantly, the pain doubles and I am the disappointment. It is my fault. I wanted more. Somehow, I am to blame. It's the sting of impossible desire and my response to it, finding me here at the fair.

I keep walking. I am so glad to be walking. I start to feel a light touch of sensory awareness, breathing through my belly and limbs, releasing me from the grip of disappointment.

It occurs to me. This pain is motivating me to do exactly what I most need to do and the one thing that I did not succeed in doing today: take care of myself. Move. Cultivate a sensory awareness of the movement making me.

I walk hard, striding, pushing, and humming with the insight. My impulse to connect with Geoff is impelling me to be present in and with myself. How beautiful! My pace eases. I laugh out loud. Last night I was so disappointed that Geoff was late. Now I am on time and no one cares! All at once, I find it hilarious. I am trying to give the gift that no one wants, unable to give what is most desired: me.

Thinking back to that moment, I marvel again. For when the pain first hit, it registered as nothing but a blaring inadequacy. I had responded as if it were true, rejected the idea, mounted walls of self-defense, and couldn't connect with Geoff across them. *Yet the added pain of being so separated from Geoff had forced me to make another move.* I had to do something, and I knew what. I had to breathe, drop into my body, and bring my senses to life. I was out of touch with a lived, bodily sense of my own movement. I was out of touch with the sources of my freedom and creativity. I wasn't present to myself and couldn't be present with him either.

What amazed me most, however, was realizing that I had been able to tolerate this distance from myself when I was alone. I was able to ignore the discomfort and function superbly, delivering the basics of work and life. But face to face with Geoff, I could no longer ignore *my sensory self.* His presence pulls me into a place of honesty with myself that goes beyond what being alone requires. He awakens my senses, and I cannot *not* sense what my movements are creating in me. When I caught up with Geoff, it was obvious: I had not been honoring my bodily self and, as a result, I had nothing to give.

I return to the ring, ready to share with Geoff what I have been thinking. I am anticipating the joy of connecting with him. He is in the stands watching the final throes of the kids' games. I decide to wait by the gate where Kai can climb the fence. I look at Geoff from time to time,

feeling bursts of pleasure. He isn't looking at me. Does he know I am here?

After the egg toss I look again. He is gone. The games end minutes later and the kids and I work our way over to the barn. I want to find Geoff.

I find him, his face folded in fury. "Why didn't you come sit with me?" he demands.

I pause. It's not quite what I was expecting. I offer, "How about: how was your walk, sweetie?"

He scowls, hesitates, and speaks. "How was your walk?"

"Good," I say with excitement. "I figured things out. I figured it all out."

He isn't impressed. "What you did was violent!" he exclaims. He repeats it. "Violent."

Senses open and breathing from my walk, I hear his pain in his criticism of me. He hurts. We talk. What is so violent for him is the thought that he might be disappointing me yet again, as he had done the night before when he was late. He doesn't want to disappoint me. The thought that he might is one he cannot tolerate. We already know: it is his number one nightmare.

I hone in on his impulse to connect, letting any defensive moves on my part fall away. I remind myself. Geoff is upset because he cares about me. He wants to be there for me. He wants to give to me just as I want to give to him. We keep talking, sharing, and finally, cracks appear. We unearth once again a persistent, mutual impulse to connect at the heart of our struggle.

"The challenge of our relationship is so different than I have been taught to expect," I confess. "It is not about two individuals who must learn to compromise by shaving off the edges of themselves that don't fit. We want the same thing! The challenge is rather for each of us to learn how to be present in ourselves, to our desire for each other, so we can stay open to one another right at that moment where we would rather lash out in ego-fortifying fear. It's about making the love that connects us more real in every moment than our fear of not getting what we want." Geoff smiles. Yes.

Walking then. Walking now. My movement once again is drawing happiness and hope back into bodily range. At the same time, the sun is getting hot and I am looking forward to the shade of the barn. "Come on, Kai. Let's see how Jordan, Jessica, and Kyra are doing."

I think again about the challenge of partnerships. On the one hand, a partnership can heal our childhood wounds.[7] We find and choose a love whom we believe will help us satisfy the desire for more that our caregivers stirred to life in us. On the other hand, this healing is never a question of filling some gap left by caregivers. Rather, a partner helps us heal by quickening an impulse in us to connect with him or her. This impulse chafes against the patterns of sensing and responding to others that we have created to protect ourselves from the sting of impossible desire. We want more—more for ourselves and from ourselves—than our fears of not getting what we want allow.

To succeed in connecting with a partner, then, we need to release our impulse to connect from patterns of sensing and responding that we have created and become in relation to our caregivers; and create new patterns of sensing and responding that affirm this potential partner as a cause of our being. As we do, healing happens, for we are allowing the openness we share with this person to become more real for us than our fears of not getting what we want. We no longer feel the pain of this fear. We are present, instead, to the impulse to connect coursing through our singular sensory selves.

It occurs to me. *Geoff and I aren't two becoming one. We are one becoming two.*[8] Our impulse to connect with one another is demanding that we each become the singular persons we have the potential to be.

As Kai and I near the Youth Barn, I reflect on the difference this shift in experience makes. For one, it recasts the meaning of any apparent conflict in a relationship. If we are two persons trying to become one then, when a conflict arises, we set out to

sacrifice our differences for the sake of the relationship and assuage our separated selves over the losses. We, as individuals, take the hit, and in the process we reinforce patterns of sensation and response that we created with our caregivers to deal with the sting of impossible desire. No healing happens.

However, if we perceive a partnership as a shared love that grows as two persons, then we can sense and respond to such moments differently. We realize that part of who we each are *is* a desire for the other—an impulse to connect with that other as a cause of our being. We want to be who we are with that person, because of that person. As a result, our challenge is to remain present in our singular, bodily selves, in touch with this impulse to connect and then *welcome* whatever tangles erupt as expressions of our desire for more. Such frustration or irritation is guiding us to *move* in relation to our selves and one another in ways that will bring that more into being.

Total presence is not what it initially seems. It is not a static state. It is not a once-and-for-all vow. It does not imply a merging of persons, or even a tell-all attitude. Rather, as we were learning, total presence is an ongoing *practice* in which each person attends to the bodily rhythms of his or her own impulse to connect with the other, and is willing to trust whatever shapes those impulses take as signs pointing out the path to a stronger connection—even if it means going for a walk.

Total presence is not about blurting out every thought we think; it is about being willing to move with whatever our openness to one another is allowing us to think, feel, do, and become. It is about asking, once and again, how the movements I am making in this relationship are making me. *What am I creating? Is it who and what I want to be*?

I am looking forward to Geoff's arrival. I have no idea when he will come or what will happen when he comes. All I know is that, whatever happens, I will be learning what I most want to learn: how to live in the flow of my love for him. For our love

nourishes my singular bloom, enabling me to become who I want to be. That is why I am here, waiting, open, vulnerable at the fair.

Earth Within

12:30 p.m. Kai and I round out our walk and enter the Youth Barn. It's lunchtime. I take the kids behind the barn where there are some more picnic tables, crack the cooler, hand out plates, dole out pasta and bread, peanut butter and jelly, and pour some water to drink. We sit around the table, toes dragging in the dirt, and contemplate what we are doing here. Kai pulls out his bag of trucks and begins plowing gravel into piles.

"What do you think, guys? How is it going?"

"Fine," the three older kids respond, nearly in unison. They are exhausted, and not wanting to admit it. They want to be here with an intensity that I admire but cannot really understand. I surely wouldn't be here without them. Caring for cows is not exactly part of my mission. I am on the farm to dance and write, not process milk and muck!

The kids nourish themselves in silence.

Jordan is finished eating. He wants to go back to the barn to give Daisy some water before the show. She is often reluctant to drink from the large tub used by the other cows. She prefers the sweet water of Hebron Hollow to the chlorinated variety offered here. Jordan is sympathetic. I am too.

I wrap up the leftovers and turn to put them into the cooler just in time to see Kai dump a shovel full of dirt into the cooler as well. I am about to explode when a thought stops me: Kai wants to load the cooler too! Oh Kai! I empty the cooler of all its contents, and ask Jessica and Kyra to carry it to a nearby spigot where they can rinse out the dirt.

How is it that these kids are enabling me? Sitting at the picnic table, waiting for the cooler to return, my belly softly holding a familiar lunch, my experience suddenly shifts.

Perhaps being here at the fair with my children is not so far from my mission after all. Perhaps my kids are enabling me to have the exact experiences I need for my work but would not have sought out myself.

The thought seems absurd. Could it be true? I unroll it. Central to my mission from the beginning has been to cultivate a relationship to the natural world as a source and context for my work. I have wanted whatever I think and write to "remain faithful to the earth" [9]—an earth within and without, in which every moment is connected to every other in a complex, interdependent web of life. I have known this, believed in this, and written about this. But what exactly did I think this relationship with the natural world would entail?

Well, I imagined admiring nature, its wonders and beauty, alone. I imagined appreciating the changing of the seasons, the cycling of the moon, the turning of the day. I imagined walking and dancing in the woods, along the pond, on top of the hills, alone. I imagined writing in any corner of the land I chose to visit. I imagined shopping at the grocery store for milk, eggs, and other provisions.

I didn't imagine spending a week with my kids at the county fair.

Yet our experience at the fair is reminding me how thickly entwined our relationships to the natural world and to one another are. The fair is all about the practices we humans have developed to maximize our survival success; it is about the technologies we have developed to help us save time and energy along the way. But it is also about the relationships we have created with other humans that enable this engagement with the forces of fertility. It poses a question we in the twenty-first century need to ask: what kind of relationships are we creating with one another through our means and methods of relating to the natural world? What kind of relationships do we need to create if we are to support an ecological consciousness?

Jessica and Kyra return with the cooler, a technological invention that is enabling me to feed my family and survive the week closer to the natural world than the fair would allow. Packing it back up, I marvel at my ignorance. The *nature* with which I imagined connecting before I moved here was not nature at all. It was a cultural product—harvested, packaged, marketed, and delivered. It was palatable, useful, and tame enough for an individual to manage. Not anymore.

Nature is the cow my kids wrestle in the ring, the milk she makes for me, and the manure I shovel from her stall. Nature is the food that nourishes, the water that quenches, the air that inspires, and the ground that supports. Nature is the disappointment I feel in relation to my parents, the frustration I feel in relation to my partner, and the worry I fear in relation to my kids. Nature is the wilderness of sensory awareness, and the changes in our bodily selves that awaken us to our impulse to connect with the persons, practices, and elements that nourish our becoming. Nature is the dirt in the cooler.

Here at the fair I am exposed through the bodily desires of my children to a "nature" that is not some romantic ideal, but a reality we are creating in every moment of our lives, in everything we do. With every breath, beat, pulse, and step, as we relate to the elements around us and within us, we participate in the ongoing act of creation. *We are nature too.* It is what we tend to forget when we think of ourselves as individuals and set out to connect with the natural world as if it existed out there, apart from us. We are always already connected, always already participating in the rhythms of our bodily becoming, the rhythms of creation. The question is not whether but how. *What are we creating?*

Can you drink milk straight from the teat? Can you lift a warm egg out from under a hen and crack it over the pan? Can you look the animal you eat in the eye before saying goodbye? Can you open to the significant others in your life and embrace them as causes of your being?

1:45 p.m. Jordan's class is finally about to begin. He is in his whites, ready to go. His golden hair spills down over his ears, closing like curtains around his temples. His Red Sox hat rests on top until the last possible moment.

Daisy is the calmest of the three cows, the mature mom. It is rather ironic that Jordan will be leading her, as he is the strongest of the three cow show-ers. In the ring, he stands with ease and Daisy does too. I am sitting on the bleachers, thankfully in the shade, watching. Daisy is the only cow in her class this year, another irony. A medal for Jordan.

Daisy, Precious, and Dandi are back in their stalls, enjoying a peaceful afternoon of munching and slurping. The kids are hanging out, hanging on the stall bars, chatting with friends. What's next for me?

The afternoon simmers in the heat. The sound of fans whirring gives the barn the feel of an airplane hangar. The halo of yesterday's work is wearing off and I am getting ready for some time to myself. I want time to think, to go deep, to open to the life-giving creative flow somewhere in me. Maybe Geoff will be back soon.

6:30 p.m. Geoff arrives, dinner in hand. I smile. He has containers of pasta and steamed broccoli to go with the bread and cheese and salad we have in the clean cooler. He has tempeh and bananas especially for me. We sit out back on the picnic table we now call ours, and count down the hours until the end of the fair.

8:30 p.m. Jessica and Kyra are working at the 4H Food Booth tonight. They will be there until 9 or so. Jordan decides that he wants to spend his last evening in the barn. Geoff and I stroll over to watch the girls at work. Kyra can barely see over the counter, yet she bustles back and forth with purpose, filling cups of lemonade and handing out potato chips. When we place an order, she delivers it with a priceless grin. *Keep the change.*

9:30 p.m. We are all back in the barn for a final cow check. The beasts have clean beds, plenty of hay, and are lying calmly in their stalls. We tidy up the show box and say goodnight.

10 p.m. Jordan, Jessica, and Kyra are sound asleep. Geoff and I snuggle into our sleeping bags. Night-bird Kai crawls on top of us, under, around, and through. The boy never nods, so Geoff and I talk. What a week. How was it possible for us to trigger so many old patterns? Why has it been so hard to stay connected?

Geoff doesn't have an answer. I don't either, but many things are clear. We see how far we have come in learning how to live in the spaces opened up in us and between us by our impulse to connect with one another. We feel how we are recreating, at a deep sensory level, the patterns of perceiving and responding that we have each harbored for years as our primary defense against the sting of impossible desire. We know too that in this process of recreating our relationships with caregivers and each other, our kids are playing a vital, enabling role. We are giving our kids this week at the fair; they are giving us the opportunity to be here with them, learning how to live in love with them, each other, and the natural world. The perfect present.

We wrap ourselves together, raw, humble, and happy to be doing the good work. As for the rest, we will figure out it out tomorrow, at home.

4

Egg Hunt

[T]he highest affirmation, born of fullness, of overfullness, a Yes-saying without reservation, even to suffering, even to guilt, even to everything that is questionable and strange in existence. –Friedrich Nietzsche[1]

September 2008. "Where are the eggs?" I ask Kyra for the second time. I am not sure whether she hasn't heard me, or doesn't want to hear me. "The eggs?" I repeat.

She shrugs. Kyra is in charge of the chicken chores these days, and for all of her six, nearly-seven years, she does a terrific job. She gives our four laying hens, one rooster, and one duck scraps and grain twice a day. She changes their water and collects the

eggs. Lately, there haven't been any.

"Did you check the coop?"

She nods.

"Did you check the barn? Behind the cat carrier? The hay loft?"

She shakes her head, looking a bit forlorn.

"I'm not mad, Kyra, really. You are fine and doing a great job. I just want to find those eggs! That is why we have those hens, for their eggs! And now we have none!"

Once content to lay their eggs in the boxes we arranged in their own cozy coop, the hens have decided that they need to lay elsewhere. They are undoubtedly searching for the best nest. The only problem is that we have no idea where that nest is. The quality they prize most seems to be secrecy. Unless we want to spend the day tailing chickens, the nest will be hard to find.

Are the hens seeking to protect their precious orbs from us, the voracious egg-eaters? If they spent any time sitting on the eggs, I might think so, but they don't. They simply sequester the eggs, returning to the same spot to lay another, until the pile of rotten treasures prompts them to find a new nest. Why do they care whether or not we gather them?

I vow to go looking for eggs once I have finished cleaning up the breakfast mess.

Hide and seek anyone?

This is not our first egg hunt. Before the horse or the cow, the cats or the duck, there were the hens—or rather, the hen and her eggs.[2] In our first month here, a petite Bantam hen arrived along with the four eggs on which she was determined to sit, gifts of Farmer Harold. The hen had not laid the eggs. Harold had given her fertilized eggs laid by the larger laying hens who had been pecking her down the order. She did not seem to mind. Whatever maternal switch there is inside of her had flipped and she knew: she had to sit. She would raise her tormentors' babes. She couldn't have been happier. Gorgeously feathered, orange-

flecked and red-brown, she fluffed her small appendages into a warm blanket that covered every curve. Twenty-one days at her 100 degrees and we would have chicks. The kids named her Amber.

Since then we have had hens and roosters, though not the same ones. Our bird count has risen and fallen like the numbers on a dieter's scale, subject to the hunger of various predators: weasel, fox, rat, and the metal monsters cruising by along the slim black strip of hard ground in front of our house. Along the way, we have learned life lessons and death lessons, and blazed trails through the wilderness of our barnyard.

We have also learned to play hide and seek. The first time our hens hid their eggs, it took us over a month to find the nest, by then packed with frozen ovals. The nest had been resting a mere fifty yards from the coop, right under our noses. We found it just in time for Easter.

Where is it this time?

I finish the kitchen chores and head out to the coop. Sometimes the eggs can be tucked under the hay in a corner, or alongside the outer edge of the nesting boxes. As I enter the coop, a familiar smell stands to meet me. Chickens poop all the time and all over the place. Give them a clean room with sweet smelling hay and in a matter of days they will transform it into a smelly hovel. When released into the garden, this particular trait is a virtue of the highest order. Chicken manure is a boon to growing plants. The chickens even eat the pesky insects that compete with us for those plants' fruits. For this reason, we let our chickens roam around the yard during the day. Still, they don't stop pooping at night. This coop needs cleaning. As fastidious as she is, Kyra never seems to mention it.

The lingering smell reminds me of the time my parents stayed at the farm for four days to take care of the three older kids while Geoff, Kai, and I traveled north for a scholarly conference in Banff, a resort town tucked amidst the Canadian

Rockies. I was to receive an award for an article I had written. While we were away, the chicken scene impressed my father. He pulled out our book on barnyard animal care and used a highlighter to mark the sections that deal with using antiseptic wash and a scrub brush to clean a chicken coop. He bought the birds a new water feeder, so the water would not spill into a fetid manure mess. He admonished the kids with stories from the book about possible infection and harm to animals and humans. He also rounded up a spare tire to hold our heifer's tipsy water bucket in place, purchased orange plastic fencing to hold her in, and highlighted the book sections on the danger of flies. He was right, of course.

Geoff and I returned from Banff shrouded in a honeymoon halo, so wrapped in love that we were daring to consider conceiving a fifth child. ("Perhaps we should remain open to the arc of our fertility?" Geoff had asked, as we walked under dark green firs down a deep slope towards a dusky blue glacial pond.) Hitting me in this glorious state, my father's good words and actions took on a life of their own. They entered my consciousness effortlessly and began to burn. While I was happy to see my parents engaged in farm life and grateful for the new supplies, I could not shake the shrill internal shriek. *You are not enough! You are not doing enough! You can't clean the coop, de-fly the cow, or care for your kids.* How could I even imagine wanting more?

For days after my parents left, I suffered. I couldn't find a way to make the same experience shift from disappointment to gratitude that I had managed to find months before, around the birthday gift-giving impasse. I lurched to and fro, shifted and shafted, unable to dislodge the piercing rays of my parents' gaze. I knew I should be experiencing my life through my eyes, but I couldn't make it happen. I was furious with myself for being so weak. I felt so trapped, so exposed, so inadequate. I railed against myself in anger. *Why can't I feel gratitude to my parents for awakening in me a desire for more than they can provide? Why can't I*

feel any appreciation of my incalculable debt to them for quickening my impulse to connect? What is wrong with me?

A small voice responded: *You must have something more to learn.*

I breathe through the memory, as I scour the corners of the coop and toe the hay looking for telltale flashes of tan. Nothing. Kyra was right. No eggs anywhere. Our duck, Pikey, is tucked into her nesting box. She often lays one big white egg. I am looking for several brown ones. I vow to return that afternoon when all the kids are home. They will help me clean, if not by lifting a shovel, then at least by cheering me on for doing what they should be doing but don't really want to do. We will do it, in this way at least, together.

Outside of the coop, the chickens are walking around, pecking at the ground here and there. I smile. I never imagined that I would get so much pleasure from having chickens. Like many avian creatures, they have a quick jerky movement that reminds me of a type-A train conductor prodding people this way and that. They always seem so worried. One hen's large lidless eyes, ringed with gold, stare intently at me as she cocks her head to size me up. The red comb on her head wobbles a bit as she turns back again to continue pecking at the ground.

What most intrigues me, however, are the chicken's legs—not the edible part, but the scrawny spindles that stick like stilts from beneath their well-puffed rounds. While a chicken's body is small and bony, all joints and ribs, the feathers grant this illusion of fluffy fullness. A seemingly heavy load teeters on fragile twigs. To maintain bird balance, the chickens launch their sturdy necks and small heads forward and back with the rhythm of their gait. Watching one of the hens run in a toe-tapping, neck-pumping, breast-thrusting, tail-wagging, zigzagging burst of color, I laugh.

I stroll into the barn where the hens have laid before and peer into a small niche where I know they like to sit. One egg appears

before my eyes, small and brown, a slight wobble in the middle. It is still warm. There should be at least two, but for now I shall settle for one. It is a beauty. I carry it inside.

A warm egg. It is smooth and round, pointed at one end and blunt at the other, perfectly shaped to enter the world and yield to forces of life growing through it. Within this protective shell, a bodily being, liquid, golden and clear, if hummed and warmed by a feathered friend, can become something other than it is. It can take shape, burst free of what has enabled it to be, and unfold, leaving behind the shards of its former self.

An egg exists to become something else. It consumes itself from within, surrendering to the life that it is becoming. An egg is what it is by overcoming itself—even when I eat it.[3]

I set the egg carefully in the refrigerator and return to my study. Thinking back to that summer of 2006, after our trip to Banff, I sigh. I did find what I needed to shift my experience of my parents to a life-enabling gratitude, but not for another six months. It wasn't until a colleague, mentor, and friend of mine invited me back to Boston for a meeting that I learned what was preventing me from doing so. What was it?

I lie down on the floor, pull out my journal, pick up a pen, and begin to write.

Back to Boston. It was my first time returning since our move a year and a half earlier. I did not want to go. I felt as if I was ripping out the fragile roots I had been working so hard to grow. At the same time, I didn't want to say no. I left Kai with Geoff and piled my three older children into the car as human shields, comfort objects, and fellow transplants. Half-hour shy of my destination, I dropped the kids at my parents' house, knowing how happy my parents would be to have them for a couple of days.

While in town, sleeping in a hotel across the street from the Harvard office where I had worked for six years before moving to the farm, I had a dream that soon cracked open to reveal a balled up desire holding me back—and ready to grow.[4]

The Green Dream

December 2006. I am watching this woman, a stuntwoman of sorts. She is preparing to jump off a high, grey-rocked cliff with a sheer face that plunges down into bright green water. The cliff is at the edge of a continent. The water is a piece of the ocean, an emerald pool somewhat enclosed by long arms of land, yet open to an endless horizon. She will leap off the cliff, fly through the air, and land at the far end of a peninsula that juts out into the water for nearly as far as the cliff is tall. It is not an easy feat.

Suddenly launched, her shape cuts across the sky. She is small and lithe, muscular and strong, wrapped in a strapless bathing suit with a V-cut neck that is green like the water. Her dark hair is slick and tied. She is Madame X aloft. Her right leg is bent under, her knee pointing forth like an arrow. Her left leg is outstretched behind her, pointing back towards the cliff. Her arms are in reverse, left bent and right outstretched. Her chin is tucked. I can't see her face. Graceful and athletic, she holds her position firmly as she slices through space.

The crowd gathered to watch is large, rapt, and silent as she soars. A bird! A plane! She plummets toward the water and enters cleanly, head first, with a small double splash. The crowd explodes in rousing cheers of relief. They are giddy with pleasure at the thrill she provides. They crave the worry, the anticipation, and the flush of success, however vicarious. She will not disappoint them. She doesn't.

I am watching too, from high above. Below the water, I see her unfold and swim quickly to the surface. As she raises her hand to wave to the crowd, a cramp doubles her over in pain. Her belly! It must be an air bubble. She tries to work it out. She fixes her grin while stroking gently towards the dock at the end of the peninsula.

She waves again. The pain stabs again. She can't bear it. She won't bear it. She grits her teeth and drives herself down into the water as hard and as fast as she can.

I see her sleek, torpedo self plunging, then slowing. She readies for her inevitable return to the surface. As she bends her neck upward, a large white face, somewhat shark-like, with huge red eyes and a round gaping mouth, leers up in front of her. She screams. Everything goes black.

She wakes up in a white room, in a white bed, wrapped in a white gown. Her head is slightly raised. She is tubed and tied. The face of a masked doctor appears before her, bearing no small resemblance to the shark. She is resentful, angry, and unapologetic. She feels fine. She wants to get out and go home. Watching her I know: she is me.

The effort to write down the dream makes me hungry. It is time for a snack. I get up from the floor and head into the kitchen. I grasp our smallest frying pan and the egg I found this morning, now cool in my palm. I turn on the stove and prepare to crack the egg.

As I lower my arm towards the pan's edge, a slight tremor passes through me. It always does. What is inside? Smashing this piece of life, this work of art, seems so violent.

Shell meets metal and shatters into pieces that cling together, barely held by a thin inner skin. The yellow orb slides out onto the pan. Half of a globe, an island of gold, rises above the whitening sea. Subject to the heat, the clear ring bubbles and crisps. The yolk gels. I flip the egg and load the top with cheddar cheese. I wait until the fluid congeals into a firm, teeth-resisting thickness. I want something to chew on, something that will land inside of me and bring me back to writing life.

Ever since the miscarriage this summer I have craved a mid-morning egg. Why? Is it to make up for the one I lost? Even though I prayed mightily that my golden nest of a uterus would hold, it didn't. The fertile egg cracked and slipped out of its cozy tissue web. Gone. Without me.

A fifth child. This bodily self my parents gave me wants another baby. Still. My mother thinks that five is too many. She

has told me so several times. She cannot imagine it. I can.

Back at my desk, I reflect on the green dream and how surprisingly significant it became to me. In those nighttime images, I found a haven for my growing gratitude as well as the nourishment I needed to flex free of my sting-safe shell.

A few days after dreaming the dream, at home again, I began to write about it. What snared my attention was the woman's response to her post-dive cramp. She was angry with herself, I thought, bent on cracking herself open against the hard edge of her pain. She was rebelling against that pain, turning the full force of her will against the felt limits of her bodily self, determined to win. She would prevail over her bodily self. She would do it for the crowd. She would not disappoint. I *knew* the feeling. It was my own response to the sting of impossible desire.

In the weeks following, however, as I wrote about the dream some more, its meaning morphed. Pushing pen across page pulled new perspectives into view. I saw.

She loves the water! Her plunge is not directed against her bodily self. It is a move towards healing. She loves being in the water; she loves being under the water. Under the water she is weightless in the embrace of its whole-healing deep green. The water allows her to disappear from the crowd and silence its roar. Diving down, her bodily self, almost in spite of her, is seeking the health and well-being beneath her pain. She is diving to find herself.

Perhaps. The thought provoked another question. Then why the cramp? What is causing her so much pain?

I kept writing, wanting to know.

It happens when she waves. It happens after she has completed her dare-devil, death-defying act of precision and grace. Safe in the water, she is in control. She has proven so beyond a doubt for herself and the crowd. Yet this control is what is causing her self-doubling pain. For she knows: it is an illusion.

Wrapped in her fat-free skin, pretending to fly, she knows: she is merely falling. She is surrendering to forces that pull her down. She is

falling for the crowd. It is why they love her. The crowd loves her for her mastery over her own body that she leads them to believe they too can have. She is enacting what they do daily in order to survive—holding themselves immobile, stifling their vital energies, free-falling through life, while making it seem that she and they are flying and in control. She holds herself hard for herself and for them.

Recognition exploded. *They don't really love her. They don't really care about her. They only care about the pleasure that she allows them to feel.*

My experience of the dream shifted. What seemed obvious, no longer was. I realized that *the cramp was a gift.* As painful as it seemed, the woman's cramp was a call from her deep green silent, silenced self, the one who really could fly. The cramp was calling her to dive far deeper than the roar of the crowd could penetrate. It was calling her to find the pleasures of honoring and moving with the rhythms of her own bodily becoming.

I breathed through this realization. The dream wasn't about a self-harming violence after all. Still, I wanted to know. Why does she dive so hard? If the cramp is a gift, why does she seem to reject it?

As I continued to write, feelings bubbled up between the lines of the page. I felt her fear. *She tries to stay and wave because she is afraid that if she reveals her weakness, the crowd will hate her. They will reject her, and if they do, where will she be? Who will she be? What will she do? The crowd has given her a task, a challenge, a goal, a reason for being, and a sure path to affirmation. As limited as it might be, the "love" of the crowd is the only love she knows.*

It was as if a shell cracked open before me, revealing a knot of tangled desires.

She plunges hard because she wants more. She wants to be free from the crowd and the illusion it requires she maintain. Yet, at the same time, she wants to be the masterful self that the crowd has enabled her to believe she is.

She feels the bind: to lose the love of the crowd would be to lose the

confidence and strength that funds her desire to find her freedom from its claims on her life.

I ached with empathy at her conflict; I looked beyond. The cramp-fleeing plunge was not what mattered most. The monster was. I decided to try to write myself back into the dream to learn more.

Just as she is about to return to the surface of the water, the woman sees a face in the deep, the face of the deep. She passes out. I wake with her on the bed and remember. In the instant after taking that fear-driven underwater breath, she realized that the monster was not scary after all. Its eyes were cheerful, its terrifying leer a friendly laugh. The monster was welcoming her home.

She wants to return. She wants to go back to the dock alone and dive again, head first, but she is stuck in a hospital bed. Her displeasure and resentment are palpable. The doctor hovering over her knows nothing of who she is or what she needs in order to heal. He does not see her. He is one of the crowd. His care gives her wounding a false meaning: she "hurt herself." It is not like that. She hurts because she wants more of the connection with her own sensory self that diving for the crowd has helped her to feel as hers. She wants to break the illusion that has protected her embryonic life and grow through it.

Wrapped in her white bed, she hears the call. She must hunt for her own bodily truth, creativity, and well-being. Her cramp is pointing the way. She is ready to face her fears of losing the crowd, and laugh.

Which comes first: the chicken or the egg? Which comes first: the voices of those who judge us, or our habits of critically judging ourselves? The chicken lays an egg; the egg becomes a chicken. The voices we hear turning against us become us. Soon, we hear a judge in every voice. How do we learn to hear and sense and respond to ourselves differently? How do we learn to welcome the monster who is calling us home?

The eaten egg settles in my belly and dissolves, the perfect protein. Its presence in me, light and firm, buoys me on. Nutritionists advise people to restrict their egg consumption to

two or three a week. It is the cholesterol, they say. Just wait, however. Soon scientists will find that some chemical in the egg helps metabolize the digestion of its fats, putting those fats into practice not plaque. An egg is pure potential, fully formed. Life complete; life becoming itself.

A Stretched, Stretching Self

I keep writing and remembering. In the wake of the green dream, I looked for the move I could make to help silence the crowd and set me firmly on the path of overcoming my attachment to it. While I could see how my patterns of sensing and responding to the sting of impossible desire were cramping my style, I remained rippled with discontent, unable to dissolve a sense of apprehension at my parents' disapproval. Why? Where was the visceral hook holding me fast to these old patterns?

Less than a month after the dream, I finally took my discomfort to the yoga mat.

January 2007. I begin. After an initial warm up on the floor, I rise for the sun salutation. One cycle, two cycles. On the next pass, as I bend my head back towards the sky, a sweep of sensation arcs through my bodily space. A clearing clears, across my torso, shoulder to shoulder, down the front and back of my abdomen to my belly button, nipples to navel, forming a long, oblong rectangle. The space is pure, empty, and instantly, I know: this is the space of self, of my self, a self that existed long before my parents walked this planet and will continue to exist long after they die.

In quiet ecstasy, as I move through the postures, revelations move through me. *There is a part of me that my parents have never touched and can never touch, a part of me that extends through them, beyond them, carried by them, from generations preceding them. I existed before being born. I will exist after I die.*

It is a parent-free part of me. A stretched, stretching sensory self. Deeply green.

More thoughts follow. *I chose to come into the world through my parents.*

The idea is challenging, though I recognize its trace. It is a Nietzschean call to will backwards and say yes to everything that has enabled me to be in this time and place.[5] Could I take the cue and make this move saying: yes, I willed it. I willed my birth in this time and place? I consider the idea.

Perhaps I chose to be born to these parents because I knew that they would be the crowd whose demands would enable, and even force me, to plunge into my sensory self and discover this space of my own connection to a world wide web of others stretching before and after me in space and time. I couldn't breathe in the life my parents wanted for me. I couldn't eat. I tried. I waved. I felt the cramp. I also felt their love for me. I heard the cheers. I wanted more. I had to dive.

I move from my standing postures to the floor. Breathing down into the ground, I find the place where my disappointment and fear—those sticky shards of my shell—still attach. I feel the sharp edges and the fragile membrane skin.

Even though I know I want my freedom from the self my parents have helped me to be, I still want to connect with them; and my impulse to connect is still expressing itself as a desire to do what I think will please them. *I love them!* I want love from them! I want to give to them! I tremble when I imagine their disappointment. So what do I do with this impulse to connect? Moving into gratitude, because it opens me to them as causes of my being, seems to make that impulse to please them all the stronger, and my disappointment at not doing so that much more acute!

I breathe back into the space of my eternally extended, stretched and stretching self, calling it into sensory awareness. It is what I want, who I am. I fill it with my attention. This self is safe. This self is big. I inherited this self through my parents and because of my parents. But I did not inherit it for my parents.

My experience shifts once again.

I love my parents when I honor this gift they have given me—the gift of my bodily self. I love them when I continue the good work of nurture they began along the trajectories of unmet desire that they helped me to discover. I love them when I create the relationships that will support me in becoming who I have the potential to be, including a relationship of life-enabling distance with them.

In that session, I made the shift I had been wanting to make for six months; or rather, the shift happened in me. The yoga moves coaxed into consciousness a sensory space of self that gratitude quickly filled. The physical moves enabled emotional and mental ones. I knew that I would be able to find my way to this place of gratitude again, sooner and more easily than before. I rehearsed a word-path to it anyway.

When my parents' doubt, disapproval, or disappointment threaten to topple my sense of well-being, I can remember: I love my parents when I receive the gift of this bodily self that they have given me in all its cresting currents and infinite reach; I love my parents when I continue the good work of nurturing myself that they began.

I pondered the implications. What if becoming an adult means cracking open to acknowledge that in our innermost bodily selves, we are *not* individuals first? What if it means learning how to open with gratitude to our caregivers *because* they have no idea of what they have given us? What if it means learning to live in the tension of wanting love from them even as we act in ways we know they will not understand or appreciate, and doing so *because* we have received enough love from them to know that we want more?

I look out the window and watch as the chickens parade by my study: all four hens and the white cocky-tailed rooster. Pikey must be in her box. Did I miss the egg-making moment? Perhaps the hens are hiding the nest to protest Kyra's egg-hatching efforts. Several weeks ago Kyra was at her wits' end. She really wanted chicks or ducklings. Either would do. She wanted soft fluff-ball baby birds and lots of them. For days in a

row, she tried to get one of the hens to sit. She would lock a hen in the coop for the day with a nest full of eggs and cross her fingers. Every time, when Kyra went to open the door, the hen was nowhere near the nest, wanting nothing to do with anything maternal, and would quickly hop out of the coop to join her band of swinging singles.

I was not surprised. These girlfriend hens had spent the first months of their lives together in a bathtub at a local farm. After a traumatic encounter with a dog, they had been set apart from the flock, left with intact bodies but shortened wings. We adopted all four, saving then from their longer-winged comrades who would have demoted them to the bottom rungs of the pecking order.

Ever since arriving, these four have moved together in a clump, to the left, to the right, and away from any human or animal who tries to approach, including our rooster, Brooster. Brooster arrived sometime after the hens, another hand-me-down from Farmer Harold. Scrawny and nervous, he would crow constantly, often while chasing the hens. Since the hens would have nothing to do with him, however, he resigned himself to traveling with our duck. While the four girls giggled and fussed, Brooster and Pikey stuck together, pecking and feeding. Brooster even climbed on Pikey's back to mate, much to her delight or dismay. I was never quite sure.

When none of the hens would sit, Kyra was despondent, but not for long. About a week ago, she went into the coop and there was Pikey, slunk down in a nesting box, sitting on eggs. The eggs weren't hers, they came from the hens, but Pikey didn't seem to care, and neither did the hens. After hanging out with Brooster for so long, Pikey must have come to the conclusion that she is a hen too.

Kyra was delighted. Me too. Pikey to the rescue! Our duck was sitting on chicken eggs. Kyra would get her babes. What would we call them? Dickens? Chucks?

Now that I think about it, it was about the time Pikey began sitting that the hen eggs began disappearing. I can understand why Pikey is no longer laying. Her sitting switch has flipped. Her body changed overnight from ovoid producer to ovoid warmer. But the other hens—where are their eggs? Were they experiencing some kind of non-laying empathy? The kids are hooked on recipes I have concocted requiring many eggs and much milk! Besides, I need my daily fix. We have to find those eggs.

My daily fix. At the thought, a feeling of desire blazes through my sensory self, doubling me over. A fifth child. I do want one. As the cramp of emotion subsides, I marvel at the tenacity of this returning idea. It won't let me go. I will be looking around the kitchen when words flash: *there is someone missing*. I will be walking down our mountain, stumble and catch myself, knowing: *a fifth child wants to come*. I will be tucking in the sheets, tidying the pillows, and hear an inner voice loud and clear: *I want a fifth child.*

At the same time, I resist the idea. I cannot say yes. But why? Don't I want to hatch another egg? I do!

As I turn back to my writing, the green dream reenters my mind and I see. *It is the crowd again*. The voices screaming no in my head are voices of the crowd. I am afraid that if I say yes to this desire that wells within me, the crowd will judge me for wanting too much, having too much, being too much and never enough. Yet when I listen to them rather than my own desire for more, I feel the cramp. I try to fight the cramp into submission with my will, waving and smiling, but it doesn't work.

I breathe through the insight. I am fighting my own desire for another child because by some filament of a membrane, I am still attached to the love of a crowd that I don't want to lose. Yet as soon as I try to resist my desire, in order to please the crowd, I reinforce the felt sense of myself as an individual, still smarting from the sting of impossible desire.

The coast looms clear. I see the challenge. It is right here, in the swell of my desire for a fifth child, that I am going to have to put my yoga-stirred sensory self to work. The bodily self my parents have given me wants another child. The more I open in gratitude to them for stirring in me a desire for more than they can provide, and the more of my bodily self I let live, the more strongly I want this child, and the more I fear their criticism.

Somehow, then, I need to make a move that will enable me to feel gratitude to them—not just in general—but for this particular desire that puts me at odds with what they want for me.

It is not enough to be able to think that I am loving my parents when I honor this bodily self they have given me. I want to feel it.

How do I embrace this desire of mine, anticipating their disapproval and disappointment, without balling up once again in a self-protecting, self-annihilating fear?

What other moves are there to make?

Radical Self-Affirmation

I am restless. It is time to get up and move around. I walk outside into bright sunlight. Since I have been writing about the chickens, I decide to visit them again. This time I am determined to tell our four hens apart. To the kids, they are Roxanna, Ginger, Streak, and Featherwhite, and have been since the day they arrived nearly five months ago. To me, they all look the same: they are prime layers, a cross between Rhode Island Red and White Rock. Their red bodies are flecked with a soft white that bursts open in a fan of tail feathers. Until now, I have chalked my lack of discernment up to what Geoff and I fondly call CSD: cumulative sleep deprivation. The excuse is wearing thin.

On the way to the coop I ask myself, why I am doing this—why does it matter whether or not I know their names? They are chickens! Well, I reason, it is for my daughters. When one hen escapes or runs across the road, I need to know which girl to call to bring the bird back. For Roxanna, I call Jessica. For Streak,

Kyra. On the other hand, I could just call Kai. He is a terrific hen-catcher. As he is just their size, they don't run away from him. He can get closer than the rest of us, which he does, before grabbing a fistful of tail feathers and holding on tight. He reels the hen in and scoops his catch into his arms. "I do it self, Mommy!"

Or maybe I am making this effort as a sign of gratitude to the hens for their egg-laying favors. The least I can do is thank them individually. If I do, maybe they won't be so determined to hide their eggs from me.

I approach the quadruplets and watch carefully. I loved pattern games as a kid. This should be fun, right? The kids have told me many times where to look; I have just never been able to see what is so obvious to them.

First, I look for the hen with an all-orange neck. The kids, thoughtfully, named her Ginger. I see her! OK, next. The remaining three, I am convinced, are carbon copies of one another. Brooking doubt, I look again. OK, it does seem that one of them might have a larger crown, but which? They are moving around one another, in and out. I keep getting confused about which one I am observing. Suddenly I see it: a larger, floppier, redder crown. That must be Roxanna. *Good*! I encourage myself, trying to keep the two I have identified clear in my mind and apart from the remaining two. I focus again. I look to the back ends of this pair and yes, just as the girls said, one is whiter. She must be Featherwhite, which means the final hen is Streak!

A feeling of triumph carries me along. I did it!

All at once I feel a rush of affection for these birds. What great birds! I like them much more than I had moments before when I felt limited by my inability to tell them apart. Sure, I need to have them all together in order to make the distinguishing comparisons, but I can! I like them! The thought shimmers: I like them because I like myself for being able to see their nuances. I like them because they are

giving me a momentary experience of moving beyond my own limits, and opening a new sense of myself. I can be a bird observer too.

I trip into the house and trumpet my success to my smiling daughters.

"I did it! Ginger has the orangest neck; Roxanna has the reddest comb; Featherwhite has the whitest butt; and Streak has none of the above!" My pride dims a bit as I realize that the words I have just uttered are the very same words that Jessica and Kyra have been spoon-feeding me for the past few months. The girls nod appreciatively.

As I pad back to my desk, I think about Kyra's attachment to the hens. I understand it now. She has a fierce desire for more and I want her to have what she wants. At the same time, I feel a familiar cramp. I am her caregiver. If she wants more, then there will be moments when she wants that more from me when I cannot give her what she wants, and not just because of CSD.

It has happened before. In fact, it was an encounter with her that gave me the push I needed to find the move to make that would land me in gratitude towards my parents for any desire that exceeds their sense of enough. Kyra was the catalyst.

I think back to that day. It was in the middle of January 2007, over a month after the green dream. Geoff was away at a yearly music convention. Dinner was over, the kitchen a mess. Every kid needed Mom; Mom needed Dad. Kai wanted to nurse. Jordan wanted to sit on one side; Jessica was on the other.

Kyra piped up, "I want to sit next to Mommy too!"

As Kyra finished her words, in the tiniest fraction of a moment, I hit an invisible limit and cracked. I was instantly awash in despair. I was trying to be everything to everyone and I was failing. A beastly howl of frustration escaped from my throat, freezing every child in his or her tracks. The roar left me moaning. "I am going to give up! I just can't do it!"

Jessica, always calm in moments of other people's distress, responded: "What would you do if you gave up? Where would you go?"

"Nowhere," I mumbled.

"Courage, Mom!" She exclaimed. "Faith! Courage! Hope!"

I smiled reluctantly. Where did she get that optimism? From me?

I arranged myself to allow Kyra to sit near. Then after a few minutes, I rallied everyone to tackle the kitchen mess together.

The eruption was over as quickly as it came, but it left its tracks in my heart. The visceral feeling of hitting such a limit in my ability to give causes me an acute curdling pain. My inner flesh rolls and cramps. Every tender, vulnerable point in my sensory self that I have ever felt in my life flares red. I hate myself for feeling so inadequate, so unable to deal. I am sure I will explode. I wish I would. I don't.

Later that night, while lying in bed trying to heal my scratches, I asked myself the question: Why does it hurt so much when I reach a sense of limit?

I wait with the question, pulling awareness in with my breath and letting it go. Releasing the length of my sensory self into the comforting hold of our soft futon, I soon recognize the print of my emotional ache. Of course. It is the sting of impossible desire. As soon as I feel a limit in my ability to give to my kids, I am convinced that I cannot have what I want. I cannot give what I want. I want what will not be. My kids are living proof.

I see the irony. It is my kids who are not getting what they want, not me!

Even so, the feeling is raw, pulsing. I keep breathing, looking to the ceiling and deep inside myself, waiting to feel an impulse for another move to make. I can't stay here. It hurts too much.

A whisper of a thought appears. I hear the roar of the crowd. Again. This time it isn't my parents. It's my kids. I am afraid that I will disappoint them (so I roar in their faces?!). I am afraid that if I disappoint

them, they will no longer love me. Who could blame them? I am surely woefully inadequate, a disappointment to all.

As I watch, the cramp of fear shades into visceral patterns of pleasure-denying protection, tried and true—my vain efforts to manage the pain of this inner wrench. I see myself clamping down any sensory source—no feeling, no pain. I hear familiar words: I am too fat. I don't deserve to eat, or be touched. I am suddenly surrounded by a ring of monsters whose ugly faces leer at me. I grit my teeth, fix my grin, and keep waving, waiting for the cramp to subside. It doesn't.

As I stayed with the discomfort, the shape of the bind appeared: I want to please my kids. I want them to love me. When what they want is me and I cannot deliver, my own desire that they get what they want triggers the sting of impossible desire. I feel the cramp and curl into myself, suddenly unable to give anything to anyone.

What am I supposed to do? I wondered. *How can I sense and respond to my own sense of limit in a way that lets me stay connected with my kids?*

I waited, open, inviting. Words rushed forth from who knows where in a crescendo chorus. *I am OK. Who I am is OK. What I want is OK. I am OK.*

The words bounced on the surfaces of my self and faded away. I invited them again. They sank in a bit. My love for my kids pushed me on.

I am OK, even at my limits. When I hit a limit, I don't have to turn against myself. Ever. I just don't. I am OK. Really? I could barely believe it, but I could feel it. Relief rushed through me and splinters of frustration lodged in my flesh slipped out into its healing flow.

It was a moment of radical self-affirmation, and as it happened, I saw a sight that astounded me. It was the path of my pain, and it was not really about my kids or caregivers at all. The cramp I felt when hitting a limit led straight to Geoff.

It was as if the missing piece of a treasure map fell into place.

What do I fear most? Losing Geoff's love. Why? Because somehow I know: it is his love that has the potential to liberate me from the crowd. It is the love I feel from him, the love I feel for him, the love I share with him that enables me to know and be a self that touches and releases my own desire for more along the trajectories of unmet yearning my parents helped me discover. It is with him that I conceived these beautiful bodily selves that extend my being and bring me so much joy. I want to be the self, the partner, the person, the mother that being with him brings forth in me.

As soon as I open to this possibility, however, past patterns bite. *What if I am too much and not enough... for him*? I respond to my own frissons of fear by lumping Geoff in with the rest of the crowd and running away to fortify my individual self. *What if I fail to perform the daredevil acts that will secure his faithfulness*? The mere thought is enough to turn me against myself in a blind fury that shuts down my sense of anything but the pain.

Lying there, warmed by the golden glow of the nightlight, I searched in my sensory self for a way through. *What other moves are possible*? Gently pressing against the fear, I dove deep into my sea green self, ready to face down the monster. Words rushed in.

I am OK, and if I am not good enough for Geoff, if he isn't getting what he needs, then he can choose to leave. That choice is his choice. Nothing I can do can take it away from him. I don't have that kind of control. Nor do I want it. No. I give him his freedom. He is free because I am free. I am free because he is free. That is how it should be. I am OK. I am that OK.[6]

I lay there, staring at the ceiling, my bodily self buzzing with activity. I felt tension release in my limbs, my jaw, and around my heart. On the one hand, I was accepting my limits—and that I have them. On the other, I was completely free. Free from fear. Free to love. And in feeling both together, I was changing. My

bodily self was changing; I was creating and becoming new patterns of sensing and responding to the cramp of impossible desire. No longer were these cramps of disappointment and despair signs of my inability to get what I want. The reverse was true. The cramps were expressions of my own impulse to connect, guiding me firmly to what I wanted most: *total presence* with Geoff, yes, and with my own life. *I am OK*. The movements I was making were making me.

The shift I made that night felt enormous. Giving Geoff his freedom to choose me opened me to *feel* gratitude towards my parents for nurturing a desire in me for more than they could imagine; it opened me to appreciate my children for reflecting my limits back to me. I had nothing to fear.

In the crucible of these relationships, I was discovering the power and joy of being nothing more or less than an impulse to connect, born to live in love, and able to learn. I was discovering my own ability to create the relationship with Geoff that I wanted to support me in becoming who I am.

I meditated on the moment, not wanting to forget, knowing that I would, and vowing to remember to remember again. *Because of my impulse to connect—because I want to connect with my children and my parents and, most of all, with Geoff—I can and must make a move of radical self-affirmation. I must make it once, then again and again in response to the merest whiff of impossible desire. When I do, I will stay present to the forces of creation pulsing through me, open to gratitude, spilling over with joy, living in love.*

I repeated the words over and again. *I am OK. My deep green bodily self is OK. I want more. I want to become. I want to give.*

I want to have a fifth child. I am OK.

My open heart swelled with love.

Thank you, Kyra.

It is almost dinnertime. I call to Kyra. "Time for chicken chores!" Or as Kai says, "Jiggin' jores." We call them chicken chores in

spite of the duck. Somehow it falls off the tongue more easily than "domestic bird chores." Kyra gets the scrap bucket and the grain and heads out. She will probably need some help with the water feeder. In no more than a minute she is back.

"Mom, I found the eggs!!"

"You did? That is wonderful! Where are they?"

"Under Pikey. She is sitting on them."

I am confused. Pikey is sitting on the missing chicken eggs?

"What do you mean?"

"I decided to chase Pikey off her nest. She finally got off—after hissing at me. All the eggs are there! Under Pikey. She is sitting on *lots* of eggs!"

I have to see for myself. I slip on my boots and march behind Kyra into the coop. Pikey is agitated, pacing back and forth in front of her nest. I don't want to disturb her, so I move quickly. A great pile appears before my eyes. Eggs!

"Twenty eggs!" I count, about five days' worth! How did they get there? For all we knew, Pikey had not budged from her nest.

Grinning with our good fortune, Kyra and I decide to leave the bottom six for Pikey's sitting pleasure. I mark them with a permanent pen for good measure, and we return to the house. Hopefully Pikey won't mind the interruption. Kyra is counting on those eggs.

I am still counting.

5

Too Many Tomatoes

[E]ven the best is something that must be overcome.
—Friedrich Nietzsche[1]

September 2008. I am standing at the sink, washing the last of the tomatoes that we picked yesterday. Each one is so beautiful, so perfect, so different. Some fruits are as round as a globe; others are dimpled by the effort of separating from the branch. Some have grown flat edges in response to a nearby vine or companion; others are joined at the hip. Some bear the remaining stains of youth, and others yield the deep purple juice of age.

Each one is delicious.

Until last year, these glorious red orbs, succulent and sweet, familiar to many a backyard gardener, had eluded us. Back in our suburban life, we always planted too late, watered too much, picked the wrong variety, or wound up with mysteriously withered stalks. Moving to the farm we were determined: we would grow our own tomatoes.

The summer we moved, 2005, there was no time. With a house in severe disrepair and a baby on the way, we barely had a moment to shower let alone plant a garden. The tomatoes would have to wait.

Summer number two, we started early. In April, weeks before planting time, Kyra and I spent a day cutting toilet paper rolls into inch-high pods, filling them with dirt, and carefully fingering in miniscule bits of organic potential: peppers and beets, carrots and corn, zucchini and, of course, tomatoes. We lay a cookie sheet full of them in a sunny window and watered regularly. From time to time we blew on the growing sprouts, as we read we should, to increase the plants' resilience to wind and water.[2] When the weather warmed, we planted our pods in plowed earth, and watered and watched some more. When Geoff and I went to Banff, my parents watered and watched too.

After we returned, disaster struck. Farmer Harold offered to come over with his bushhog. I wondered: was it a type of pig? A small tree? No. A bushhog, I learned, is a large lawnmower blade pulled by a tractor. While Geoff was sitting on the tractor's fender, guiding Harold where to mow, that bushhog accidently ran right through the vegetable garden, gobbling up every shoot in a one-two pass. No more tomatoes.

Summer number three, 2007, we were more determined than ever. We would plant *only* tomatoes and bought lots of them already started. Enough of the toilet paper rolls; we wanted visible, guaranteed success. As we put the plants into the ground, we realized that our gardens were a bit too small to leave the

recommended spacing between plants, but we squeezed them in anyway. They were so tiny; surely they would have enough room to flourish. We figured that the instructions must be wrong. We added lettuce and carrots around the edges for good measure.

Growth was slow at first. Rainfall was light. We started watering in earnest. Soon tomato tops swallowed the stakes that had once towered above them. Branches of neighboring plants tangled in ferocious knots. We could not tell one plant from the other. It was one big, green, hairy mess. We weren't concerned, at least not until the tomatoes started popping out.

Tomatoes were everywhere, visible and invisible, high and low, inside and out. As fast as we picked and ate, they ripened and fell. We regularly discovered a juicy red one right after it had tumbled to the ground, split, and filled with ants. We gathered as many as we could, making sauces and ladling the red mush into sterilized glass jars.

When frost crept down the hill, we got serious about our harvesting. We yanked stalks by the roots, exposing hundreds of green balls, tiny, hard, and dark, to large and light-white. The books said these stragglers would ripen too, so we put them in paper bags and cardboard boxes, ready for the blush of edibility to appear. We loaded the boxes into the basement and promptly forgot about them until we were sure it was too late. In the springtime, we gingerly carried the boxes, now strangely light, into the trash. We didn't dare look.

2007 was the year of too many tomatoes.

It was also the year that Geoff and I recreated our relationship.

My journals from the year of too many tomatoes are a tangled mess of revelations. Insight after insight appears in the pages, produced by the force of love growing through Geoff and me. Inch by inch, we untangled the knots of self-protecting behavior we had so carefully wound around ourselves, and staked out new trajectories for the vines of our desire. We recreated the

shapes of our relationship from the ground up, allowing our love to become what we each wanted it to be: the most important thing.

The path wasn't pretty. It was strewn with dead and dying fruits. Not only were we creating new patterns of relating, we were necessarily letting others fall. Some refused to drop easily. Encounters with caregivers, children, and each other revived the very patterns we were working so hard to leave behind. Nevertheless, we came to realize that such moments of seeming resistance to our forward progress were alerting us to potentials we had overlooked for finding more freedom and more love than we had known before. There were seeds to discover.

At first, when we felt such resistance, it took us months to find a new move to make. We were more likely to complain to one another about how hard it was to live in love. Over time, as our experience with the rhythm deepened, finding the seeds took us weeks, then days, then forty-eight hours, and finally minutes. We began to trust the process: whenever an unproductive shape of relating refuses to die, it is *because* a new one is yearning to be discovered. Every fruit was sweeter and more succulent than the last, until the vine topped out in a flash of leafy green.

We had so many resources nourishing us along the way. At the heart of our respective frustrations, we had discovered a desire for more (chapter 2). At the heart of our desire for more, we had discovered a desire to become the person that our openness to each other enabled us to be (chapter 3). I had had the green dream, an expansive experience of my stretching self, and felt the surge of radical self-affirmation that was propelling me to make new moves in relationship to my parents and our kids (chapter 4). I had vowed to give Geoff his freedom so I could find mine. I just no idea what doing so entailed. Geoff didn't either. In that year of too many tomatoes, we learned.

Resistance is Always Right

January 2007. My experience of radical self-affirmation is days old, a mere sprout, still tender and new, and I am eager to share it. Geoff returns from his trip. We are dazzled by each other's appearance and heartened in each other's embrace. My desire stirs within, but on its way out bumps up against a taut skin of resistance. This feeling of resistance is familiar. I know it well. I thought, however, given my palpable joy at Geoff's homecoming and my newly energized inner *yes*, that I wouldn't feel it again. I do. Something inside me remains shut to the man I know I want. Afraid. I don't know why.

A wave of frustration passes through me, followed by another of anger, and a third of guilt. I am feeling frustrated at not having what I want, angry at him for making me want, and guilty for wanting what he must not be giving. We are not connected. Why not?

Perhaps it is that he doesn't yet know that I have made my move to radical self-affirmation. *I am OK.* I want to share this with him, but I hesitate. An old pattern quivers, ready to release: I am afraid Geoff will take away my pleasure. I decide to wait.

Later we are making dinner, discussing his trip. I casually say, "I know what your first follow-up should be, billing Bob!" I am proud that he earned so much money. The reward makes our separation worth it. I am imagining that this fact is something we can celebrate together—a place where we can connect. I am wrong. Geoff disappears. He is standing before me, but his face is blank, motionless, as if he cannot see me. It is a response of his we know too well. We call it "the wall."

"What's wrong?" I ask quickly trying to call him back. "What did I say? Where did you go?" I then add, "Sometimes Bob takes a while."

Clipped words shoot sideways from a crack in his mouth. "Bob always asks me to ask him. He is always prompt with payment." He is defensive, belligerent. I am really confused.

"What's wrong? What did I say?" Silence. I continue, "If I don't know why I upset you then I can't *not* do it again."

He inches closer, almost in spite of himself. "It is so hard for me to ask for money."

"Yes, OK," I reply. "But you don't have to push me away."

With that he lashes out. "I'm not pushing you away!" After releasing a few more choice words, he closes with a hook, "Where is that coming from?" It feels like a deliberate attack. Not good. I pull back and try again to meet him wherever he is.

"OK, a distance opened up, you retreated, maybe I wasn't pushed, but suddenly I felt locked out. What could I have done? I don't want to be locked out." I wait for a reply, hoping for a rush of reality. I want his trust in us to toss whatever fears are strangling him high to the sky so that we can shoot them down together. Instead he digs in, blames me, and tells me I should respond differently to his distance. I let that go and try to approach from a different angle.

He cuts me off. "I know what you are going to say and you are going to tell me that I am wrong." It's worse than I thought. He is really stuck.

"No, not at all!" I protest. "I am just trying to call our attention to a moment before you got upset. Tell me what to do before you retreat, not what I should do after I've been hurt trying to connect with you!"

Standing there in our kitchen, as the conversation continues, a new sensory awareness blasts into view. I feel it for the first time: a visceral link between this feeling of facing Geoff's wall, on the one hand, and a sensation of resistance to him on the other. I hadn't felt this link before as a sensory pattern in my bodily self. Now I do. I have come a long, long way to be able to stand like this, in front of the wall, without retreating behind my own strategies for avoiding the sting of impossible desire. I feel strong, clear, and open. I am asking for his help in meeting him

and caring for him. Yet, I also know: I can't kiss. Not now, and not until we heal this moment.

As the sensory awareness of this visceral link between his blame and my resistance settles, my experience of that resistance shifts. A wave of radical self-affirmation spills through me and I know. It is not my fault that I feel resistance. In the past, if I felt such feelings, I would berate myself for them and set out to determine why I was so screwed up. *What is wrong with me?* Not now. The shift of affirmation holds. I know: this feeling of hitting a limit is not my fault. *I am OK.*

Still standing, wondering what to say next, my thoughts spin forward. *I am OK.* This visceral resistance is not some arbitrary or willful withholding. Nor is it simply a well-worn pattern of sensation and response etched years before in a protective stance against caregivers against which I must fight. *This resistance is what I feel when Geoff is trapped inside his own fears. It's not just about me.* This resistance is a call to us and for us that happens to be coming through my sensory self. My resistance is calling Geoff to find his freedom—the freedom I want for him.

My thoughts wind around a common stem. *Resistance is always right.* The resistance I feel is my ally; it is our ally, alerting us through me to the places where we need to grow. I vow to trust it.

Seeds of Fear

I need some more tomatoes. Kyra and Kai are our principal pickers. Jordan is milking Daisy. Jessica is tending to Marvin. I send my two K's on a tomato mission: "Round up the red ones and bring them home!"

As I look out the window, I see Kyra probing the deepest, lost among the greens, reaching her small hands between knitted branches to retrieve her prizes. She hands some out to Kai and stuffs others into a sack she makes with the front of her shirt.

Minutes later I hear a call. "Mom, YOOK!" I go to the door. There is Kai, smiling widely, his lumpy belly leading the way.

Behind him is a trail of tomatoes, leading back toward the garden, one squished flat. Kyra comes soon after, with another belly batch. I gather up the balls to replace the twelve I just chopped for tonight's dinner.

Each fruit sits in my hand as I carry it from kid to counter. For a moment I feel the livingness, soft and firm like a baby's skin. (Yes, a baby.) I sigh in gratitude and despair. If only we could keep these worlds of goodness all year and have a couple per night, this freshly picked!

It's impossible. In days, these beautiful Big Boys and Celebration specialties will be ugly mounds of tangy, bubbling bacteria, laced with seeds. It is the way things grow. Even relationships.

February 2007. Geoff returns from a day of substitute teaching at the local elementary school. I am tired after slogging through chores and the kids' riding lessons all by myself. I feel the need for energy coming toward me. He is subdued. I brace against him, feeling a familiar closing of my bodily self. Resistance.

"How was your time alone?" I ask. He responds as if I am challenging his productivity. I fear the need in his response. My own puff of power fades as soon as the words reach my lips, leaving despair in their wake. I try to share my feelings.

He erupts: "I know you are sad! And I'm not going to be the cause of it. I refuse. I won't go to teach. I won't do it. I quit!" He closes with a complaint. "Your emotions are so big!"

"Don't be angry with me," I reply.

"I'm not angry with you, just frustrated!"

Even though I am exhausted, I am amazed at how free I feel of my usual slamming self-criticism. It's where I now am, thanks to the move of radical self-affirmation. I don't want to confront him. I want to connect with him. I move sideways.

"I am saying the opposite of what you fear. I am not blaming you! I am expressing my *faith* in you. I am inviting you to help me!" I have a new move to make, I remind myself, because I

know I am OK. I can stand, present, waiting to be seen. I don't have to run away or hit back, for I know I want to be here with him. I want his freedom. I trust my resistance. Even so, it hurts to stand.

I want to encourage him. I try reminding him of what he often says to me: *I want our love to be the most important thing.* I continue: "What you say you want to be true all the time is only true some of the time, and it needs to be more true." An impulse arises in me to try a direct approach. "You need to do some work, Geoff. You need to find a different place in yourself, other than your fears, from which to respond to me—a place of trust and love."

It works. He gets it. He grasps the seed of hope in the current mess. He realizes that the place in himself where he is feeling resistance to me is calling out to him: *heal me here.*

My day is forgotten, yet I feel OK. I am OK. I am trusting my resistance.

Later, Geoff and I talk some more. It's a rousing full-body hug of a conversation. He affirms how my bodily self has become a barometer, acutely sensitive to our degree of connection. He sees too: when his fear dominates his actions towards me, my desire flees to a distant planet in some subterranean galaxy. We agree again: the distance is intolerable.

He affirms: "Your body is a gift to us both, guiding us to more love."

I am dazzled by his beauty and by the beauty of what he is saying. I listen. He goes on. He admits that he carries around a burden that depletes his energy and separates him from me. He is always trying to anticipate what I want and wanting to make sure I get it. Before now, he wasn't aware of how much of a burden it was. He feels it now.

We see the dance of desire that has brought us here. By breaking my own habit of blaming myself for his unhappiness, and beginning to trust in my resistance, I was breaking the

pattern that had enabled him to continue his own well-worn strategies of deflecting blame onto me to protect his individual self. My move to freedom was thrusting him face to face with his own fears of impossible desire.

"I am afraid," he confides, "that I won't be the person who can give you what you want."

I smile. There it is. Because I want to be connected to him, I fear I am too much. Because he wants to be connected with me, he fears he is not enough. Neither of us would feel the fear if we didn't want the other so much. Feeling my fear, I turn against myself, trying to make myself smaller; feeling his fear, he turns against me, blaming me for his sense of inadequacy. In so far as I blame myself, I don't challenge his dynamic. I feed it. I feed his fears of not being enough by doing what I think he wants me to do.

No longer. The old pattern is dying, rotting away, and in its dying shape, we see a new possibility. We see that the fact of our relationship—the lived sensory experience of the world that opens up in us and between us when we are together—has the potential to become more real for each of us than the worlds of impossible desire that have been real for each of us before. Each of our fears is a seed, wanting nothing more than to die to itself and come to life in a world where love is more real.

"You are a new woman," he says. He is channeling now. I bask in the warmth of his words. "We are artists in our studio, working together to bring our vision of love to life. *Total presence.* We are struggling to realize a new philosophy of living. We are figuring out how to communicate our vision, and we need time and space together to do so."

I see too. Geoff isn't going anywhere, and I need not fear that he will. Geoff wants my pleasure. He realizes that if I get what I want, he gets what he wants—me.

He says again what he has said before and I hear it anew. "I am the one to go all the way with you," to the end of time, to the end of who we can be, on a never-ending journey of bodily becoming.

I meditate on his phrases. They feel like divine gifts, heavenly balm. I worked hard for them, persistently and patiently. He did too. He feels the pleasure of his being able to say them. I do too. The work and the wait was worth it, for both of us.

I wake the next morning overflowing with an intoxicating brew of honey rich sensation. Love, new and renewed. Did I know this was possible?

Visions of a fifth child hover like a halo, beckoning me. *This is who you are.*

From Pleasing to Pleasure

I lift a tomato from the basket and stare at it. It is so perfect, its surface smooth and clean. I don't want to rip into its circular shape to tear out ragged chunks. Or maybe I do. Then again, maybe it wants me to. Perhaps this tomato wants me to eat it. Its luscious bounty is calling me to become a vessel for its seeds—to carry those seeds into new territories and plant them along the surface of the earth. I might as well oblige. It is my pleasure. This tomato and I are locked in a life-enabling embrace. It must die so that we both can live.

April 2007. It breaks, and I don't just mean the lamp. I am feeling guilty again for not giving Geoff what I think he wants. Again. I thought I had moved beyond this place. Why do I constantly fear that I am failing—ever too much and not enough? Why am I racked with guilt? I don't want to be. The guilt kills my desire. It drains my joy. I pull in. I don't want to feel what I am feeling, yet I can't manage to transform my shame into a different sensory shape. I can't find another way to move in relation to Geoff, and I have no idea why. What is blocking me from moving toward the total presence I know I want?

I try to remind myself: Resistance is always right. Find the seeds. But how?

I drag myself out for a walk. As I begin to stride, my lungs open and my heart pounds. My striding motion, the play of the

breeze, the touch of the sun, and the strength of the earth pull on my emotional knots. My senses wake up. High above the meadow, I sit down on a rock, suddenly aware of how encased I have been by unhappiness. Sobbing gasps of oxygen release me to feel the shapes of my tangled, yearning desire. I am still hurting from something he said to me. I need to talk about it. I need him to touch me in this place where it stings so that I know that our love is more real.

Back home, I try to share these insights with Geoff. I begin to explain. Within seconds he is screaming at me, mouthing my words in a sneering tone.

"I can't please you! I can never please you!! I can't satisfy you!!" He knocks over a lamp. The bulb shatters. His pain is as jagged as the shards of glass. I am crying, apologizing, telling him he can and does please me. Young Kai, in my arms, bursts into tears. I leave the room and seek refuge on the couch. I wait for Geoff to calm down and come find me. I trust that he will.

My mind is racing, still nimble and light from my breath-enabling walk. New moves pulse to life. He is right. He can't please me. It's not his job. It is not his burden to carry. Only I can please me. He can love me, and work with me to help me find the pleasure I seek, but pleasing me is not his job. I am not his vocation.

I am not Geoff's vocation, and I don't want to be.

As I clutch Kai tightly on my lap, the logic falls into place. Geoff's vocation is what I have been ever since the dark times, seven years ago, when we recreated our relationship once before. At that point, we were inhabiting a pattern of relating to one another where I took care of him, took care of me, and took care of us. It couldn't last. I was unhappy. When that pattern broke, he turned to me with a new longing and determination, wanting to please me. I loved the attention. We healed many hurts. We opened more deeply with one another than ever before. As we did, our love grew, and because it had, we were now persons for whom the degree of connection we were living wasn't enough.

We both want more. The pain and frustration were letting us know what. If I am Geoff's vocation, then I am always under pressure to react to him in ways that let him know that he is doing a good job, that he didn't do anything wrong, and that he isn't disappointing me. If for some reason I am not happy, he blames me for making him feel inadequate. It is my fault, once again. It is indeed time for this fruit to die—I want freedom from such pressure—but I am reluctant to let it go. *I like it when Geoff is focused on me!* I don't want to go back to a time when he wasn't! I want his attention!

I look for the seeds—what potentials are here for a more potent pattern of relating to one another than we have known before? *What is it that I really want from Geoff, even more than his attention?*

Words branch forth within my sensory self. *I don't want to be Geoff's vocation; I want to be his partner.* I don't want him to be worried about pleasing me; I want to be moving with him to a place of deeper pleasure. Yes. Relief washes through. I want to be Geoff's partner in finding and fulfilling his vocation and mine. I can't please him and he can't please me. We must move together, side by side, of our own free will, all the way.

The words double back, picking up force. *What I want most from Geoff is his freedom—his freedom from needing to please me and his freedom from fearing that he cannot.*

Geoff comes in, subdued. We are both raw, quiet, careful. We agree: we need to find ways of moving in relation to one another that express our impulse to connect with one another, rather than expressing an excruciating fear that such connecting might not be possible. We want to live open to one another as a cause of our being.

"What would the new paradigm look like?" he asks. We explore some possibilities and come to the same conclusion: we don't know. We will have to improvise, experiment, and then evaluate how well any new movements we make are moving us towards total presence.

We are breathing again, side by side. He is no longer carrying the burden of my satisfaction. I am no longer carrying his. Deep in the mystery of our bodily becoming, we come together in waves of love and gratitude.

It occurs to me. If I hadn't been willing to share my feelings of lingering hurt, we would never have found this potential for more. I like it here. *Resistance is always right.*

One Becoming Two

A seed is a desire to live. It is also a desire to die. It is a desire to create more life by becoming something other than it is: a sprout, a stalk, leaves and fruit, seeds of its own. It is a desire to destroy what it has been so that it can.[3]

A seed is movement, ever absorbing earth, air, water, and sunlight, and transforming these elements into its own flesh and fruit. A seed is an impulse to connect.

Desire is a seed, and the freedom to love is "the flower and fruit of a man."[4]

April 2007. I am waiting for Geoff to claim his freedom in a more consistent manner. I want it. He wants it. We discuss strategies. I offer him a threefold practice to help shift his experience of me whenever I ask for something and he feels himself slipping into fear of my anger or disappointment.

First, *mirror me*. Just let me know that you hear what I am saying.[5]

Second, *greet whatever I say as information about how to go deeper*. Don't take it personally. It is not a judgment on you. It is only *me*, coming to you, wanting to be with you. Hear the desire in what I am saying—hear my impulse to connect. I am sharing with you who and where I am so you can succeed in doing what I know you want to do too: connect with me.

Third, *take care of yourself*.[6] Know that you are OK. You are OK. You are OK.

As we are discussing these moves, Geoff confesses. "I just want

to be able to control my emotional environment." I am shocked. He has never admitted anything of the sort before. I hadn't even guessed that he had that awareness about himself. He can seem so relaxed and easygoing. Yet when he says it, I see it. Maintaining such control is of paramount importance to him: it is how he protects himself against the sting of impossible desire.

Even so, he sees the limits of this strategy. In trying to secure his safety, he is not getting what he is realizing he now wants even more than control: connection with me. Instead of getting that connection, he finds himself constantly crashing into his own walls, combusting in anger, and lashing out at the apparent cause of his pain. Me.

The fruit is decaying; we see its seeds. Geoff won't be free to be with me until he makes a similar movement to the one I made in January when he was away, a move of radical self-affirmation. He needs to know that he is OK, that his desire to be with me is OK. He needs to find his freedom by giving me my freedom to choose him. For only when he is free of his need to control my "big emotions" will it be safe for me to drop my fear and unfold with him as we both want me to do.

The implications spiral through us. Because our relationship is giving us each so much, we each want more—more of the self we have the potential to be when nourished by the openness we share. Our impulse to connect with one another is pushing us to grow as two persons into two persons who agree that the reality opening up between them is far more life-giving than patterns of boundary building they have known before. Our impulse to connect with one another is pushing us to name and claim and make real a world in which we each are who we are by virtue of the relationship we are creating with one another.

We gaze at each other, confounded by the paradox. The nearer we draw to one another and the more open we are to each other, the freer we are to become our singular sensory selves and

the more necessary it is that we do. It's the paradox of total presence.

Making an I-Moment

Ginger. The dish I am making needs some. I go to the spice basket to look. We are all out. I mention it to Geoff. "I forgot to put it on the list, and you didn't get any more at the store."

He replies, "I did get some—a real ginger root—about the size of your thumb."

It hits me. Here I am, thinking that he hadn't gotten what I needed and feeling disappointed (and at fault), when in reality, he had remembered what I needed without my asking and had gotten something even better than I would have asked for: the real, raw thing.

I decide to remember: *go for the root.*

May 2007. Geoff is working hard to find his freedom. I see the effort. He wants it for himself and for us. He begins a conversation with an affirmation: "You have to know that I want you to ask for what you need."

"Yes. Thank you. I hear you." I pause. I don't want to say any more, but the words tumble out. "But it is not always that easy, for you say you want me to ask and then when I do, I often feel a lot of resistance from you."

"Resistance? I don't resist you!" My heart plummets. I wish he were joking. He's not.

I stay calm, low, quiet, hopeful. "Well, you stop responding. You grow silent and the more passionately I ask, the more you withdraw, so that when I ask, I end up working my way into a situation that is the opposite of what I want—and not getting what I want."

My words trigger the wall. It rises instantly between us. I see the silence in his face.

I cry out in frustration. "Three minutes ago you asked me to ask you for what I need and I said it is hard because I face resis-

tance, you denied it, and then here we are!" We have broken through the wall again and again, yet old patterns of sensing and responding are still too strong, too close to the surface, too ready to activate. We have learned so much! What more must we learn to be finally free? Why this resistance?

"I just don't have anything to say," he replies coolly.

"I don't believe you are being honest with yourself," I blurt out. "I don't think you want to be where you are, feeling what you are feeling."

"No," he says quietly. Maybe he isn't so far away after all.

"So what can I do?" I implore. "How can I help you not slide behind the wall?" It hurts to watch, hurts to stand. I am yearning, remembering, affirming: *I am OK. My impulse to connect is OK.*

He offers, "Even when I am present and empathetic, it isn't enough."

"That's not true," I reply, wanting to encourage. "You are enough. What I want is always the same—I just want you to be with me, to move with me where I am. Sometimes you are kind and nice but detached. You are so interested in doing the 'right' thing that you stand back, without taking the risk of engaging. I feel your distance. I am all alone to wrestle with issues that concern us both. All I want is to feel the flow connecting us." My words fall into a black hole.

"Well, what is there left to say?" he retorts. "You say it all. You say it and there is nothing left. I am just looking on, watching you play tennis with yourself."

I shut my mouth. He has always appreciated what I have to offer, my hard-won insights and rays of clarity. Not now. I let go. He is right. He has to do his own work. I can't do it for him.

"OK," I say. "You figure it out. How can you get what you want?"

"I'll think about it."

Later that evening, I am stretching by the side of the bed. The kids are asleep.

"I have an answer," he begins.

"What?"

"Radical self-affirmation," he states.

I nod. "OK. What does that mean to you?" I ask, still stinging from earlier in the day.

"I was going to ask you!" he says, laughing. "I keep thinking about what you went through with your parents."

"I went through the radical self-affirmation part with you, actually. With my parents, that time doing yoga, I discovered the sensory space around my heart, beaming out in time through them and beyond them. I knew that I existed before them. I knew that I chose them as what I needed to find my own capacity for creating relationships that will support me in becoming who I am. Is that what you mean?"

"No."

"It was in relation to you that I had to affirm myself in the face of my greatest fear."

"That I would leave?"

"Yes. I had to give you your freedom. I realized that I had to let you have a choice and make a choice in every moment about whether you want to be with me."

"As if it is an issue," he laughs, with a touch of sarcasm. He doesn't feel like he has a choice, I know. I grin. Loving me is who he is.

I go on without invitation. "So, radical self-affirmation is about knowing that you are OK." The words spill out of me. "It is about affirming yourself completely in the moment as OK. It is not about accepting or justifying your actions as good or worthy. It is about *not* having to justify your actions. It is about being *free* to move *with* another person, in response to him or her, *because* you have nothing to defend or prove. It is about being *honest* with yourself about who you are and what you are doing so that you can be open to the impulses to move differently that are always being born in you, impulses that are guiding you to get what you

want. To become who you want to be. To connect—to love!" I am spouting, sprouting, hopeful. He listens.

"I get it," he muses. "But it will be really hard! It means adjusting a part of all of my interactions with you at that point where I am wondering whether you will like what I'm doing."

I go to fill my water bottle, feeling gloriously empty. We crawl into bed. Lying there, I realize that something is still curled in me. What he said was so wonderful but I feel resistance in me to opening. It doesn't feel safe yet. I don't feel safe yet. I don't want to feel what I am feeling, but what can I do? I decide to trust the resistance—I have to—so that he will be free.

"Can you say, in your own words, what we've been talking about?" I ask, hesitantly. I am hoping beyond hard that we don't lose our connection. He starts describing the events of the day, and I hear exactly what I fear. He is talking about "the dynamic" but not his role in it. He is talking about "it" from a distance.

It hits me: *There is no I-moment in what he is saying.* There is no moment where he is taking responsibility for what is happening. Because there is no moment when he sees his role, he cannot see mine either. He can't see how what he was doing hurt me, or how much courage it has taken me to keep standing in the face of his anger and withdrawal.

I breathe down into the resistance that has now gelled in my stomach and try another tack. I ask, "Are you sorry for saying the things you did to me when you were behind the wall?"

Geoff erupts in fury, tosses back the covers, leaps out of bed, and goes downstairs. I roll over, head in pillow and let him go.

Some time later, he returns. "I can't say sorry. I don't feel like saying sorry. I was thinking about how brave you have been, but I am not feeling sorry." He is adamant.

"I think you don't want to say it because it would mean admitting that you had done something you would rather not."

He is furious again. "But that's not true!"

"OK, but if you ask me to ask you for something, respond by shutting down, and then deny that you are shutting down, what am I supposed to do? How am I supposed to trust you?"

"I can't hear this. You are just playing tennis with yourself again."

I roll over and am silent. He rolls away from me. The pain bounces back and forth. We are both in it.

"Do you really want to go to sleep feeling this way?" I ask finally.

"No."

Something about the "no" releases me a bit. "You don't have to say you are sorry. But I had to ask." He nearly explodes again and then checks himself, as if he had been expecting me to say something else. He asks me to repeat it. I do. Feelings of love rush through me. "I love you," I add. He bursts into tears.

I continue, "I know you are working hard. I know that it is hard. I am so proud of you." He quiets down.

"Can I spoon you?" I ask.

"Yes, that would be lovely," he replies. We fall asleep, shedding tears of sadness and relief. We are not there yet, but we are closer.

Plants and trees grow towards the light. They never make it. If they did, they would burn. Yet in the effort, they unfold incredible beauty—life-enabling beauty.

Affirming the We-In-Me

May 2007. Geoff and I begin talking about our love as a river. Like a river it flows, not between us but through each of us. It lives in our bodily selves, because of our bodily selves, always pulling and pushing us towards one another. It is a river that flows along the trajectories of unmet yearning that our caregivers helped us discover. It is a river with the power to heal the sting of impossible desire and wash us free of our self-immuring fears.

Nevertheless, even though we want nothing more than this freedom and healing, we also know that there are times when we allow our stress or worry or fear to grab us by the collar and yank us out of the rivery flow. We retreat from our bodily, sensory openness to one another, keen to protect our individual selves. We gaze at each other from opposing banks, yearning and frustrated, apt to hurt one another without intending to. We imagine that the other sits there judging us—determining in some court whether or not we are worthy of love, whether or not we will get what we want, namely one other. Hounded by the sting of impossible desire, we are bound spirits, unable to move with our own sensory flow.

Nevertheless, our impulses to connect refuse to lose: they are who we are. Every move we make to block them expresses them. We don't want to be bound and banked. We want to be frolicking in the fertile flow. We want to affirm the resistance that registers in our bodily selves as an invitation to heal whatever wound has triggered our defensive response. We want to share that hurt, immerse it into the flow of our love, and allow our love to be more real. We each want to live open to the other as an enabling cause of our singular sensory self.

I get a new idea and share it with Geoff. "When I ask for what I need, it is not *me* who is asking something of *you*. Part of me is a *we* and it is this *we-in-me* that wants more. I am not asking you to do the right thing. The we-in-me is asking the we-in-you not to allow your fears of doing the wrong thing to suffocate it!"

We find ourselves exploring a strange new proximity. At every turn, radical self-affirmation is essential, yet the self that we are each affirming is not an individual nomad, existing over and against the other. *The self I affirm as me is no longer, nor was it ever, an individual first. I am nothing more or less than an impulse to connect, who I am by virtue of the relationships I create with those who support me in my bodily becoming.*

Especially you.

We affirm what we are creating. We are not two individuals, sharing an orbit, who need to compromise or sacrifice in order to move in line with one another. What Geoff feels, I feel. What I feel, he feels. This emotional entanglement is not a problem to fix with psychological strategies of increased differentiation or self-soothing. Part of who I am *is* a fierce desire for Geoff. Part of who he is *is* a fierce desire for me. I *am* an impulse to connect with him. He *is* an impulse to connect with me. The challenge then for each of us is to learn to trust our coming-together—the "we" alive in each of us—as the reality that is enabling each of us to grow into the singular sensory selves we have the potential to be. We wonder how. How can we allow ourselves to be so vulnerable to one another, so exposed and so bare?

Radical self-affirmation is radical self-negation. It is seed work. It is the movement that frees us to become both different than we were and more of who we are.

Practicing Presence

May 2007. We continue to talk about Geoff finding his freedom. Geoff asks me what to do. I am wary. If I answer, how will I know that he won't accuse me of playing tennis with myself again? How do I know he won't blame me for blaming him? How can I speak in ways that prevent the wall from going up? What do I do if his fears threaten to grab him from the flow of our love?

I breathe deeply, remembering, telling myself: *resistance is always right*.

Rather than answering his question, I decide to share my concern.

Geoff says he is sorry. I appreciate his response. I also realize in that moment that saying sorry is no longer enough. I have to say so. Kai wakes up and I rock him back to sleep. I gather myself, trying to shrug off my fear of triggering the wall.

"Thank you. I hear you. I really do. So, now I want more! I want to transform and heal this dynamic. I want to do the work

we need to do so that I don't have to fear that the wall will ever appear again." I wait, expectantly.

"I get it." I breathe again. He summarizes with a concise beauty that astonishes me: "You want me to care a bit more about you than I care about my own fears."

While we've been here before and we both know it, something moves at a depth that has eluded us. He is making an I-moment. He is affirming the we-in-him and his desire to be free to live in love with me. He is present with me. I hear it. It is what I want.

"Yes. Yes! That's it!"

He drives off to a gig, and I ponder the exchange, knowing that the we-in-either-of-us won't be satisfied with anything less.

Finding Freedom

I gaze at the pile of tomatoes in front of me. Even this year, there are almost too many. I think about what more they want to become. How do I preserve them? How do I preserve the pleasure that I want to get from them? How do I keep them safe from the ravages of time so that they can nourish our family whenever we need?

I am amassing recipes and generating my own. To preserve these orbs takes sugar or salt, or some combination of the two; hot water, glass jars, and lots of pots and pans. What you get is familiar to all—sauces, salsas, and soups, or just plain stewed, chopped, and dried. When you begin to explore the range of options, you know why our culture eats as we do. Overtime we have cultivated a taste for the recipes we have learned to concoct in an effort to save the fruits of our labor. We have learned to want what we have learned to make in order to keep what we can't through the winter months. How many staples are there that represent this desire in us to hold fast to what is good? We cultivate a taste for the preserved. We invent recipes of death. We eschew the wild globe, preferring to render it tame.

In our relationships too, we develop a taste for preserved patterns of relating to one another. It's our comfort food. We work so hard to plant the seeds, grow the bond, and gather the fruit. Then we store it away, holding on to our jars, wanting the security of knowing that we will have enough. We will be enough. We have our life in our hands, locked in glass. "The finest qualities of our nature, like the bloom or fruits, can be preserved only by the most delicate handling. Yet we do not treat ourselves nor one another thus tenderly."[7]

What we succeed in preserving is not as nourishing as what we set out to preserve. Eager to please, we forget the pleasure of getting as close as we can to the growing. We forget to plant more seeds. We forget that we won't have any more tomatoes unless we let them live though us, in our planting, picking, eating, and eliminating.

June 2007. I ask Geoff how it feels. The virtual instrument he has been designing for months is finally out! "Looking back on the experience, what are your thoughts?"

He replies, matter-of-factly. "I came up with an idea and carried it through, pretty much as I intended." Stop. He doesn't say anything more.

I wither inside and feel a familiar skin of resistance forming in me. There is no mention of the tremendous anxiety that wrung him dry, nor of the radical doubt he wrestled at every step of the process? No reference to the hours I spent encouraging, supporting, and helping him through? No attention to the difficulty managing the emotions coughed up by such a lengthy, risky entrepreneurial venture, and how they had forced us to grow in our love for one another?

I share my thoughts and watch a veil slip across his face. I can feel it. He doesn't want to have said anything *wrong*, anything that would make him feel that I do not like him—as if it were an issue. I see him struggling. The wall threatens, but Geoff is trying hard not to let it form. I keep plunging ahead. I have to. The

rising up in my bodily self won't stop. I know I won't feel connected to him without working this through.

He apologizes for his anxiety.

The we-in-me needs more—an I-moment, an affirmation of the we-in-him, a sense of what he has learned from the experience about finding his freedom, about us. At every turn I am positive, hopeful. I press on, trusting my resistance. Finally it yields a revelation.

I share it: "You know, the story of your work on this project is the story of *us*! It is the story of how we have been learning to be present with one another, to trust our resistance, and allow our love to grow stronger than our respective fears! *We* did it! The product exists because our love won!"

I am so deeply glad to be seeing this view. I needed to know. The resistance in me to what he had said was key to opening it up. I marvel, resistance *is* always right! It is a potential for pleasure, waiting to unfold. He nods. We sleep.

The next morning, he spontaneously gives back all I said and more.

"What has happened in this past year has been a huge shift for me," he relates. "I learned that when you are telling me that something I did hurt you, you are doing it because you want to get closer to me. You just want to get closer to me. My tendency is to deny that what you are saying is true because all I feel is: why did I do that? She won't like me! Now I know something different." He pauses. I revel in the rays of his words.

"When I remember this," he adds, "I stay in touch with my freedom. I have things to say."

This year, Geoff and I are reaping the fruit of our experiments in tomato-growing. We bought the right kinds of plants, set them eighteen inches apart, and watered as needed. As their legs grew long and their load heavy, I replaced outgrown stakes with longer ones, and retied the vines. The tomatoes are now turning,

and we can see them, reach them, and enjoy them.

So too with our relationship. We are working with, rather than against, our impulses to connect, each becoming more of the sensory selves we have the potential to be as we spiral towards the light of total presence.

The last tomato falls beneath my knife. Slight serrations in the blade score the tender skin, releasing the meat beneath. Juice drips, seeds splay, chunks pile up. As pleasant as it is, I am ready to finish this part. I have almost enough mass for my sauce. Onions and garlic are sizzling. Fresh parsley and basil wait their turn. I slide the red mess into the pot, add the spices, a couple of bay leaves, and stir. The sauce will be delicious, fresh and freshly cooked.

Too many tomatoes, or just enough?

6

Falling Away

Perhaps what we have always called intuition is merely a nervous system organized by training to perceive.
—Martha Graham[1]

October 2008. I wake up and gaze out the window. Mist swirls softly on the beaver pond, skimming across glass. A rose glow reflection of sky stretches across the surface, broken by swarms of lily pads and framed by a tousled cattail fringe. Along the far side of the pond, a row of early turners sets the bar. Brilliant red bushes flecked with gold stand forth against a background of more leisurely turning green. Their flame is a herald: autumn is here.

Through the wispy mist, other messengers appear. Canadians float in handfuls, leaving slow wakes. They take turns reaching black beaks beneath the water to replenish their flight-worn bodies.

As the sun rises round and warm, the cooling vapors glide away leaving air that is crisp, dry, and eager to be breathed. Solar rays crawl down into the heart of the valley and suddenly all is aglow, radiant red and green, living and dying at once.

Is fall the most beautiful time here on the farm? I want to say yes, though I know my answer will change with the seasons. Still, there is something exquisite about this span of time where life flares in a peak of passion and falls away.

After a morning of work, I lace my sneakers and tumble out the door ready for an adventure. Breathing deeply, I taste a sweet tang of decay. The first leaves to fall crunch beneath my feet. I climb steadily up, up towards the hayfields. All morning I've been going over my journals from last fall, taking notes, and reliving the story of what happened after Geoff began to claim his freedom. It wasn't the end. Memories of memories tumble around inside of me.

As I continue up, the valley drops below me and the hillsides draw near. Sensations randomly pop into view: a foot, a hand, a shoulder, a hamstring, a heel. My movement pulls at my awareness, stretching my inner gaze down and out, up and around, bringing my senses to life, and making me whole again. There is a world out here too.

I brush through tangles of grass and flowers. A last bright white blossom of Queen Anne's Lace appears flanked by older grays whose stalks are stiff and brittle. She won't be long for this world either, but she blooms up bravely, oblivious to her dying comrades, her eyes only for the sun.

I stop and finger one of the elderly heads, wise to the ways of the world. My thumb flips tiny urchin pods into the air that cling instantly to my sleeves and shirt. I am seeing the generations here—and the process of generating. *Use me*! I smile as I walk on, carrying my small travelers, proud of my bit part in creation itself.

Enabling One Another

Walking on, splattered by seeds, I think back to last fall, when these shedding plants were seeds themselves and Geoff and I were savoring the first fruits of total presence. Who knew then that there were so many shapes of our relationship that still needed to fall away, so that new expressions of our impulse to connect could come forth to support the weight of our mutual desire for more?

September 2007. I am sitting at a piano concert being given by my mate. His playing is extraordinary. It is clean and precise, passionate and dynamic. He is playing what he knows and loves: a collection of songs that have poured through him over the last fifteen years. He is better than ever.

I am aware too that he and I are not presently in a great place. An encounter earlier this morning left Geoff high and dry on the banks of our love, out of the flow, and behind the wall. I had been trying to share an experience I had the night before of a sensory openness that seemed new. The experience had me wondering: what would it take to sustain this degree of openness, this depth of awareness, this thickness of the moment, this possibility of pleasure in all moments of my life?

As soon as the words left my mouth to travel towards Geoff, I felt absolutely bare. Fear flashed. My span of inner exposure contracted forcefully. I was suddenly terrified of his response. *Would he take advantage of my openness? Would he see me and move with me?*

In an instant, he caught the whiff of my fear and jumped to the conclusion that I was judging him for not immediately saying the right thing in response. He left. He was right there next to me, yet gone. I had rebounded quickly from my spasm of fear, but he hadn't come back.

We had spent good portions of the day talking, with little resolution. Then it was show time. There we were, cordial but not connected.

The tilt of his head catches my eye. He is dancing now, bobbing up and down on his stool. Brilliant notes stream flow.

Suddenly, my experience of him shifts. I see myself. I am watching him, but what I see is *myself in him*. I see a *Kimerer-enabled Geoff*. I am everywhere in this concert, in his narrative, in his organization of the material, in his playing of the songs, and as the inspiration of some of the songs themselves. Of course, Geoff is out there, I am sitting here. He is on his own, alone with his instrument, playing. Even so, in every moment, at every level, what he is doing he is doing with me, enabled by me, as an expression of what his being with me has opened in him.

The thought is gratifying and humbling. What an honor to be given the gift of participating in this man's life! What a responsibility too. He has so much beauty to unfold and so much divinity.

My experience of him rebounds back to me and I also know: he is enabling me to unfold what I have to give too. There is no question in my mind that the depths of sensation, pleasant and not, to which I go with Geoff open possibilities of movement in all areas of my life that I wouldn't otherwise have discovered. It is happening even now, as I sit receiving Geoff-enabled thoughts. Without him, I muse, I wouldn't be learning such hard lessons about how to stay open to the wild mysteries of an ever-evolving love.

What I see buoys my faith. Even so, I sigh. It's not easy. I feel it now, the slight closing in me, like the lowering of a blind. I open and close in response to Geoff like the pupil of an eye in response to light. Because we are so connected, every move registers a response. With the slightest word, I release wide; with another, I contract in self-protecting spasms of irritation. Love flows, trickles, and flows again. Why? Why can't I just stay open? Why the resistance?

I step back from the cliff of self-incrimination, rehearsing the moves I have learned. I am OK. I want to connect. And the big one: somehow this frustration represents a possibility for

pleasure that we have yet to unfold! This feeling is calling me to learn something new about how to make our love more real than this. But what?

The concert is a rousing success. Song after song, the applause is warm and enthusiastic. Afterwards, we meet interesting people and collect a few addresses for our mailing list.

Back home, our simmering separation breaks out in another conversation. He apologizes for his reaction to my sharing that morning and for getting stuck in his fear. I appreciate his words, but I don't hear him making the I-moment that would move him and us forward. He is shut down by the thought that he did something wrong. I try to convince him that he didn't do anything wrong. I try gently, sternly, playfully. My words keep triggering—and then hitting—the wall. The thought that he might have done something wrong sends him spiraling in agony. Again and again he responds by digging in his heels, making excuses for his behavior, and hoping something will change—namely me. *Sorry*. I gave up that move when I made the move to affirm myself. He knows it and I know he is glad, for it means I am not giving up on him.

Finally, it occurs to me that nothing I can say is going to persuade him that he didn't do anything wrong. The feeling of being wrong sets him gnawing himself to bits; the feeling of being right reinforces his need to be right again. Either way, he loses. I lose. We lose. There must be another way. What?

As I breathe through the question, a small insight waves. It forms out of a memory of my experience watching the concert: *Geoff is Kimerer-enabled*. Geoff is afraid of being wrong because he wants to connect with me. It is the *we-in-him* that is forcing his fear to the surface, demanding that we heal this place in himself where he can't bear to be wrong. The we-in-him wants to emerge from its protective shell and become stronger and more real than the fears of not getting what he wants. But he will get what he wants. I am right here. Could the issue be this simple?

I am dazzled by the thought and try to communicate my enthusiasm. I don't have much luck. Every time I try, Geoff hears me saying, yet again, that he did something wrong. So far, the wall is winning.

Beyond Right and Wrong

I enter the hayfields to a blast of fresh green and exhale the memories into the ground. The pain of being so separated from him still trembles, threatening to trigger my own self-isolating fears. But I am here, in my meadows. I pause. My gaze rests for a moment at the tips of my toes then slowly rises, following the grass to where it hugs the hills and meets the horizon. A recently cut swath curls down to the left behind some trees and up to the top of Moon Rock to my right. I smell it. I see the touch of wind rustling though the growing green whose shoots are making up for time lost to the cutting weeks before.

Only then do I spy them—tiny miracle wing moths, beating rapidly through golden rays. The creatures are white and yellow, darkly edged and sporting an occasional decoy eye. With every beat of their translucent sails, they disappear, only to flash open again, like living strobes.

I watch two nearby moths, one yellow and one white, chase each other to a local red clover head and fly off, darting left, right, and circling one another, together and apart, together and apart again, like Geoff and me. For how long?

September 2007. The day after the concert, Geoff and I have lunch. He is still not present with me. I joke: "Well, at least the wall is short and we can smile at each other over it."

The comment shoves him further away; the wall instantly inflates. He thought he was being good! He hears me telling him he is not.

We slog on, tracing our tracks around again. He sees the ruts. He wants to give me what I want, but when I say I am not getting it, he doubts that he can give it, retreats in pain, and pushes me

away. Bang. He loses his freedom—the freedom from having to please me. The freedom I want for him; the freedom of living in love.

"How can you not let your fears yank you out of the flow of our love?" I ask.

He titles the tools we have invented. He remembers that my asking and sharing express my impulse to connect with him; he knows to greet every situation as an opportunity to grow that connection. He can affirm the we-in-me and the we-in-him and acknowledge his own role in it all. Yet despite having practiced and made all of these moves, the thought that he is not doing the right thing still arrests him.

"All the tools in the world will do no good if you get stuck there!" I protest.

We keep talking. A new move begins to unfold in my sensory self, as my sensory self. I share it. *"Beyond right and wrong!"* I cry. "We need to move beyond right and wrong! It is where we need to go. In our relationship, there can be no right and no wrong! There is only love wanting and needing to grow. The we in each of us!" [2]

Geoff nods. He likes the idea. *Yes.*

"It is really hard for me," he adds, "I'll have to work on it." He doesn't sound confident. He knows how deeply lodged in his sensory awareness this fear of being wrong is. He cannot just let go for it is a shield welded to his heart that serves as a protection against the sting of impossible desire. It grants him an illusion of the control he craves. The crowd loves him for it.

We keep talking.

"Do you know what Thomas Edison said?" I ask. *"I never failed. I just discovered one hundred ways that don't work."* It is a slightly desperate pitch, pulled from the page of a *Magic Tree House* book that I recently read to Kyra, but it works. I continue, "So what if we discover one hundred ways of connecting that don't work! Every time we do, we can simply gather more

information about the connection we do want. We can learn from such moments how to give and receive a touch that releases us into the flow of our love!"[3] I am excited by the possibilities.

All at once he is back. He sees me. He sees how I have opened so deeply in myself in order to be present with my resistance and thus with him. He takes responsibility for himself. His face softens; tears well. He admits: "My ego is a bigger part of this than I imagined. Everything I do well that succeeds feeds it."

Welcoming the Wall

I keep walking, seeing, inhaling. My hearing is the last sense to come to life. I feel the hum before I hear it. Crickets are bowing in rhythm, sounding out reedy tones as sweet and clear as the air itself. I close my eyes and stop. The vibrations pulse against my skin, then under, then through. I become the sound, transmitting its radiating rays. Other players enter—a single cricket close by, a chirp of a bird in the nearby tree.

I open my eyes and walk on. The crickets are strumming their legs madly in this last blast of warmth, looking for their mates. They are eager to create beyond themselves and give their lives to a next generation. Me too.

September 2007. The conversation is terrific. Geoff and I go further than we ever have in understanding what we want and how to get there. Even so, I am not done. Feelings of sadness weigh heavily; I am raw from the experience.

I share the feeling, wanting him to touch it and heal it—no, I clarify, wanting our love, the we-in-you and the we-in-me to touch it and heal it.

As I share and Geoff listens, I hear in my own words, something I haven't heard before. I hear the wisdom in my sadness. I am sad because there is a further I-moment I must make too, one that mirrors Geoff's. A move beyond right and wrong. What is it? My thoughts rub together.

It's about the wall. I need to welcome the wall. I need to embrace it, with gratitude, as enabling me to become who I am.

The thought lands with a punch in my belly.

Welcome the wall? Affirm the pain that being separated by it brings? I am incredulous. I hate the wall! When it goes up, I just want it to go away. I want to go away. I open a backdoor in my heart and mind and flee into visions of my independence. I creep up the riverbank of our love, prepared to bolt if Geoff doesn't come through. *I hate the wall!*

Yes, I realize, I hate it. I hate it because it scares me. I am afraid of what it means (Am I too much? Not enough?). Yet, because I hate it so much, I try as hard as I can to tread lightly to avoid triggering it. I hold myself back from Geoff, putting more faith in my ego-hung ability to manage his emotions than in our relationship.

It dawns on me. This wall is not just his. It is our creation. It is the shape our relationship is taking. I am not beyond right and wrong either.

The move I must make opens within me. I need to be able to welcome the wall, and I need to be able to welcome the wall as a sign that Geoff and I have what it takes to go all the way. The logic is all there. The fact that we both feel the wall as a wall means that neither one of us can tolerate the lack of connection it represents. Because we feel the wall as a wall, we thus have what we need to learn how to make moves that won't recreate it. Easily said, but how do we do learn to make such moves?

Beyond right and wrong. The significance of the phrase hits me full on. It doesn't mean that there is no right or wrong. Nor does it mean that we will never act in ways that hurt one another, however earnestly we try. It means that the *meaning* of whatever happens between us is not given in its happening. It is not yet determined. The meaning in any moment is *up to us;* it will emerge over time based on how Geoff and I sense and respond to that moment and what we create out of it.

In this sense, even the wall is beyond right and wrong: its meaning is not yet determined. Even the wall has the potential to become a catalyst for new understanding, greater freedom, and more love, if I can welcome it.

The insight lands: when Geoff and I are beyond right and wrong, no exchange between us is complete until we both feel grateful to it as a step on the path to total presence.

Feel gratitude for the wall? The possibility, even though I can think it, feels far away. I hate the wall. I can't help it. I hate it with every ounce of my sensory self.

Perfection in Process

A monarch glides by, queen of the flying folk. Back from a long journey, she will soon lay her eggs on a milkweed plant whose waiting pods are bursting with fluff-lifted rounds. Then she will die.

September 2007. Days later, despite such clarity about needing to welcome the wall, I am sad again. It seems that every time Geoff and I scramble out of a pit, we end up crashing back in, with Geoff down a tunnel, behind the wall. I feel devastated. Hurt. Ignored. Resentful. I don't want to stick around for more. I don't want to try any longer. I want it to be easy! Yet, I yearn to connect with a pull that sickens me and will not let go.

Most of all, I am angry. I am mad at Geoff for reasons that are new to me: he has created me. His love for me has enabled me to grow into someone who wants total presence with him. So why won't he come along? Why is he so stuck in his own resistance to what we both want?

I want to share this anger with him, but if I do, I am certain that I will flip the wall switch. I shiver with horror. But if I cannot talk about the wall after it is gone, then it isn't really gone. And if I can't share, then I can't be open myself to the place where I sense and know our connection.

Slowly, I come to the inevitable conclusion: the only way out is through. There is nowhere else to go. I cannot not share. I have to give Geoff his freedom—the freedom to choose love over fear. I have to give him the opportunity to recreate with me the meaning of the wall. I have to honor the we-in-me. *I am OK.*

I bring up the issue, reluctantly, gingerly. I talk about how I need to get to a place where we can talk about the wall without triggering it. I share with him how I need to be able to talk about it with him so that I can know it is safe for me to stay open and present with him.

This time he is here. He responds from love, with love, making more love. He affirms everything that the wall is teaching me, teaching us, and teaching him. He makes a new move.

"Our experience with the wall is giving me what I need to grow," he offers.

I am amazed. He realizes that he needs my need to talk. He needs my resistance. When I trust my resistance and share it, I pull him into the river of our love right at the point where he has a tendency to split off against himself. I am giving him a chance to heal and his gratitude flows.

We are the perfect match, we affirm, sharing in an insistent, frequently frustrated desire for more. Love is our moral compass. What keeps us open to one another is what is right.

Geoff says it again, "We are going all the way."

"There will be a moment," he confides, "when we unite so perfectly and so completely that the universe explodes."

My body is breathing now. Limbs rocking back and forth float my feelings to the surface and tug my thoughts into line. I make my way to a glen where Geoff and his brother made a bench from a log. Thanking them, I plop down on its span.

My eyes float upward, peering into the trees and through a pocket of bright blue. These sky-circlers are locusts, planted by farmers for their fence-post potential. Some red pine tower too, their telltale bark peeling in hand-sized sheets of papery red.

Rippling splotch patterns, made by the most penetrating beams, travel up and down along the trunks. I can't quite see through the trees to the horizon, but soon I will. For now all the blue I can see is through my leaf-lined ring.

The wall. It has taken me a long time to grasp the idea that what seems like an act of deliberate pain-inducing indifference is actually an expression of Geoff's deep and abiding need to connect with someone he knows, at some level, is enabling him to be present and free. Me.

I want to believe it. I get up from the bench, letting the sting of impossible desire evaporate through my pores. So much hurt. So much hope.

I continue up to Moon Rock. As I pass through the gateway to the headwall, a new sound fills my aural arena: the whirring wings of countless buzzing bees. The sound is less rhythmic than that of the crickets, smoother and lower. Not as tuned or toned, the drone is equally persistent. It vibrates in time with my breathing and beating, bringing to life my sense of every surface that responds, presenting me.

The bees are everywhere, but difficult to see. They fly among the gray branches of flowers whose purple bursts coated the hillside a mere month ago. A few puffs remain, their thin petals fingering the air. The bees must be finding something here. Their hives are down the hill and over a crest. Our beekeeper took most of the supers yesterday to harvest the honey. These bees must be busy trying to replenish their stores for winter, working together to transform dying flora into life-giving nectar.

I stride to the top of the hill, pressing hard through hamstrings and quads. My steps are firm. I sink my soles into the earth so as not to lose my balance, breathing deeply into the core of my abdomen, the center of gravity, the center of life. I am shedding cells.

I pause at the top and breathe deeply. The work makes the view so much better. My parents taught me that. Life with Geoff proves it true. My kids help me enjoy it. Will there be a fifth? I am

open to it. I wonder. What if perfection unfolds in time? Can we know perfection as perfection before it is so?

October 2007. The process is intense and ongoing, and I still can't welcome the wall. Geoff and I invent new practices to share what we shirk from sharing. We *confess*: the shame at our actions; the anxiety that covers like a rash; the fury at being stuck; the hardy fears that keep returning even when we are sure we have dug up the roots. We *drop all attempts to measure* what we say in an effort to please one another, knowing that such placating acts enable the other to remain bound by past fears. We insist on *giving each other the freedom* to respond from a place of love. We know: there is no refuge from a love that calls for the best of who we are. We *practice changing the meaning* of whatever arises within either of us, dividing us, into one more occasion to connect. We talk about the wall.

Geoff affirms: "More and more, I will take longer to go, not go as far, and come back sooner." Every cell of mine swells in response. I have been waiting my whole life for someone to love me like this.

We learn that beyond right and wrong has other meanings too: beyond ego, beyond the individual, beyond you versus me. We realize again that we are not two persons, shaving off awkward edges to fit more or less together. We are one love growing as the two singular, sensory selves whose living this love is enabling.

I still can't welcome the wall.

I begin to wonder: is this resistance right?

Befriending the Monster

I walk on over the edge of the hill, gazing out at the mountains beyond. Fall is perfect for walking, not too hot or cold, not too light or dark. My gait is not hobbled by mounds of crunchy ice or by snarling strands of thigh-high grass. I move easily and comfortably over long distances.

What I love even more about autumn walking, however, is that every day is different. At first the color shifts ever so gradually. A slight auburn glaze crosses the forests. The shadows deepen. Then a few trees single themselves out, catching fire quickly, or receding into darkness. The sumacs go in a group; their maroon finger-leaves point down, leaving their crimson bananas arching up.

The maples stage a more elaborate tease. The outer edges of a few leaves take on a parchment-look, singed around the edges, while the leaf heart pulses green. Yellow yields to orange which yields to red, slowly consuming the entire leaf. Then the fire spreads along one branch. A length of leaves flares, while the rest hold onto summer wear. But the color is contagious. Within days, it catches and slowly spreads inward, upward, and through.

If I miss a day of walking, I miss a day of knowing.

Take today. It is no different in being so different from the day before. Overnight, the balance has tipped from green to jazzy hues that blare louder than before. I brush my eyes across the horizon. Impressions left by the texture tints sink into my skin.

I remember Kyra's recent comment: "When you are looking at something, you can never see all of it." It's the paradox of total presence.

January 2008. I didn't see what was coming. We are having a conversation like so many we have had in the previous year. Old patterns seem to have a hydra-like tenacity. Every time we cut off a tentacle here or there, the beast grows back even stronger. Are we making any progress at all? We remind ourselves that we are, for every screaming death throe of an old way convinces us even more that what we want is to live in the flow of our love—to know it as more real than any fear, any doubt, or any stressor. More important than the ego needs and wants to which we once clung in a vain effort to get what we most desire.

Still, the tsunami of a moment catches us unaware and consumes us both. We are stuck in a rutted, circular conversation

that stretches for seven hours. We are pulling back and forth, struggling mightily to find the movements that will release us into the currents of love, when suddenly we see it. It is the monster. Geoff's monster: a seething whirlpool of self-condemnation, rising from his depths, dredged up by our frustrated impulses to connect.

Geoff shares what shames. Everywhere and anywhere he lives—not just with me—he feels as if he is at fault. He always feels as if he is being accused, always wrongly, and so is angry at being blamed. He doesn't want to be framed as someone who doesn't or can't or won't care, because he does!

His words tell of a sickening sucking vacuum void that catches wisps of my words and transforms them into an amorphous howl. Regardless of what I am saying, all he hears is a barrage of false accusations attacking him. He has no recourse or resources to do anything but lash out at the source. Me.

I am groping to understand. I think back to all of the times when I have tried to share my pain with him, and that pain has come rushing back at me as his anger at me that I feel that way. For so many years, I went along taking the blame, turning against myself, fearing the loss of the crowd's love. I now see what happened when I did. Every time I turned against myself in an effort to please Geoff, I condemned him to his own private hell. I fed the monster that builds and defends wall after wall after wall. By breaking my own patterns of self-incrimination, however, I had forced Geoff's monster to the surface where it was screaming in protest at being so exposed to the healing power of my open sensory self.

We keep talking, unwilling to stop for a moment. We see what spooks Geoff's monster: stress with work and money; guilt at not supporting me enough; fear that I am not getting what I need, or feeling wrongly accused for something he could have done but is not doing.

We see how the monster responds: defending himself, blaming me, denying the reality of my pain or my right to feel it, accusing me of having done too much, withdrawing and going numb, getting angry at me for making him feel inadequate, twisting every word-string into a death sentence, and building wall after wall behind which the Geoff I know disappears.

We see how my efforts to dismantle the wall have tickled the beast who howls: *I already did that! Look where it got me!* Or in desperation, *I never get it right!* We see my response again, as I try to hear in those words a desire to be with me.

We see how each time the monster appears and the wall goes up, we keep reaching and rowing, until we land some understanding that promises us less wall. Fewer walls. More freedom, more presence, more love.

Before now, we were not strong enough to land this leviathan, or live without its protection. Now we know what to do: we haul the monster out into the open, remove its fangs and claws, and render it one more harmless expression of our mutual desire for more. For that is what the monster is: the last gasps of impossible desire. A thwarted, traumatized impulse to connect.

In the middle of the conversation, we almost get stuck. I remember our New Year's resolutions, made weeks ago. "Total presence! Total freedom!" I gleefully cry. "Oh I wish I had said these words earlier!" Geoff scowls and nearly slips behind the wall. He is convinced that I am criticizing him for not living up to these ideals.

"No!" I profess, "I am just calling into presence a point we know we share, so we can affirm it and make it real *now*—more real than whatever is pushing us apart!"

"Which, of course," Geoff replies, "means that it's not more real." He is protesting loudly, but I know why: he wants our connection that much. Round and round we go. He finally drops his shield and yields to his own desire. *Yes! Total presence is what we both want and now!* We move again.

"I ask you for what I want," I affirm, "because I *know* you can give it to me. Because I *know* you want to. Because you and I want the *same thing*: to be open to one other as the cause of our being. *Now.*"

We are learning more about total presence. Total presence is a willingness to move beyond right and wrong with one another. It describes a way of being in the moment, for the moment, that must be recreated in every moment out of whatever memories, habits, experiences, and challenges that moment gives.

What are we creating?

Geoff sighs with relief. He feels as if a huge load has been lifted from his shoulders and from his heart. He is free. He sits quietly. A boulder moved. The plaits beneath are curled and yellow, but they will grow.

Today I notice the berries. They look decorative in their color, shape, and size. To potential pod carriers, they must seem attractive indeed—tangy bursts of vital nutrients with secret seeds stowed within. There are white berries on brown stalks and red berries on green stalks, all on display. *Eat me!*

The asters too are calling attention to themselves. Each type chooses a different ploy—white petals emanating from a yellow core, lavender petals from a white core, and purple petals from a gold core. Something for everyone.

These plants are dying, yet in such a glorious glow. Then again, I muse, they are not dying at all. What looks like death is a sign of the plants' vitality and their responsiveness to the changes of season. As the light dims and temperatures drop, they are demonstrating their resilience by pulling their lives inward and leaving self-contained seed-packs of promise swaying on their drying twigs.

These plants are dying because they are alive; they are dying to live again. They are creating the relationships with the setting sun, the cooling wind, the freezing water, and the hardening earth that will enable them to grow into spring-new shapes of life.

That same impulse to connect lives through me.

January 2008. The next day, despite Geoff and my shared glee at having landed the monster, I am mad. I am angry at the monster. I am flat out furious that it has deprived me of so much happiness and leisure over the years. I want it to die, once and for all.

Yet in between internal eruptions, I note how different this anger is from anger I have felt in the past. *This anger is not directed at me!* It feels good and pure, righteous even. *Nor is it directed at Geoff.* It is specific—zooming in on a pattern of sensation and response that has prevented us from opening to what our love can create through us.

As soon as this thought forms, my experience of the monster shifts.

Perhaps Geoff's monster, like the monster in my green dream, is, in the end, a friendly monster, a big oaf of an imposter, pretending to be a ferocious terror when it is really a wounded kitten. Perhaps it even *is* the monster I saw in my green dream—the red-eyed, white faced, smiling mien leading me into the depths of myself.

Think about it. Without Geoff's monster, I wouldn't have had to break my own patterns of self-incrimination. His monster triggered these patterns in me in such a way that I was able to see them, grasp them, and know that they weren't working to get me where I wanted to be—closer to him. Because the monster was his monster, I had to learn how to stand up and speak to it, honest with how I was feeling, asking for what I need, trusting in our connection more than my ego-protected self.

When I began to stand up and speak, of course, I sent the monster into a building frenzy. Wall after wall appeared, and I kept running smack into them. Even then, however, this pain forced me to step back and see, in what I didn't want, a mirror image of what I did. I had to keep asking for more. And I kept going because every time, eventually, Geoff would come around

to agree with me completely: what I wanted was what he wanted too.

As this arc of the process appears, fraught as it is, I see something else as well: the sting of impossible desire is losing its color. My fears of being too much and not enough to love are falling away. New patterns of sensing and responding are budding to life. *We are going all the way.* The monster is learning how to play.

Geoff listens as I knead my rage at the monster and its walls into a mystifying gratitude. "Yes," he responds, "you should be mad at anything that gets in the way of your pleasure." He affirms too how necessary it is to him that I keep coming towards him.

"I want you to be someone I am afraid of losing."

I welcome the wall. That night I feel my desire as love.

Bringing Sense to Life

Total presence. Of course, I know, it is an impossible ideal. We humans are never fully present to ourselves, not to mention present to one another, and we can never be. We are multidimensional creatures, always in process, always becoming someone else with every movement we make.

Yet, this impossibility is what makes total presence a desirable and fruitful *practice* over time. Because we can never be present once and for all, we can cultivate a willingness to be present *now*. When we do the work of bringing our senses to life, we can find an impulse, in the pinch of an instant, within our sensory selves, to move in ways that sustain this openness. When we are attentive to what love is creating in us, we allow love to grow through us.

Seasons change. We shed our leaves, bare our branches, and welcome the new leaves that grow in the spring. We die and are born again, more able than ever to live in love.

I make my way back to the house by way of the wild apple trees. Where other trees turn red, these trees make red: solid

rounds dimpled by stem and core. This year is bountiful. Our apple trees could pass as Christmas trees, so decked are they along every branch with glowing globes. I want to pick some. I want to eat some and become some. While most of the trees around here have grown so big that it is impossible to do so, I spy one tree with a few low branches whose burden I am confident I can relieve.

I pop into the house for some bags, and bring Kyra and Kai back out with me to help. Jordan tags along too. He climbs the tree and tosses apples down from above. I reach the reachable gifts. Kyra finds whole fruit on the ground. Soon we have a bulging bag full, enough for now. We take it inside. Abundance. What can we make with these?

I opt for the most basic of storage media: sauce. Besides being delicious to eat, good at any meal, and tolerant of bruises, applesauce is a versatile food filler, excellent for baking into breads and muffins, cookies and brownies. It will go to good use.

First, however, we should collect some raspberries. On the way in, I noticed their weighted stalks, heavy with purple-red, plumped prizes, so sweet and tart to the tongue. We all tramp back outside, pint-sized yogurt containers in hand, to pick some berries. Bags won't do for this job.

We make our way around the outside of the bed, pulling off the stray grapevines that are threatening to take over. I pull up a raspberry branch and find a hidden jackpot. I drop the seed-laden fruits one by one into my container. It quickly fills. I share some with Kai. His container quickly empties. Chances are that most of what we pick today will end up in his belly.

What better place could a berry be?

7

Pumpkins in the Compost

All change is a miracle to contemplate.
—Henry David Thoreau[1]

October 2008. I have been hearing the rumors for days, whispers from the outdoor-chore doers. *There are pumpkins growing in the compost.* Pumpkins in the compost? I decide to investigate.

I sink my feet into the squishy comfort of my forever-warm-and-dry, anti-muck Muck boots and trudge outside. The afternoon sun is softening. Its rays melt golden. I walk around to the back of the barn, next to one of the two white-washed silos that stand sentinel over our farm.

To call our festering pit a "compost pile" is a bit of wishful

thinking. We dug a hole in the ground and into it we dump whatever indoor food scraps we cannot feed the chickens—banana peels, coffee grinds, corn cobs, and onion skins. We don't tend it or turn it. We don't layer it as we should with materials that will keep it simmering at a weed-killing heat. Still, technically speaking, the matter there is decaying. Composting is what we would want to have happen, hence the name.

Sure enough, wrapping in, through, and over our peels and rinds are pumpkin plants, at least three of them. Elephant ear leaves and flashy orange blossoms sprout from a tangled weave of vines. I follow the vines under and through, looking for the hard green rounds that form at the base of each flower cup where it sits on its stem. I find a few golf balls, then a tennis ball, and there, one the size of a small soccer ball. We may have a pumpkin yet!

A rush of joy startles me. It gives me so much pleasure to see these freckled green globes. So much pleasure. Why? The pumpkins are growing here, pregnant with possibility, a complete surprise, where we would least expect them, using our dumped and neglected waste to make something beautiful. It is magic! It is a miracle! It is what farming is all about.

Perhaps I shouldn't be so astonished, but I constantly am. Such magical transformations are *natural* on the farm, expected, and even counted on as necessary. Molding mounds of manure transform into fragrant fertilizers. Scraps from kitchen plates morph into perfect light brown eggs. Grass clippings and cornhusks become light-spilling milk. The dirt feeds the plants that feed the animals who feed us, all of whose waste feeds the earth again. It is an endless and endlessly creative cycle of life in which every death—even that of pumpkins tossed the year before—harbors a potential for supporting new life.

As I see these pumpkin plants growing hearty and resilient over bumpy terrain, I *know* this endless rebirth in my sensory self. I feel it *viscerally* as hope for the surprises that life can bring, and

the joy I feel moves me to want to participate. I want to be a part of this miracle! It's the connection I moved here to find—this open sensory awareness of the earth within. *I am a part of creation and creation is a part of me.*

Pumpkins in the compost. The same logic, we are finding, holds in our life as a farm family. Those fraught encounters with caregivers, partners, and progeny that we would prefer to cast away as irredeemable refuse provide us with the vital nutrients we need to sustain our life. They nourish our capacity to love. In fact, such moments are exceptionally fertile. A peel of disappointment or crust of desire can catalyze a shift in our experience of our bodily selves in which we come to a *visceral knowledge* of our impulse to connect. We can realize that we are feeling these aversive feelings *because* we want to connect and be connected with those whose support we need in becoming who we are.

We know in our sensory selves that *we are nothing more or less than an impulse to connect, born bodies who can and must learn to live in love as the enabling condition of our best becoming.*

When this experience shift happens, we have the conceptual and sensory resources we need to compost our discomforting emotions into black gold. The magic is undeniable. With caregivers, we can transform the sting of impossible desire into a boundless gratitude to them for awakening in us a desire for more than they can provide. With partners, we can transform the desolation and despair we feel at the walls between us into the delight of practicing total presence.

Nowhere is this alchemy more evident, however, than in our relationships with those we choose to raise: our children. With progeny, we can transform the flares of furious frustration that they ignite in us into a healing energy that propels us to live for ourselves the lives we would want for them. Our children are primary enablers: they require us to grow along the trajectories of desire quickened by our caregivers and stoked by our partners *in order to succeed in connecting with them.*[2] So too, the changes

they provoke in us feed back into our relationships with caregivers and partners, providing us with added resources for making moves of gratitude and presence.

Since Geoff and I first conceived, I have learned the lesson again and again: our children need us to become who we are for their sake. They need us to unfold our capacity to love for their sake. Children are not black holes demanding attention; they are creatures born of connection, who need and want to feel the power and pleasure of their own impulse to connect, giving, growing, and creating the relationships they need to support them in becoming who they have the potential to be. Said otherwise, children want nothing more than to love their caregivers.

As parents, then, our greatest challenge in learning to love our children lies in learning to receive our children's love for us. It is a task that requires that we let go of the expectation that we can or should meet all of our children's needs. It requires that we let go of the sense of ourselves as individuals in control. It requires that we acknowledge our children as causes of our being, and so welcome the emotions they stir in us as opportunities to make the openness we share with them more real than our ego-protecting patterns of withdrawal, defense, or attack. If we can and when we do, we see anew our relationship to our own caregivers as well, for we are children too.

Choosing to Participate

This evening, the outdoor chores fall to me. Usually, the kids lead. However, Jordan and Jessica are playing an away soccer game and won't be home until 7:30. By then it will be dark and dinnertime, homework time, and bedtime. Now it is chore time.

Kyra and Kai are in the yard pretending their tricycles are tractors when I head out to take care of Marvin. They decide to come with me. While they hang out in the barn, I enter the new pasture we made for Marvin over the weekend. It is horse

heaven, grass galore. Already he is making a dent in what seemed like an endless quantity of crunchy greens. He comes to me quickly, a friendly look in his eyes, knowing well what time it is. I reach high to put the halter over his ears, nearly hugging him in the process. We are face to face. He could knock me over in a heartbeat. He doesn't.

I lead Marvin into the barn, fill his grain bucket, connect the water hose, and turn it on. I pull out a rubber-nubbed currycomb and cover his body in circles. My hand moves round and round, behind his ear, down his neck, across his back, under his belly, around his haunches to the tops of his legs. He stands there without constraint, seeming to enjoy his full body rub. He nuzzles me as I cross in front of him to his other side. Horses need this rousing touch. They aren't the only ones.

Kyra, eager to help, dumps an armload of hay in Marvin's stall and goes to get another. Kai adds his handful and follows Kyra back to the bales. At this rate we'll be here all night. Still, every little bit helps.

I take out a stiff-bristled brush and begin again, going over the same span of Marvin's hide, and brushing away all of the fluff and dander stirred by my first skin-scratching pass. A rush of joy passes through me like the one I felt moments ago at the sight of the compost pumpkins. This time it flows through my arm, down my legs, and out into the ground. Why?

My movement pulls thoughts into its wake. *It's my impulse to connect.* My brushing is creating a connection, animal to animal, that is not only pleasing Marvin, it is transforming me. I can feel the change in my sensory self. My own grooming movements are making me into someone who is open to this fellow creature as providing her with the pleasure of this action—someone who feels love for this beast.

Words that Jessica uttered on a recent ride pop into my mind: "I could live on the back of this horse," she said. Tonight I understand. As I brush, I am aware of Marvin's strong shape and

powerful build. I feel the desire to climb on him, walk, trot, and canter with him, aligning myself with the force of his beauty.

No wonder Jessica loves Marvin so much. She must feel the joy of creating a relationship with him that supports her in unfolding what she has to give. The pleasures of caring for Marvin and of becoming who she is are inextricably entwined. In caring for him, she not only confirms how much she loves horses, she knows that *she can*. She can open to Marvin as a cause of her being, and as she has, she has become both a better rider and more of the singular, relational bodily self that she is. This horse is enabling her to experience her own impulse to connect.

I smile remembering her last riding class. Jessica was so impressive—erect and strong, posting with the trot, rolling with the canter, and craning forward to jump. It was a dance.

As for me, I surely wouldn't be here in this barn brushing a horse if it weren't for Jessica. Jordan and Kyra love horses. Kai does too. But Jessica is the one who begged to have a horse, found this farm for a horse, and has read every book she could get her hands on about how to care for horses, train them, ride them, and heal them.

I wonder. If it weren't for Jessica's passion for horses, would Geoff and I still be waiting to live our dream of moving to the country and creating our center for arts and ideas? Did we birth her to enable us to unfold in this farm-fed life—for her sake?

I finish brushing. There is some crusty crud under Marvin's right rear fetlock. I administer *White Lightening* gel as the farrier recommended, give Marvin some pats, plant a kiss on his velvet nose, and turn off the hose.

I wait for Kyra and Kai and we all cross back over the street together. This snake of a road winding through our pastoral Eden constantly reminds us of how dependent our farm family remains on the grid for electricity, oil, and food. It is a constant reminder as well of the dream that brought us here: to connect with our earth differently than the vast majority of people in the

western world. We want to live off the grid, using renewable energy sources to heat our air, water, and food. We want to recycle every wad of waste into someone else's food. So too we want to create the relationships with one another that will support us each in sustaining this life-enabling connection with the natural world. We want to be our own earth-friendly farm family.

I slip into the kitchen for a small pail of soapy water and a milk bucket, call Geoff to tell him I'm milking, and leave Kyra and Kai under his care. As kind as our cows are, they are too big for our small K's. Daisy has knocked Kai over too many times with an innocent scratch of the belly, a shift in weight, or mere swat of the tail. To milk, I go alone.

The heifer barn is dark. Scant sunlight penetrates at this hour. The smell is rich, and the long corridor no longer as pristine as it was when we spent the afternoon shoveling a mere two weeks ago. These cows are big, and so are their cow "patios" as Kyra once called them.

The cows follow me as I open the door to the hayloft where we store the grain bags. I turn to put down the bucket and pail. In a flash, Precious, our heifer Houdini, is out the door and into the hayloft, brown eyes boring in on the plump sacks of sweetness. I rush behind her thousand-pound frame waving my hands, slapping at her behind.

"Hey! Stop!" I yell. As a strategy, it is highly effective. Precious ignores me.

OK. Hurry. *Think*!

Precious pauses at the first sack of grain. Stepping in front of her, I quickly fill a scoop, thrust it under her nose, and take a small step back into the barn. She takes a step toward me then hesitates. Behind her the hayloft door stands open to the wild green yonder. I take another step back, she follows, and again. Finally she passes through the gate and back into the barn. I slam it shut and exhale relief. I am well aware. My sole power in

relation to Precious lies in her desire. Fortunately, when given the choice between food and freedom, she always chooses food.

I pour grain into Daisy's bucket, click her into her stanchion, give Precious her grain, pull an overturned crate beside Daisy, sit on it, and go to work washing her teats with the soapy water. It's an easy task today, not much muck. I pull on each of the four teats to start the milk flow and point the first few bacteria-laden squirts into the hay. Then I put the gleaming stainless steel bucket between Daisy's back legs under her udder and begin.

I watch in silence as slender streams of milk pulled by my hand fill the bottom of the bucket. This milk is beautiful. It is a foamy golden color, creamy thick and translucent at once. It is not like milk you pour from a bottle bought at the store. Store-bought milk is flat, opaque, and chalky white. Once pasteurized and homogenized, bottled and shipped, milk is inert. That is the point. No bad bacteria. No good bacteria. It is done becoming anything but sour. This newly pulled milk, by contrast, is luminous and alive. It is capable of becoming so much more, cream and butter, yogurt and cheese, and our staple, ice cream.

The bucket fills a couple of inches. I am squeezing and pulling down, closing off the top of a teat and pushing the milk out of its hole. With two hands, it's two teats at a time. The back teats, half the length of those in front, require some finger-warping dexterity. I move my hands to the far couple, front and back. Maybe these will go faster. Eventually, I know, the milk will rise to the top of this two-gallon pail. All it takes is time. It is what we call a Jordan job, demanding patience, attention to detail, and the creation of something beautiful.

I wonder how Jordan does it. I haven't asked him recently, but I am sure he has worked out a new and improved system of teat tugs. Milking is his passion, his quiet time with the cows, his contribution to family life. He double-handedly secures our dairy independence every day.

Dandelion and Precious, having finished their grain, gather round to watch. Dandi comes up behind me and touches her nose to my ear. I smile at the sound of her warm breathing. Precious sticks her nose under Daisy from the other side. I point a teat at her and squirt.

The level of milk no longer seems to be rising. I take a deep breath. Patience. Time to start singing. I try one song and then another. Daisy shifts back and forth restlessly. OK, I sigh, "Edelweiss." I don't know why Daisy likes it. Perhaps it's those visions of Alpine splendor, where *Heidi* meets *The Sound of Music*. This cow before me, however, is no dream. The bucket won't fill unless I squeeze and pull, and sing to keep myself sitting and sane. The sound of my voice echoes off Daisy's side and reverberates round the bucket.

The level of milk is rising again. As it nears the top, Daisy's milk flow slows to a trickle. Her udder is soft and empty. She has not kicked the bucket today. Nor has she plunked her muddy hoof into it or swatted my face with her knotty tail. I will leave with a full bucket of gratitude, this evening's catch.

Jordan has made me into a milker, and one who is acutely conscious of our current cow culture. It used to be that every family had a cow, or aspired to have one. The rhythm of milk making was as much a part of life as day and night. Once out in the open, milk can't be kept for long. It has to be drunk live, or curdled, creamed, churned, and cheddared. Every day.[3]

Yet now, the simple action of milking a cow seems exotic. What seems "natural" is to walk into a warm kitchen, open the refrigerator door, and lift out a carton. We consume milk from the masses for the masses, pulled by machines from anonymous cows. Most people in our culture no longer know the animals who feed them or quench their thirst. We can pretend that such animals don't really exist. Yet when we lose this link to the sources of our nourishment, what have we lost? We lose a sensory awareness of our impulse to connect with the natural

world. Factory farming and the local grocery store support us in believing that we are individuals first. Jordan is enabling me to know otherwise.

As I lift the bucket of Daisy milk, a thrill of accomplishment passes through me. What she gives is more than nourishing, life-enabling elixir. Daisy is enabling me to feel the pleasure of connecting in this way with her. I thank her, scratch her neck, and place the bucket safely over the fence away from curious noses. I release her from the stanchion, spend a few minutes mucking out, and make my way back outside. Picking up the bucket I walk towards the house, noticing. The clouds are swarming in elongated clumps of pink and blue, stretching across the horizon. The sun is tossing its last red-yellow rays along the valley, preparing to pull back and over the hills. I am in awe of this earth.

I muse. If it hadn't been for Jordan wanting a cow, and if I hadn't been out here doing chores for him, I would have missed this moment. Bearing witness to this beauty, I choose to participate.

I enter the house with my glowing pail. Kyra and Kai are already inside, scrambling about the kitchen. Geoff is chopping vegetables for dinner. On the shelf, I see Kyra's pumpkin—the lone round that had been growing in her garden (not our compost pile) a mere hour before. She picks up the pumpkin and trots over. Days ago we discovered black bodies gathering on her vine's one viable fruit. Jessica identified the visitors as juice-sapping squash beetles. They had done their work.

"Mom! I was trying to clear the squash beetles off my pumpkin and it fell off into my hand! It is all squishy!" I ache seeing the lingering strains of her disappointment.

"Good for you, Kyra." I say encouragingly. She has been so excited about her pumpkin and its jack-o-lantern potential. I know she is working hard to be brave. "What a great pumpkin. So that is what those beetles do!" A flash of gratitude races

through me for those pumpkins in the compost. We have options.

"Have you done the chickens yet?" I ask. She shakes her head. "Let's do them together," I suggest. She picks up the scrap bucket and heads out the door. I follow. We are soon joined by four hens and the rooster. I pause and watch as the five birds bound after Kyra up the slope towards the coop. They recognize her as their caregiver. She feels the love.

Stopping at the door, she announces, "Mom, we have to clean out the coop tomorrow." Ah, she noticed. Is that my job? At least she said "we."

Letting Love

Returning from coop to house, I send Geoff back to work. He might as well get in another half hour before picking up the tired soccer stars. I am happy to make dinner on my own. Kyra and Kai will play, I hope.

I never was much of a cook. I didn't catch a love of it from my parents. It was something my mom did. I wanted to be a bread-winner, like my dad. Before Geoff and I married I made sure that he knew: if he was expecting someone to cook his meals, do his laundry, and clean his house, he had the wrong partner. Being in the kitchen meant losing myself. Period. I had greater ambitions than that!

I chuckle. Here I am cooking away with immense satisfaction. It has something to do, I think, with the colors and shapes, textures and tastes. It is has something to do with working with my hands to turn a hodge-podge assembly of ingredients into a mouth-watering, soul-nourishing communal experience. But it also has something to do with the mental space the movements enable: when I cook food, I cook thoughts. The manual moves enable mental ones. I sort problems along with the spinach leaves. I cut issues into pieces with the tomatoes. I find solutions with the right spice.

It occurs to me. I wouldn't cook like this if it weren't for the kids. I wouldn't cook like this if Geoff weren't working in the next room towards our vision of an art-inspired farm family. I wouldn't think like this if I didn't cook. I like how I think, and it's all because we are here on the farm. *My kids are enabling me again. They are letting me live.* With a rush, I feel the joy of connecting with them in this way.

I pick up at the cutting board where Geoff left off, slicing onions, peeling and pressing the garlic, and mincing fresh parsley and basil that Kyra snipped from the garden. I set pasta water to boil. We are having pasta again, mostly because Jordan loves it so. Given the chance, he would eat mounds of semolina, stretched, rolled, cut, and cooked, at least twice a day, every day. He promises me that in three years we'll be growing our own grain.

I follow the pasta path back through my memories of him. The kids enable me in so many ways—and not just by giving me the opportunity to cook for them or care for animals. My kids push me to open to love beyond where I have gone before; it is my children, even more than caregivers or partner, who mirror back to me the sensory impress of my own actions. They are the ones who can release clods of rage that threaten to bury us all. It is rich compost.

The water is boiling. I open the cabinet to six pasta types, long and thin, short and fat, and everything in between. Tonight it will be linguine. I dump the pound. Soon a pound won't do.

Just this morning Jordan and I locked horns and I found myself far down a path of furious frustration, madly scrambling for a way out. Jordan was late for school. I did not want him to miss the bus.

"You have to be outside now, Jordan. You only have fifteen minutes to milk!"

He tosses his head in frustration. "Don't say that! It stresses me out!" Suddenly everything is wrong and he is blaming me. "I don't have any clean socks!" "Who took my jeans?" "Where is my hat?" He

is slowed by the stress, which makes me even more anxious and even more defensive about my right to be anxious.

"You have got to get out there now. Wear any socks! Take Dad's!" He won't. "OK, here is one clean one and one dirty one, now go!" He is downcast, moving slowly. I turn and wipe the counter with harsh strokes. The atmosphere is thick. Finally, finally, he leaves for the barn in a huff, gruffly asking me to close the door behind him.

He is gone. I breathe a sigh of relief. In its wake rides a shimmer of despair. I don't like this scratch of stress between us. It feels horrible to me. I feel horrible about myself for riding him so hard. It wasn't just about him.

I breathe down, open, and out, pulling my self back into my body as I pack Jordan's soccer bag and unpack my emotional state. Why this calm-cracking flood? Where is the desire in my sensory swirl? Where is the desire in his?

Soon after the exchange, as I breathed open my sensory awareness, an image formed in me of Jordan's impulse to connect. I do know: Jordan wouldn't be upset if he didn't care. He wouldn't be upset with me if he didn't care what I think. He wants to connect and be connected with me. I should recognize it by now. What he is resisting is our *dis*connection, as he has always done. At age two, he would respond to my disappointment or disapproval with newly minted words: "Please don't say that, Mommy. When you say that it makes me very sad." He cares.

In this respect, Jordan hasn't changed. Even if it seems to me that he is oblivious to my concern, and oblivious to the time he has to be in the car and on the way to school, he isn't. Not only does he care about milking on time, he cares even more that *I know he cares*. He not only wants to do the good thing, the right thing, he wants me to know that he can do the right thing. He wants me to know him, to believe in him, to see in him the person he is and wants to be—just as I have always wanted from my parents. He wants *me* to see *him* as loving *me*.

At that point, a connection formed in my mind between congruent shapes of sensation and response. I remembered the walk we took with Marvin (chapter 2). When Jordan is not connecting as he wants to connect, he responds as I have modeled for him. He takes the blame himself and then resents how heavy and unjust it is.

The implications landed with a solid thump. *Jordan wants what I want. We want the same thing. What frustrates him is the distance he knows I perceive between us—a distance neither one of us wants to be there. So if I respond to him in anger, I prove him right: I obviously am not understanding him. I make his predicament worse: he feels as if everything he is doing is having the opposite effect from what he wants! Because of my response, he feels the sting of impossible desire.*

Because of my response. So why do I respond as I do? I rehearsed what I keep relearning. *It is my impulse to connect as well. When I see Jordan making moves to protect himself from the sting of impossible desire that I have been working so hard to recreate in myself in relation to my parents and Geoff, I am instantly flooded with the sense that I am failing in my desire to connect with him, for he is stuck in the same hell I was. All of my own fears come roaring back: I will not get what I want. The universe is intent on taking my pleasure away. Jordan is proof.*

I know now and I knew then, it isn't true. Jordan, in sounding out this moment of disconnection, was giving me exactly what I need on an ongoing basis: the opportunity to find my freedom from the last grip of my self-denying, self-protecting stunts. I have learned to affirm my stretching self and welcome the wall; I have tasted boundless gratitude with my parents and total presence with Geoff, and I can find ways to move in relation to my kids that open me to them as causes of my becoming too.

How? I followed my breathing, down, around, and out, inviting a sensory awareness of my own impulse to connect—the desire at the core of my emotional knot. *What do I really want in this situation? It's not that Jordan be on time for school. I want Jordan*

to let himself live. I want what I say and do to register with him as catalysts for his own bodily becoming, and not judgments on his worth. It's what I want with all my children, all the time.[4]

My lingering frustration dissolved and a new sensory space slid into view. *Jordan and I are so connected! We want to be. So how can I help him succeed in loving me?*

A new move sped into view: "How can I help you, Jordan? I know you care. What do you need? Tell me what I can do."

I stir the pasta, add tomatoes and spices to the sauté, and cut, butter, and spread garlic on the bread. No two meals are ever the same. We have some basic dinners, but with each preparation, there is a novel twist—a new combination of vegetables, spices, and flavorings of varying sizes and shapes. Otherwise, I would get bored. I can't stand being bound by a recipe. In my book, the only way to prepare a perfect meal is to do it differently every time.

Geoff leaves to pick up the soccer stars. I add carrots, cucumbers, and more tomatoes to the salad. The tomatoes are for Jessica. I mix some in and leave another pile right on top. Inevitably, the stash will be gone soon after she enters the house. One by one, the red chunks will disappear. I rarely catch her in the act, but the correlation is strong. I want a few left for me.

My raw thoughts drift from Jordan to her. Jessica triggers a different, overlapping range of sensory responses in me, though no less savory. She has this uncanny ability to imagine all possible eventualities to any suggested course of action and point them out—as obstacles. Sometimes I find it infuriating.

It happened just the other day. I was trying to encourage her, unsuccessfully, to ride Marvin, as I had been for a half hour. She was folded into a book, half perched on a stool, lost to the world. I was feeling the weight of responsibility. Marvin needed his exercise. It was her turn to ride him. I finally made another suggestion, offering her an easy way out: a flat and forgiving

dirt-road ride, on a strip of land visible across the pond from our house.

"Why don't you ride Marvin up Lang Hill Road?" I asked.

"I don't think Marvin likes Larry's dog."

She replied without hesitation, without lifting her eyes from the page, shooting down my idea in an instant. I was trying to help her get what she says she wants (riding her horse), and trying to get what we both want (a well cared-for horse), and all she could say was "no, that won't work."

My ire rose in sheets and coils into biting pronouncements poised to strike. Although I held my tongue, I imagined myself saying all kinds of horrible things: "Well, I guess you just don't want to ride your horse." Or, "You don't care about your horse!" Or, "Why do you have a horse if you aren't going to ride him!" I have said such words in the past, much to my regret. I know what happens when I do. Jessica will either burst into furious tears, or argue vehemently no and dig in even more, defending how Marvin, in this case, really doesn't like carnivorous canines. Unlike Jordan, she doesn't turn against herself. She stands and fights.

I worked hard to breathe calmly, down and out, around and through, to give this seething mass of frustration time to transform into something else. *What do I want here?* I wanted Jessica's happiness, of course. Jessica wanted her happiness too. She wanted my happiness, and I wanted my happiness. *What move can I make?*

Looking for a way through, I saw where I was getting stuck. I reminded myself. *Jessica's propensity to predict the future is not a problem. It is not a judgment on me or my suggestion. It is a gift; and this gift is a potential that I can and want to help her develop. She might be right. Even now, she has a point. The dog is a barking terror, lunging at the end of a clanking metal chain. So?*

As I freed Jessica from my whirlpool of self-incrimination, I was able to see her and her impulse to connect anew. The thoughts that

surfaced were shocking. *Perhaps, in this very moment, she is using her gift in order to connect with me. Perhaps she is trying to share with me how much she cares about Marvin and me, not how little!* The insight hummed. Even if it wasn't true, the possibility of imagining another interpretation of her resistance alerted me yet again to how primed I am to sense and respond to her comments as if *I* am being denied. *Why am I so primed? Why so irate?*

It was not hard to discern another fold of my own unresolved desire for more. At some level, I was afraid that Jessica too was blocking my happiness and preventing me from getting what I want. If, in such a moment, I respond to her as if she is blocking my happiness, and then she responds back to me as if I am preventing her from getting what she wants, then she is simply mirroring the move in relation to me I have just demonstrated in relation to her.

Seeing her make those moves in relation to me infuriates me, because the reverse is true: *I want to help her get what she wants!* I don't want to be someone who is blocking her. I feel unseen and unappreciated. *Her response in unjust! But is mine unjust as well? Is Jessica really preventing me from getting what I want?*

No. I recognized the dynamic, so similar to the one with Jordan. In resisting me, Jessica was giving me exactly what I needed so that I could find my freedom from fear and succeed in helping her get what she wants. She was letting me see myself in a way that was inspiring me to make a change in my patterns of sensing and responding for her sake as well as for mine. *I want to let her live.*

That afternoon the play of mirrors resolved into a new view. *I can connect with the power of Jessica's gift. I can affirm her desire for a relationship with Marvin and with me. I can help her get what she wants, by knowing that I am getting what I want. We both want more.*

I finally speak. "You take good care of your horse, Jessica. You anticipate what he needs and how he will feel. So what would you propose?" She has an answer.

I put the salad on the table, drain the pasta, give the sauté a final stir, and take out a block of cheddar to grate. I wish it were homemade. We haven't gotten that far in our cheese making skills. We are currently stalled at mozzarella.

"Kyra! Can you please set the table?"

"I am playing with Kai." Her voice registers a slight protest, but I can't complain. Technically she is doing one of the tasks she knows falls into the pre-dinner category. Kai must be entertained.

"OK, three more minutes." Jordan, Jessica, and Geoff are not home yet anyway, and once they enter the house there will be some organizing to do. As long as Kyra and Kai are enjoying themselves then I am happy as well, free to do what must be done. I continue grating the cheese, putting on napkins, thinking my thoughts.

Kyra, in all her sweetness, can also rocket me to that place of inner rupture with a similar catalyzing effect. I have her to thank for my moment of radical self-affirmation after all. She doesn't mean to—none of them do—but it happens anyway. It is inevitable. The dynamic is the same: when she practices patterns of shaming and blaming that I learned in relationship to my caregivers, and does so in relationship to me, it strikes me as a judgment on my ability to get what I want—her freedom from those same patterns—and so triggers those dis-connecting patterns in me once more. It's a trap. The only way out is to create new patterns of sensing and responding to my own pain, for I can't connect with her or any of the other children until I do.

Kyra can whine, especially when Kai does something that she doesn't like—pinching, poking, or punching. While I don't like what he is doing either, it is her whining that somehow floods me with fury. I slide to end of my rope faster than a firefighter down the pole, and then cling for dear life, hoping the knot will hold. It happened recently.

"Stop whining," I pleaded through gritted teeth. "Just stop whining. I can't take it. Why are you just sitting there letting him

pinch you? Get up! Stand up for yourself! He is only trying to connect with you!"

I knew I should be compassionate. Kyra was hurt! But I was angry with her for being hurt; for letting herself be hurt, and for pitting me against Kai. I didn't want her to be hurt. I don't want her to be a victim. I have no patience for either. I heard myself talking sternly to her. I saw her crumple in tears. *She is hurt and I am blaming her.* As the horror of what I was doing sunk in, I quickly stopped myself, hugged her tight, and waited for my rage to compost into something more fertile.

Why so incensed? I didn't want to react in the way I was reacting. She was obviously weak, and I was scolding her. But it was not just a matter of having more patience, though I clearly could use some. There was something else at stake.

With Kyra on my lap, I consciously breathed through the curdled rage until my deep love for her was streaming through my bodily self. I reached into the corners of my consciousness, groping about for similar, potentially illuminating experiences with Jordan and Jessica, Geoff and my parents. Unlike Jordan in his self-incrimination or Jessica in her defensiveness, Kyra in her whining seems to suck away all of my vital energy. I feel powerless, unable to act, and afraid that I can't. My rebellion against her wells as a ferocious roar against everything in my life that would make me smaller and less of who I am. She too challenges me in a place where I have not fully alchemized the sting of impossible desire.

What do I want? I want to help her get what she wants; I want to live in a world where she thrives. I want to connect with her in this way, and because I do, her resignation stabs. I refuse to let her give up! I will fight for her, even when it means turning against her.

I remember what she said to me a few nights ago. Ever wise beyond her years, she pointed out: "My body is not meant to protect me from anything that hurts me." She is right. Mine isn't either, and it hasn't. There is no way to protect myself from pain,

Kyra's or my own. Her pain is my pain; at some level we are and always will be one extended sensory surface, folding and creasing through time and space.

Because there is no way to protect myself from my child's pain, I must learn how to respond to it as a potential for pleasure that has yet to unfold. I must—in order to connect with her.

With Kyra calmly on my lap, I called her whine to mind. Its echo made me shudder. Nevertheless, I took a breath and tried to shift my experience of it.

Where is the impulse to connect?

It occurred to me: maybe Kyra's whine was a sign that she was protesting, not giving up. *Perhaps she is seeking comfort when and where and how she can. She is taking care of herself by wanting to connect with someone who will help her, namely me. She is asking me for what she needs, and in doing so, she is expressing her openness to me, her love for me! That is what I want for her—and what I want for myself—to be able to connect with a source of comfort when needed! So if I can be there for her at this moment when she needs a squeeze of support, then maybe I will have nothing to fear in my own life either.*

The paradox reverberated. *I can take care of myself. I know this. I am OK. Kyra is helping me feel it, and because I feel it, I can teach her how to feel it too.*

I made a new move in relation to her. "Kyra, I am so sorry you are hurt. You must feel extremely frustrated. Kai should not pinch you. It is not right. What can I do to help you take care of yourself?"

The car pulls in the driveway. "Kyra, Kai! Time to set the table now!" Dinner is almost done. My small K's help place silverware and drinks, tofu, salad dressing, and Parmesan.

I watch Kai as he works, placing forks at odd angles on the napkins. He is doing what the older kids do, exactly as we have taught him, and doing it completely differently. With Kai, this dynamic happens all the time, intensely. Kai, in all of his three

years, is uncannily adept at mirroring images of Geoff and me back to us in ways that demand that we find our freedom from the fears that hinder us from moving in faith along the trajectories of our unmet desires.

I think back to the moment when he catalyzed in me the concept of an impulse to connect as the truth of who we humans are.

A toy whizzes through the air, whistling past Kyra's ear. It is a hard metal truck and it is way too close to soft flesh whose pain I share. I gather like a storm swirling, waiting to burst forth in a hail of no's. That behavior is absolutely not acceptable in this household!

Suddenly I stop. Something stops me. Kai is not upset or vengeful. He is not trying to tease or annoy or frustrate. He is just doing with his toy what he sees me do with a washcloth into the sink, or what Jordan does with a ball. He is feeling the thrill of releasing matter into space. He wants this pleasure, and he wants to share this pleasure with his sister. Look! I can do it too! He wants above all to connect. He wants the glee of it, the shared laughter of it, the surge of white-hot vitality. I am alive! Don't we all?

If I say no to Kai, how will he know that I am not saying no to his intention (to connect), but only to his choice of how (selecting a truck as the most available means)?

I realized that I couldn't say no to Kai. I didn't want to, and besides, it wouldn't work. If there is one quality that describes Kai, it is generous. He is always giving or wanting to give, always thinking about how he can participate in what is happening. What sends him into a scalding sneer is to feel as if his gifts are or might be rejected. When he feels excluded or unappreciated, he lashes out at the injustice. If I respond to his distress by getting caught in my own fury-flooded fears of impossible desire, then I make his deepest fears of not connecting true. He flails harder and faster, wanting to break something or someone, whatever seems to be in the way of his getting the giving he wants.

I made the connection. *Kai's hurl is like the wall. What might seem like an act of deliberate pain-inducing indifference is actually an expression of a deep and abiding need to connect with a person whom you know, at some level, enables you to experience an invaluable sense of being alive.*

I knew what I had to do. *I have to help Kai get what he wants. I have to help him create the patterns of sensation and response that will allow him to connect with Kyra and with me and with all of us in the ways that bring him the pleasure of becoming the person he wants to be. If I can honor his impulse to connect, then I can release him into the stream of generosity that he is and wants to be. Sometimes, at least.*

"Here Kai, try this soft squishy ball."

Ever since that moment, I have known. Kai teaches me much more than patience. He has made me aware of my own impulse to connect—not only his—and of its power. What stopped me from scolding him in that moment was my impulse to connect with him. My impulse to connect with him overrode my habit of shutting down in response to a sense of limit. My desire to be open to him, loving him, was stronger than my past patterns of fear-protection, and I could feel why. *This impulse to connect with him is the driving core of who I am. I am not any particular patterns of sensation and response that I have created in the past—not even those I created and became in relation to my caregivers. I am the ever-ongoing movement of making new ones.*

Jordan helped me see my kids' desire to connect with me; Jessica helped me to attune to how the kids use their own gifts to express it; Kyra helped me appreciate the importance of affirming myself for connecting with them, and Kai helped me name this impulse to connect and grasp its inherent paradox.

My children have helped me to a liberating, visceral knowledge: *I am nothing more or less than an impulse to connect, who I am by virtue of the relationships I create with those who enable me to be.*

Fighting (for) a Fifth

I serve the plates and hand them to hands for transport to the table. Soon, and finally, we are all sitting around our round table. Gazing at this circle of faces, so familiar, so strange, I breathe a sigh of relief. We are here. We hold hands and sing ourselves together, winding our voices into one sound, each person lifted and calmed by the energy of the ring. Amazing Grace. Our farm family. *We enable each other to be.*

As dinner begins, the feeling that I can't seem to shake strikes again. *Someone is missing.* We are all here, but someone is missing. I know it. I feel the lack. But who? *We are not yet complete.* I ponder this thought, crunching hard on a branch of broccoli. *A fifth child*?

It is a relatively calm meal—no spills, squabbles, or screaming fits. It ends. Jordan and Jessica retreat to their favorite homework hangouts. Kyra and Kai pull out all the chairs to help with sweeping. Geoff takes over the dishes. I withdraw into the laundry room to fold.

When you live on a farm with four children, laundry is not one chore among many you can check off your list. It is a state of being. A constant stream of crumpled clothes fills the laundry basket seeking an outlet. I am it.

You would think that the sheer volume of dirty duds would be enough to quash any lingering desire for a fifth child. More laundry? Ah, but I have a secret. It can be rather nice to spend a quiet moment arm-deep in soft warmth. I do some of my best thinking folding and unfolding thoughts as I do the same to shirts, shorts, and sheets.

A fifth child. The thought is overwhelming and irresistible. I have been obsessed with it for two and a half years, ever since that trip to Banff, when my parents were home with the kids, cow, and chickens. The mountain-made moment of imagining a fifth was so pure, so formative. It was our love, beating its wings against the shells of our preconceptions, wanting more of itself.

In the months since, even though I have been wracked with doubt, beaten down by rational arguments, and shuttered by my own exhaustion, I have been unable to squash the small, persistent, deeply inner "yes." I have lived many a moment as a referendum on the issue. If I feel tired or weak or unable to deal, my mind screams—*Aha! You can't do it*!—and I feel despair. Other times, I act weak even when I'm not in order to give myself an excuse not to do what feels too hard. *I just can't.* The yearning remains. How can I say no to the love that flows when Geoff and I open to one another?

I take out a pair of jeans, holes in the knees. Once Jessica's, they are now Kyra's and already too short. I put them aside. Kyra needs new clothes. I abhor shopping.

I revisit the reasons against a fifth child, spinning in rutted tracks. A fifth goes against the rules I have about children: stick with an even number; no more than one child per parent-hand. My four beautiful babes are healthy and well, a perfectly balanced set of nested pairs. Geoff and I have made more than enough humans to replace ourselves. The world is already crawling with people. Kids cost money, and what about my career! I am ambitious! I want to go places, do things, and enter the world as fully as I am able.[5]

Why another child? Is it just the farm fact of being surrounded by relentless reproduction? Shouldn't it have the opposite effect? Enough babies!

"Bach had nineteen children," Geoff explains.

"And three wives," I respond.

The reasons are never enough, for whenever I am feeling open and rested and alive and in love, the desire returns with a crystal clear ring. *This is who you are.*

Even if the reasons were not enough to snuff out the idea, what about the miscarriages? There is no arguing with them. Since Kai's birth, I have had three. *Three.* One was at eight weeks, one at nine weeks, and the third at ten weeks. When I would

finally dare to open, getting pregnant wasn't the problem. Yet the little ones wouldn't stay. It was absurd—a sick nightmare. *Wake up!*

You would think the pain of these losses would quell the desire, but the reality has been more complex. Each small traveler, as short as its visit was, gave me incredible gifts. Each tugged me down into my bodily self where I found new currents of creativity and love. Each enabled me to become more of who I am by pushing me further along in the work I was doing with my parents, with Geoff, and with my first four children. It was as if the little ones that didn't make it were opening the way for the one who would.

Three small deaths gave me so much life.

I take out a balled shirt turned inside out and gently separate and smooth the arms. When the clothes are hot, the wrinkles disappear with a swipe, regardless of how long they sat in the dryer waiting to be folded. A quick warm-up round and we are wrinkle-free.

I think back to the three arcs of anticipation, joy, and loss.

April 2007. No one knew about the first pregnancy. I hardly knew. I didn't take a test until seven weeks. The nausea was teasing, light, and at the surface. The appearing spots confirmed my suspicions. The day before, I had walked the property with Kai on my back, clearing fallen trees and branches, feeling fine. Even so, I was surprised by how sad I felt. I spent hours on the couch, pondering the sequence of events, hoping it might decide to stay after all. *I guess I really did want this.*

I wrote a note to my parents, feeling for some reason that I had to tell them. My dad said nothing. My mom wrote back with relief. *Good. Your life is so busy. Five would be too much.*

Reading her response, I felt the trigger cock to release the sting of impossible desire and all my tried and tired responses. *My parents do not believe in me! They do not want what I want for me! They are only interested in making me smaller—restricting*

my creativity, limiting my joy. They do not really love me—they didn't even say they were sorry! They couldn't love me and respond like this.

I waited for the sting. It didn't come. I was not blasted into paroxysms of fear that I would never get what I want. Something had shifted in my bodily self. I was in a new visceral place. Somehow I was able, as never before, to *sense the love*. I could see in my parents' responses their impulse to connect with me. My mother was parenting me as she had always done, within the limits of her comfort zone. She wanted for me a happiness that she could imagine as possible. For her, five would be too many. Five had overwhelmed her best friend. So she was expressing her love for me as a relief that I would not experience the same ordeal. *She loves me that much.*

The realization dawned, slow and strong. This move in relation to my parents that the little one was letting me make in response to its leaving was exactly the move that I needed to make in order to be able to welcome a fifth child. It was the move I had imagined that would allow me to remain in a sensory space of gratitude to my parents for this bodily self whose desires put me at odds with what they thought best.

I saw the alchemical key: because I had made my own moves of radical self-affirmation with myself, with Geoff, and with our children, I was free to perceive their ways of parenting me as expressions of their impulses to connect with me—expressions influenced in turn by their own experiences in relation to their own caregivers, each other, and me.

My parents gave me the seeds of myself and nurtured those seeds when I could not. It is up to me to discover what those seeds need to grow. As I do, I can give them the freedom to respond to me as they will, welcoming their responses as expressions of their own impulses to connect with me.

The thought boggled my mind. *Perhaps the unfolding I am doing is giving my parents exactly what they need in order to heal from their*

own stings of impossible desire, just as this child, even in its passing, is enabling me to heal from mine.

A first limb of my farm family philosophy branched forth.

It is not love to make caregivers feel as if they failed us. It is love to continue the work our caregivers began along the trajectories of unmet desire they helped us discover. It is love to embrace with gratitude this gift of our bodily becoming.

When we open to our caregivers in these ways, acknowledging them as causes of our being, we open to the flows of bodily creativity that guided us to connect with them and want from them in the first place. We find the freedom to create and become patterns of sensing and responding that connect us with what will enable our becoming.

The dryer is empty. I open the washer and haul out the clothes, wet and wrung. I lift the soggy clumps into the waiting cave, armful by armful, thinking of the second miscarriage. It was as revelatory as the first.

November 2007. I was pregnant again, and again I had doubts about whether the little one would stay. The nausea and fatigue were light, playing on the surface. I tried not to attach.

It was the day before Thanksgiving. After transforming into a human hurricane to clean the house, the spots began. I knew it was leaving. I pushed away the pain and worked harder. Geoff and Jordan and I built a ten-foot table where incoming guests could sit and eat. Our cousins arrived. Geoff left to play the organ for a local church service. The bleeding continued in earnest.

Physically, it was terrifying. It was only a week further along than the first miscarriage, but so much red. In the middle of the night, I asked Geoff to come with me to the bathroom. I passed

out in his arms. I woke up slumped against the wall looking at my feet. He was on the telephone beside me dialing 911. As we traveled together by ambulance to the nearest hospital, forty minutes away, his golden presence beamed comfort around me. It was better than the oxygen.

In the wake of the little one's leaving, another visceral shift happened. Again I saw love, this time in Geoff. Through it all, Geoff was willing to be open to me, totally present with me, trusting completely in our pro/creativity, our mutual desire, as what he needs for his life. *It is a willingness that enables me to be.*

As the insight reverberated through me, I realized that I hadn't fully made a similar shift in myself in relation to a fifth child. I was not completely convinced that the coming of another—fruit of our mutual desire—was what I needed for my singular self to unfold. I harbored worries that I would be sucked in, selling out, and sliding into a pit of unproductive obscurity. Watching Geoff move through the moment in relation to me, I knew: I can trust too.

A second arm of my philosophy arched into place.

It is not love to make partners feel as if we are compromising or sacrificing ourselves for their sake. It is love to welcome the desire they stir in us as a catalyst helping us become the singular, sensory selves we have the potential to be. It is love to trust our impulse to connect with this partner more than our fear of not getting what we want.

When we open to a partner in this way, acknowledging him or her as a cause of our being, we find ourselves able to create and become patterns of sensing and responding to all moments of our lives that express the openness to one another that we are living.

I toss a static-free sheet into the dryer and turn to the waiting wall

of clothes. The next load will barely make a dent. Ah well. I load in chore jeans and school jeans and play clothes and sleeping clothes and think back to the third miscarriage.

July 2008. The animal count was rising. Dandelion had been born in March; Marvin arrived mid-May. There were plenty of bodies to tend, so we were using contraception of a fairly reliable kind. Even so, a small passenger landed, and it felt like the greatest blessing. I didn't have to wrestle with all the reasons against having another. The one strong enough to breach the barrier of our doubt was here! This one, conceived on Mother's Day, was a gift I happily received.

I was not scared. Before there had always been some wagging dog of fear trotting by my side, barking out various complaints until the day I miscarried, once and then twice. Not this time. My creativity flowed. I was beginning this book. I wrote in my journal:

"Being full of life shifts my sensory awareness from my thinking brain into my lived experience. I could describe it as a curious lassitude—a slacking off of my whip-happy mind. But actually, what happens is that the pull downward into my body expands the horizon of my awareness. I become more present in my own self. More body, more flesh, more experience, more sensation, more potential for insight and intuition and creative flashes of brilliance… Something larger is happening and I am part of it. Whatever happens, I will learn."

I did. I was solo parenting with my four kids, together with my sister and her family at a cottage on Kimball Lake that my parents were renting. Geoff was home on the farm. I felt an ebbing and prayed hard. *Please don't go. I am ready. I am free. I am not afraid. I trust. You are a Mother's Day miracle. You worked so hard to come. What more must I do?*

For twenty-four hours, I was a threshold, a crossing place, stretched between life and death, open and available. Waiting. *I want the little one to stay.*

I imagined my uterus as a golden weave of glowing fibers.

The tissue ripped. Just after midnight, the little one left. Contractions gripped my body. Spurting, gushing, the little one slipped out from where it was in dramatic bursts of exploding clots.

I leaned on my breathing practice harder than I ever have. Earth, air, fire, water. Breathing down and out and through, I dove into the heart of the waves, circled the fire within, and flowed with the blood into a diaper I borrowed from Kai, sleeping in peace beside me.

The next day, I was due to drive five hours home. I wanted to go home. I had to go home. I had to swim first. I wouldn't make it if I didn't. The water felt heavenly, healing. My mother accompanied me in a canoe. My father watched the other kids.

"I love this lake," I said to her.

"It loves you too," she replied. I felt it.

At 1 p.m., I loaded the kids into the car. I stopped halfway home at 3:30, only to find, much to my distress that, despite all precautions, I was sitting in a puddle. I changed, cleaned up, got ice cream for the kids, and bought gas for the car. Another traveler scolded me for taking too long at the pump. I smiled back.

I made it home to Geoff. In each other's arms, I finally cried.

The third one's parting was even more bewildering than the first and the second. *This child was wanted! Why make such an effort to come if you are not going to stay? What could possibly grow out of this mess?*

As I sat with my scraps of hope, however, it all began to make an absurd sense. Again, I was learning what I needed to learn in order to welcome, really welcome, a fifth child. For I could see that even though I had been trusting in the desire brought forth in me as an expression of my love for my parents and for Geoff, I was still harboring doubts related to my four children. *Does my desire to have another child express love for them?*

Maybe honoring this desire in me for another was not the best way to love them. *Would I be a better parent to the first four? Wouldn't I be taking something away from them by splitting my attention yet again?*

In the wake of the wee one's departure, the fallacy of this reasoning cracked open in my heart. This idea that one child would take something away from the others assumed an adversarial relationship in which two parties vie over a limited number of resources, squabbling among themselves. It assumed a fixed economy in which there is only so much to go around. It was a question and a doubt based in fear, the fear that I cannot have what I want, that I want what I cannot have. It was one more haunting trace of the sting of impossible desire.

The implication was clear: *by honoring Geoff and my desire for a fifth I will become a better parent.*

Why? To say yes to one is to say yes to all. If I say no to the one who wants to come, I say no to myself who wants its coming. I say no to my parents who gave me the gift of this desire. I say no to my partner who believes in total presence with me. I say no to my children who have already come to be with us.

For if I say no to one child because there is not enough to go around, I doom us all to live in an economy where there is not and cannot be enough. It is an economy in which someone's gain is someone else's loss, an economy in which mom and dad are suppliers and kids are suckers.

Such a world is not what I want to give my children. Nor is it the world in which I want to live. I want to birth my children into an open, ever-expanding economy of surplus, where we each and all are generating more love, more life, more light, and allowing it to spill over and through us into our relationships, our work, and our responses to one another.

I want my children to experience a world full of abundance, surprise, mystery, and generosity. A world whose uncanny twists take us beyond where we knew to want to go. A world in which

we live to make more love. A world where pumpkins grow in the compost.

A third branch of my philosophy stretched into view.

> **It is not love to make our children feel as if they are burdens to bear that require us to sacrifice our dreams for their sake. It is love to help them learn how to create the relationships they need to support them in becoming who they are. It is love to do so by demonstrating how in relationship to them.**
>
> **When we open to our progeny in these ways, acknowledging them as causes of our being, we find ourselves impelled anew to create patterns of sensing and responding that open us to receive from them the love they have for us.**

Letting my children live, I find my life. Letting myself live, I give them theirs.

Three miscarriages—each one released clods of sadness and despair, doubt and distress. Yet each time, a miracle happened and I found myself further along in a trajectory of bodily becoming that was guiding me to live in love with my parents, partner, and children. I had moved to a place where I was able to welcome a fifth child with open mind, open heart, and open womb as an expression of love for us all.

I pour the soap into the washing machine, turn the dial, close the lid, and begin the cycle.

I am expecting again. The nausea is more deeply rooted in the pit of my stomach than it was in the previous three pregnancies. Vines of hope are wrapping around my heart.

Perhaps there will be a pumpkin in the compost after all.

8

Genesis

My dancing… is the affirmation of life through movement.
—Martha Graham[1]

February 2009. I am sitting on an eight-by-eight foot platform that Geoff, our kids, and I built two weeks ago on the stage-left corner of a neighborhood theater, ten miles from our farm. I am snapped into the stretchy, gray fabric envelope I fondly call "the bag." The soles of my feet are touching below my six-month mound of a belly. It is Saturday night, just after 8 p.m. A curtain softens the hubbub of people gathering in the audience. Every one of my senses is alive, though I can't see anything.

Jessica whispers in my right ear, "Almost ready to go, Mom."

Jordan is there beside her, I know, hands on the curtain ropes, ready to pull firmly and steadily as soon as the house lights dim. Geoff is to my left, sitting at the piano, ready to start playing the music he wrote for this dance. Kyra is in the audience and Kai is next to her, propped on the lap of his babysitter. We are all here, poised and waiting for *Genesis* to begin.

My mind drifts back to my first performance of this piece, eight years ago.[2] At the time, Kyra was the unknown bean in my belly. Jordan was six and Jessica four. Kai wasn't even a blip on the horizon. The idea for piece and pregnancy had come together. *Have a third child and make a dance about creation.*

I thought the idea was ridiculous, until it refused to go away. I finally stopped resisting, reserved the theater, and opened to welcome whoever wanted to dance with me. She came, two months later than I envisioned. Her timing proved perfect. I choreographed; Geoff composed the score. The experience of performing the dance—while twenty-four weeks pregnant—was a highpoint of my life. Geoff's as well.

Here I am again, filled with our fifth child, snapped into my bag, waiting to begin. Waiting to participate in the ongoing act of creation.

A spasm of fear furrows my heart. *Fear*? Why? Am I worried I will make a mistake? No, I am well prepared. I know what is coming and what I have to do. I have rehearsed the moves many times in body and brain. Am I worried about what people will think of me? No, I am no longer afraid of losing the love of the crowd. I am giving what I have to give. Whether or not people like it is up to them. I grant them that freedom.

No, these tremors are different. I soon recognize them. They are the ones that come with the act of standing, being vulnerable, and being born. This fear snakes forth from the source of myself and opens a sensory path to it. It is part excitement, part anticipation, and part awe in the face of the unknown.

As I breathe along this frisson of emotional energy, my attention tumbles into my heart, where it should be. From there, tingling energy radiates to every cell. *Wake up! Be present! Life is being born. Now!*

The audience quiets into a soft, expectant silence. The curtain rolls on its tracks. The music begins.

When we conceived our fifth child, Geoff and I weren't planning to do *Genesis*. After three miscarriages, the thought was far from our minds, or at least, masked by fears. I was afraid that this small one, like the others, would not stay and that if it did, it might not be healthy. I was troubled by my rapidly beating heart, and the reactions of parents, cousins, and friends to my news. I pulled my sensory surfaces into myself and lived moment to moment, waiting.

When the nausea-packed first trimester was winding down, and the battery of tests successfully subsided, I began to breathe again. It was the beginning of a new year, 2009, and Geoff and I were filled with hope for ourselves and each other, for our family, and for the ecstatic birth of this fifth child. *This irrepressible spirit*! The one who wanted so much to come.

One afternoon in early January, we were talking about the emerging year, my desire to share my dance, and my desire that he share his music. "Artists are people who have to keep giving what they have to give," I protested, "otherwise they get sick!"

Geoff voiced the suggestion: "Why don't we do *Genesis*?"

I entertained the thought. We could do it again and make it better. We could shrink the original hour-long piece into thirty-five minutes, and leave a second half of the concert for Geoff to play solo piano. Geoff liked the plan.

As our scheme took shape, I was delighted for Geoff: he would play a grand piano on a concert stage for the first time since our move to the farm. He was delighted for me: I would revive a dance I loved to dance. We would call our joint concert

Genesis, a concert of music and dance. It would mark our birth into this farming community as artists.

We reveled in the magic. Our move to total presence was enabling our child's birth. Our child's birth was enabling our rebirth as artists. Neither Geoff nor I could or would have performed the concert without the other; and performing it was what we each wanted most for our singular selves and for each other. Our entwined impulses to connect were at work, supporting us each in giving what we have to give.

I asked my small traveler. "Do you want to dance?"

The response rose sudden and strong: Yes.

Kyra was thrilled with the idea too. "Now I get to see it!" she cried.

A few days later, we booked two shows, Friday and Saturday, a mere month and a half in the future. Hours afterwards, my burst of excited joy evaporated, leaving clouds of uncertainty in its wake. *Can we do it? Do we have enough time? Will I be too big to move? Will my aching heel toe the line? Will my back hold up and hold on? Will anyone come? Will they laugh to see me popping out of a stretchy gray bag?*

The music is quiet at first. Cosmic threads from the beginning of time twist through space, twirl into stocky strands, reach for me, and pull. I move, slowly at first, gently, as if taking a first breath. I lift my head from the soles of my feet, open my arms, and then let all fall again. My heavy head bounces, pulses. I am beginning.[3]

I love this part of the dance, its mystery, and my anonymity. Though I can't see it myself, I know roughly what it looks like from videos taken during rehearsal. Those in the audience will sense bodily shapes without knowing which part is which. Knobs and protrusions, trajectories of action, rhythms and arcs, I am. I am the Unknown, the Unborn. The Already Was. The Yet to Be. Beginning again. My head swings to the left and my face turns

slowly towards the light, pressing my nose though the bag, as if to emerge. Almost, but not quite.

My head dips down again over my clasped feet and out to the other side. I slide to the floor in fetal position. I am safe. Yet my toe craves adventure, and immediately starts winding upward, exploring its reach. I move from the place where my small traveler is also moving. It is moving inside me, becoming itself through me, enabling me to become who I am—this pregnant philosopher, dancing with her partner, giving birth to herself.

My fear has faded, smoothing into clean planes of action. I love this dance. I call this part, "Quickening."

When Geoff and I began rehearsing for the concert, time telescoped. We found ourselves revisiting who we were when we first performed the dance, how we felt in our skins, what we knew of each other, and what we had to say. It was inspiring to note how far we had come. *We are going all the way.*

Watching the video of the original, I saw my careful control, the precise grooming of form, the reserve. I felt a tremendous respect for the piece, and its kinetic images of human experience. I also felt a deep yearning to make it more than it was. *I know more now, in my sensory self.* I found myself moving back into forms I once created and forth into new realms that those forms were enabling me to discover about who I had become.

It occurred to me. *The movements I have been making here on the farm have been making me.* Walking on the earth, dancing on the land, and doing the work of farming and family had evolved my experience of my bodily self. Impelled by my desire to connect with this corner of the planet, and in new ways with my parents, partner, and progeny, I had opened to a greater affirmation of life. *I have more to give.*

The idea entranced. *In doing this dance again, here and now, with this bodily self, I am enacting what Genesis has always been about.* I originally made the dance because I wanted to communicate

viscerally as well as conceptually that we humans are the movements that are making us. We are always creating and becoming patterns of sensation and response that relate us to the people and places that are enabling us to be; and we are always giving birth to our singular sensory selves as we do. *We are always participating, consciously or not, in the work of creation.*[4] Me too.

I roll from my fetal position onto my back. The platform seems to shift beneath me. *What?* I am confused. I suddenly have no idea where I am. Did it move? Did I move? I am still in the bag and cannot see anything other than a blur of the lights. I am used to finding my way around by touching the tape that circumvents the platform edge and binds its two halves together in a central spine. Where is the tape? I am lost, face to face with the void.

Will I fall? I don't want to fall. *What do I do?*

The question barely forms before my bodily self is already doing. I am wiggling sideways, altering the movement. My left hand is reaching for the front edge of the platform and my right hand for the middle spine. I find the spine. *Good,* I won't roll off the front. I slide my body over, so I am lying spine to spine, and gently press my right heel down beneath me. Where is the right edge? I find it—a second point in relation to me. I know my place on the plane. *I am OK.*

Geoff's music seeps through my clanging mind, calming my bodily self. Internal shrieks melt into movement. Their charge adds power to the currents of my flow. I am reaching for my own heart. The pulse of the music supports me as I let go again, surrendering to the process of being born.

Fear: it has been the greatest challenge of this whole process. Despite the clarity of the call to dance, the rehearsal process was wracked with doubt. Doing parts of the dance made me sick to my stomach. Others provoked a curious throbbing in my Achilles tendon. Others refused to take shape at all. Swamped by worry, I

kept diving into my heart for that giant *Yes*. Yes to creation. Yes to dance. Yes from my small traveler. Yes to beginning again. Every day, I took a tiny step.

Then yesterday, hours before the first performance, we were in the middle of a dress rehearsal that had been postponed from the night before. That night, we had all been there—all six of us—for five hours. The kids had read books, done homework, eaten dinner, and gone for ice cream. We weren't finished. I was a bundle of frigid knots. We decided that I would take the kids home, that Geoff would stay at the theater to work on the sound, and that we would run the dress on the morning of the performance.

The evening part of the plan had gone well. While Jordan milked and Jessica Marvin-ed and the small K's cared for the chickens, I unpacked, made a fire in the wood stove and tossed together the rest of dinner. In half an hour, we were snuggled and smiling around the stove, eating salad and tofu. Geoff solved the technical issues, and was soon home.

The morning seemed to go well too, at first. The sun warmed up. I warmed up. We began. Twenty minutes into the piece, however, something snapped—something connecting hamstring to lower back. It hurt. I kept going, gingerly, breathless with fear. *Why now? Why me? What am I to do?*

I planned to take a bath when I got home. Soon after I arrived, the electricity went out for no apparent reason. Without electricity we have no well pump, no water, and none of it hot. I crawled into bed to nap. Over an hour later, I woke up. The electricity was still off, so I stayed in bed, breathing.

I have to heal. I just have to. I have to find a place in my bodily self that is deeper than this pain, a place from which I can move through the pain. A healing place.

I kept breathing, following the wave of each breath deeper inside myself. Earth, air, fire, water: I moved through my cycle of breaths, inviting a sensory awareness of my connectedness to the earth in me and around me.[5] *I am earth-supporting-me, air-filling-*

me, fire-burning-in-me, water-flowing-through-me. I dissolved into elements, attuned to the movements that were making me.

As my senses came to life, I remembered what I always forget. *I forget that every breath is a heart breath.* With every inhalation, my heart's beating pulls oxygen-rich blood into itself and sends it forth again throughout my body. The currents carry all the elements that enable me to live. Whatever I am feeling goes forth too, fear, despair, worry or joy, and I become it.

I followed the waves of my breathing, beating self. My sensory awareness of this heart-breathing grew, and something shifted.

All at once, the pain disappeared. *It is gone. Gone.*

I lay there, not daring to adjust my position. I moved my inner gaze from brain to heart and back again, barely believing, and desperately trying to recreate what happened. I wanted to remember, to hold onto the feeling. I recognized a new pattern of sensing and responding. My heart was blooming. *My back doesn't hurt.* I pleaded with this pattern to stay.

My heart was the place from which I wanted to move, from which to heal.

My beating, breathing heart, connected in and through my bodily self, to all that is.

The discovery rang true for me. It resonated with what I always have wanted: to live in love. For when we love—when we open our sensory selves to others as the causes of our being—we find ourselves flooded with the energy of creation. We tap our bodily ability to create and become patterns of sensation and response that connect us in mutually enriching ways with all that is enabling our lives. We find the freedom to move in line with the trajectories of our health and well-being. Our dance honors the earth.

As I contemplated this discovery, my heart swelled even more with gratitude for all of those who were enabling me to be living on the farm with my family, dancing my dance, six months pregnant with my fifth child.

I wouldn't be here if my parents hadn't awakened a desire for more than they could give; if the wall had not pushed Geoff and me to pursue total presence; if my kids didn't mirror back to me my own limits and fears, or if this small traveler had not insisted, through three miscarriages, to come and be with me. I wouldn't be here if I hadn't cultivated a sensory awareness of the movement that is making me. I wouldn't be here if I hadn't honored my desire for closer connection with the natural world. I want to be a part of it all! I want to move!

It all made sense. *My dancing will express these relationships; my dancing is making these relationships with myself, others, and the natural world real as the conditions that are enabling this dance to exist at all.*

My dance is making love—this ideal of love as an openness to another as a cause of our being—real.[6]

The electricity surged on. I took a hot bath and ate dinner with my family. We drove to the theater.

I am on my knees, still in the bag, preparing to explode. The birth moment is almost here. The music thickens and swells. I circle my outstretched, clasped hands, and let my arms slide up before me across my feeling heart and thinking head until my fingers meet resistance from the downward pull of the fabric. There is nowhere else to go. I have to let go. With a final screaming rip of the score, I release my hold. The bag drops around me, collapsing in a puddle of silence. I am left on my knees, arms up, a bodily self with a blooming belly, born to give birth. *We are created to create.* It is an image of generations. The lights paint a golden halo around my emergent form.[7]

Breathing. In silence, I slowly move my arms and torso down, bending my forehead to the platform. I catch a glimpse of Kyra and Kai in the front row, transfixed. Geoff places his hands on the piano and begins playing "Jessica," a song he wrote when she was newly born.

I smile inside. I am not afraid of this section of the dance. I have rehearsed it so many times. I am the light—an act of light—

being and blessing creation.[8] I love it.

As this ease passes through my mind, the realization flashes: I just made a mistake. I did the first movement to the wrong side. Panic flares. *What do I do*? I can't repeat the same movement to the same side! It will look horrible.

As I flail, my bodily self is already moving, repeating the same movement to the same side, getting me back on track in the nick of time. Repetition is fine, and now it's over. I let go. The spike of fear crumbles into my heart. New currents of energy course through my panic-dilated cells. More of me is moving, as one.

As I begin the next sequence, it expands through me, unfolding me further in time and space than ever before. One foot finds its freedom from the bag and then the second. I bend and stretch, arch and rise, and surrender to the glorious, unfathomable medium of bodily life.

Since the beginning of this pregnancy, I have wanted to give birth at home.[9] Kai was born at home. It had gone so well. Yet the three miscarriages had shaken my nerve. *Could I do it again*? Other than Geoff, I had little support. My parents were not alone in believing that Kai's successful birth was a matter of luck. They wrote to me, begging me not to give birth at home, tacking on a list of everything that could go wrong. Strangers at the pool and on the street told me stories of births going awry. Then a doctor who worked with the midwives I was seeing sounded a brutal alarm: "If you rupture," she said, "you have ten minutes." I left her office shaking, tears welling. *I don't want to die. I don't want my baby to die. I want us both to live!*

Driving home from the doctor's office, as I passed blindly through rolling hills, I sorted through my sensations, breathing deeply, looking for a way through. I was expecting a child and the fact was that even if my first birth hadn't been a cesarean section, there was a still a chance I would rupture, bleed out, and die, no matter where or when or how I gave birth. Medical science

couldn't prevent it. *What do I do*—not give birth because it might mean death? It was too late.

I pondered the best counsel of many in the western world. Manage your risks! Hedge your bets. Authorities encourage us to parse statistics, buy insurance, and pop pills to numb our nerves. We imagine everything that could go wrong and try to avoid it. "Your chance of rupture is one in 200. I wouldn't recommend it."

I was breathing deeply, releasing my tension into the road moving under me, when my experience abruptly shifted. The fear released its grip. I saw the fertile fields surrounding me. Ideas dawned. *All of this helpful fear-fanning information masks a glaring ignorance: I have no idea which dot on the graph I will be!* When we deal with statistics, I realized, we miss the crucial piece of information: *where do I fall*? Without this piece of information, the statistics are rough estimates generalized across many differences. If we make a decision based on them, we are assuming that life is a game of Russian Roulette. Someone is going to take the bullet and it is just a matter of luck who it will be. *Will it be you?*

Life surged in me. *I am not a statistic.*

The affirmation sunk in. *Even if I want to credit the numbers, there are distinctions impossible to measure. I am supremely healthy and stronger than ever. My labors are relatively short; my babies relatively small. With every VBAC, my risks of rupture decline and I have had three. With every cesarean section my risks of rupture increase and I have already had one. So what is my risk? To whom can I compare myself?*

Can you calculate a statistic for one?

Insights sped by hard and fast. *Life is not a game of roulette. God is not some arbitrary judge out there, acting upon us. Creation is an ongoing event, happening in us and through us in every moment, including and during birth. I choose to participate in it, as consciously as I can. What do I want to create? What world do I want to bring into being?*

As I neared home, a path to my birth appeared before me. *If risks are both inevitable and immeasurable, then the best I can do is to create for my bodily self the conditions which will make the best outcome the most likely.*

When it comes to birth, all agree: nature knows best. A natural birth provides mom and baby with a precisely calibrated array of physical experiences and chemical cocktails to boost the health and well-being of both.

I knew what I wanted. *In order to give my little one such a birth, I will need to create an environment where I am able to go deep inside myself, trusting in the one infinite power that is the source of any success I could have: my living, breathing, moving sensory self. I need to surround myself with people who believe in me and who trust me to trust myself, beginning with Geoff and my kids.*

On the one hand, I wished my parents could be a part of that group. On the other, I was grateful to them for the fear that would keep them away; their fear was pushing me to go deeper than I had gone to find a place in myself from which to move beyond that fear. In their absence, they were enabling my ecstatic birth. They couldn't make it to *Genesis* either.

I switched midwives, and planned to give birth at home.

The final bars of "Jessica" lilt across the stage, pulling me up from my knees and onto my feet. I slowly round my back up; head and arms are last to arrive. My hands keep rising until they reach the highest possible point in the arc of me. Fully stretched, belly bared, neck arched back, I dissolve into the light that I am. My ray goes black. Darkness holds the space of silence.

I take a breath. Done. I scoop up my bag, step off the platform, and slide backstage as Geoff's cyber-sounds unwind. I have ninety seconds to change before I dance again. Jessica is there with my next costume.

"Good job, Mom," she whispers fiercely. I smile, still a bit shaken by my glimpses of the void. She is so good at moral

support. I breathe myself back from the brink of fear and into my skipping heart. Why is it so hard to stay there?

I touch Jessica's shoulder, take a swig of water, and walk back out onto the dark stage. I am preparing for "Playful," the song that begins this next section, "Falling into Form." This part is where I delight in desire. I ride my impulse to connect with the forms of what gives pleasure. I want to enjoy this dance fully, and beam that joy to the audience. I find my position. The lights glow and Geoff begins. His spinning bright piano tones lure me closer. I respond. We play. I feel a might shaky on my pegs, but am moving smoothly enough. I am a bead on a string of sound.

All of a sudden, the string breaks. Geoff skips a phrase and begins a new one. What? Where am I? Again I am lost, face flat to the void. I have absolutely no idea what comes next. *What do I do*? My body is still moving; my mind flails.

There it is, a familiar phrase, but I am not convinced. Where does Geoff think he is? Does he think that he is where I think he is? Are we in the same place? If I begin here, will we arrive at the end together? The final moment is important.

My bodily self is still moving, doing who knows what. My scrambling mind finally latches on to where my bodily self already is. I pull myself together in line with where I think I should be. My heart is racing and not from physical effort. Adrenaline pours through my limbs and out into the space. The fear jolted me into a new level of integration. I smile wryly, for I am really moving now.

Geoff and I hit the final bar at the same time. His fingers stop. So do I. We did it.

In the story of the dance, what I have desired and enjoyed disappears. I stand alone, bereft, waiting, rotating slowly in space. I look into nothing.

I want this dance. After last night's performance, I want it even more.

The Friday night show, after my afternoon in bed, had gone well. The kids had enabled it all, taking care of themselves and each other, so I could focus on the dance. Kai slept from car ride to final curtain. Kyra, when she wasn't helping or watching, curled into her sleeping bag. Jordan and Jessica organized tables, handed out programs, prepped the camera crew, and supported me as I dressed, warmed up, and head in heart, breathed myself through the piece without pain. It was a miracle.

Tonight, I want more. I want to give myself even more fully to the kinetic images of this dance so that I can communicate through them the power of our bodily movement to create, to heal, and to become what the experience of doing *Genesis* is teaching me.

Am I succeeding? I have my doubts.

I stop turning. My breathing is calm. The piano begins again. The song is "Pursuit" and I am pursuing what I have lost. It was during this part that I pulled a muscle yesterday, but I am not afraid. As the ardor of the chase wanes, I back up to the platform, spin onto it, and lift my empty hands to the sky. I wait for the cue to begin what is another of my favorite parts of *Genesis* danced to Geoff's piano concoction, "Sadness."

The dance is sad. What I want is irretrievable. Yet the dance is also achingly beautiful and thoroughly grounding. To dance this dance is comforting; it allows its feelings to be felt, touched, and released. For most of the dance I am sitting with my legs bent and knees clasped together. I was inspired by the Andrew Wyeth painting, *Christina's World*. A crippled young woman crawls across a vast grassland to a farmhouse in the distance. She is not afraid. I am that woman, surrendering to the ground that continues to hold me up, even when I cannot stand.

I roll towards the back of the platform. *Stop*! I am far too close to the right side, nearly out of the light. I can't make the next move with so little space in front of me! How did I get here? Even as the question forms in my mind, a small pulse begins at my

tailbone, undulates through my spine, and ripples me back six inches. I continue with the intended arch of my upper back and sense the light on my face, where it should be. *Phew.* I am OK. Relief opens my heart.

"Sadness" morphs into the final section of "Falling into Form": "Despair." In the dance, I enjoyed the object of my desire, and then lost it, pursued it, mourned it. Now I despair of ever finding it or any other pleasure ever again. I dance the sting of impossible desire. Still on the platform, I rise to my knees, then circle, fall, roll, and circle, fall, roll again. I land on my arms, carefully guarding my belly. I am getting tired. With a spin to the back, my leg juts unexpectedly off the platform. *Oh no*! I just keep going.

I make the transition from platform to floor. In the dance, I try to stand. I fall. I try to stand again, to find my balance, but I keep flailing, falling, and pulling myself up again. I love this part. I know these emotions all too well. I am splayed and given. The music blasts to a ferocious peak. It's a distorted echo of a scream—mine—that Geoff and I recorded long ago. Every time we rehearsed this part, Kai would come running to watch, eyes wide. I dance it for him. The scream pierces my heart and I fall to the floor. The stage goes black.

As I lie there, my sensations run rampant. I feel hot and flushed. My stomach is churning. What have I done? *Are you OK little one*?

The stage still black, Geoff begins to play. It is a piece we call the "Unfolding." I slip backstage where Jordan and Jessica greet me. I am so happy to see them. Jessica hands me my dress. The hardest part of the dance is over. It is time for the healing ritual.

Minutes later, I walk back onto the black stage, activating my spatial sense to avoid ramming into the corner of the platform. I step into position next to the piano. I am close enough to Geoff

that I could reach out and touch him. I don't. He is bent over the keys, on the last bars of "Unfolding." It is time.

A faint ring of light arises, casting shadows on my face. At this moment I am a voice, only a voice. I sing through the silence, a lullaby I wrote long ago for Jordan, as I walked in circles around the living room, rocking his inconsolable infant self. There are no words; it is more chant than song. I sing vowels, and have been doing so throughout this pregnancy, even before we decided to do *Genesis*. The little one wanted to hear it.

The chant fades. The lights brighten. Geoff starts a recording of himself on clarinet playing the same song. I begin to move, tracing a slow round of an imaginary circle. I lunge down, stretch my arms forward, and arch up and back. I turn sideways and pulse in a wide second position, arms fanning open again. I twist my torso and kick front, then side, then step behind myself facing out to begin the sequence once more. As I repeat the phrase, slowly, smoothly, every cycle through the sequence sinks deeper into myself and projects further into the room. The chant ends. I pause at the edge of the circle I have made—the circle that is making me.

Drums, sudden and sharp, punctuate the quiet. They are calling me, calling my vibrant heart. *Enter this space. Be born to this instant.*[10] I enter the center and start making movements I learned as a member of a Haitian-American dance company years before. I love these moves. They are grounded and sensuous, strong and full. They draw me into a sensory awareness of my hips and lower back—the pelvic cradle, rocking life, source of movement—connecting me, through my pounding feet, to mother earth. I warm up, push my fears away, and claim the safe round of my encircled self. The drums break in a percussive peak and I am free. Standing, I spin on my axis and gradually spiral outward, until I am walking the perimeter of the circle and into the beyond.

To the climbing chords of Geoff's score, I unfurl. This part

feels like soaring. In my movements, I revisit moments in the dance to this point—the movements of wanting and losing, mourning and despair. I make those same movements, yet their meaning is changed. Now they express my freedom—my capacity to move, create, and be born again. The pain and fear are gone, for I have found what that pain and fear were calling me to find: the birthing, becoming power of bodily movement. The impulse to connect. *My beating, breathing heart.*

I return to the circle and stand on its edge. I become a shaman, calling all persons to participate in the circle of creation. Halfway through the sequence, I realize that I forgot my favorite hearth-stirring move. I just plain forgot it! My phrase will be over too early! I will have nothing to do, nowhere to go! I am face to face with the void. Again. *What do I do*? I ask, and my bodily self is already answering. Before I know it, I am repeating my hearth-stirring move, making it twice as long. The music needs it. I need it. Perhaps the audience does too.

The end is near. I circle the stage once more, retreat to the platform, spin onto its welcoming surface, and curl my legs into the position with which I began the entire dance. The soles of my feet tenderly touch; my hands warm my ankles, my upper body is light. My head leads, once to the left and once to the right before coming to rest, hanging down towards my feet. I am ready to be born again.

The audience is still. No one moves or speaks. My heart expands in the silence. They got it. Slowly the applause begins, warm and rousing. I bow. I bow to Kyra and Kai, to Geoff, to all who have helped us, to all who sit watching, to all who are absent, and then I retreat. I feel horrible, nauseous and weak. Alone. Jordan and Jessica have gone up front to tend the intermission. Geoff is preparing for his set. I change quietly by myself, conserving energy. I drink some water, gobble a couple of granola bars, and try to steady myself. Hang in there small one. We are done.

I am swamped with equal parts grief and relief. It's over. I don't want to do that again. I don't think I could. But I won't have the opportunity either. It's over.

The second act begins. I watch from backstage as Geoff plays superbly. He is better than he ever has been. *Genesis* warmed him up. It occurs to me: maybe this is why I am here, to enable him to experience himself in this way, as the gifted artist he is. I feel so much love listening to him, so much gratitude. He closes the set with a song he wrote for me, "Beauty."

Back at home, the kids all settled in bed, Geoff and I meet at the kitchen table. In a wink I am gone, dissolved into heaving sobs. Effort and exhaustion overwhelm. All my vanquished hopes and fears come crashing and splashing through. I grope for words. Why did we do that? Why did I do that? What was that all about?

It is not a normal performance letdown. The ache erupts from somewhere more subterranean. Plates are shifting. The performance took so much energy and so much love. Why do it? Was it worth it? Why be born anyway?

I am too tired to think. I don't have any answers. Geoff and I tumble into bed.

The next morning, resting in warm light, I know why we did it. I know why I did it. I did *Genesis* for the sake of doing it. I did it for the transformation it works in me. I danced to be born in this community as a dancer who empties herself into movement in order to communicate a visceral affirmation of life. I did it to connect with my partner and children in a way that would nourish me in giving them what I have to give. Geoff and I did it together to let ourselves live. But it was so difficult! And terrifying! I was expecting tranquil bliss! Instead, I found myself lurching from crisis to crisis, facing the void, wrung with fear, and barely escaping disaster time and again. What was that all about?

I think back over the dance. There must be more. I decide to relive the dance in my memory. What happened? As I move through the piece in my mind step by step, remembering what I had done, I found, much to my surprise, strong threads connecting kinetic moments of shining clarity. Maybe the performance wasn't so bad after all.

Encouraged, I watch the video of the Saturday performance and I see. Every time my mind froze with fear at some unexpected occurrence, my bodily self responded by creating something new that was in itself beautiful, and sometimes, even more beautiful than what I had planned. It was as if my bodily self knew what to do. In the hours of practice and attention, cultivating a sensory awareness of the movement making me, I had created and become patterns of sensing and responding that guided me smoothly and steadily through the challenges at hand.

The realization ripples through. *I can trust my bodily self.* I can trust my bodily self to move. My practices of sensory awareness—dancing on the earth, opening to the natural world, honoring the impulses to move arising in my bodily self—all live in me as an ever-evolving capacity to make movements that will connect me in the moment, with the moment, in ways that express my open heart. *Genesis,* the ongoing act of creation, begins and ends with my beating, breathing heart.

Ecstatic birth. It is what I want and have wanted from the first moments of this pregnancy for my family, myself, and the little one to come. Performing *Genesis* taught me what I needed to know to make it happen.

The ecstatic birth I want will be like this dance. I will face the void, and when I do, I want to be present in the moment with whatever I am sensing, free to mobilize whatever I have ever felt in response. I want to trust in my bodily self and all of the connections I have made through practice and attention. I want

to transform the meaning of everything I have ever felt and known—every struggle, every challenge—into something that is enabling me to give birth to myself as a birth-giver of a new life. I want to say *yes* to life, and participate as consciously as possible in the ongoing act of creation. *I want to dance.*

We humans can't stop moving; we can't stop creating relationships; we can't stop wanting to connect with what will enable us to unfold who we are and to give what we have to give. The question is simply how.

Will we learn to open to others as causes of our being? Or will we respond to the sting of impossible desire by growing addicted to fear?

Will we cling to self-limiting illusions of being an individual self? Or will we open to affirm our relationships with other humans and the more-than-human world as enabling us to become who we are?

Will we seek to control our lives and the lives of those around us? Or will we make the move of radical self-affirmation that frees us to let others live?

Will we move? Will we dance?

The little one inside of me wants to know.

Epilogue

On June 14, 2009, at 9:03 p.m., Leif LaMothe Gee was born safely and joyously at home, into the waiting arms of parents and siblings, who were ecstatic to meet him.

Notes

Prologue

1. Henry David Thoreau, *Walden,* chapter 17, 265.

2. Henry David Thoreau, *Walden,* chapter 1, 41. Thoreau, after living for two years in a small cabin on the shores of Walden Pond, wrote about his "experiment in living" in his book *Walden.* This book has inspired back-to-nature enthusiasts, homesteaders, and environmentalists, as well as scholars of religion, literature, and philosophy since its publication in 1854. It also inaugurated an American tradition of nature writing that continues to this day.

For a useful collection of such work, see Bill McKibben's *American Earth: Environmental Writing Since Thoreau.* For a discussion of American environmental literature, see Lawrence Buell, *The Environmental Imagination.* For a history of homesteading in the United States, see Rebecca Gould, *At Home in Nature: Modern Homesteading and Spiritual Practice in America.* See Stanley Cavell, *The Senses of Walden,* for a reading of *Walden* as Thoreau's attempt to write an American scripture.

3. "Who knows but if men [sic] constructed their dwellings with their own hands, and provided food for themselves and families simply and honestly enough, the poetic faculty would be universally developed, as birds universally sing when they are so engaged?" (*Walden,* chapter 1, 36).

4. Henry David Thoreau, *Walden,* chapter 8, 142.

5. Henry David Thoreau, *Walden,* chapter 1, 2. Those who criticize Thoreau for falling short of his ideal of solitude are missing his primary message. His point is not that freedom comes from living alone. His point is rather that time by ourselves in the natural world allows us to see and evaluate the relationships we are creating in our lives, with the end of cultivating better, more life-enabling ones with ourselves, others, and

the natural world.

6. Henry David Thoreau, *Walden*, chapter 2, 69.

7. Thoreau was critical of farmers for turning themselves into machines, driven by the amount of land and work needed to sustain a lifestyle of socially competitive luxury. His call for simplicity and for attention to the "necessaries of life" was aimed at laboring men who were "plowing under" the "better part" of themselves "for compost" (*Walden*, chapter 1, 3). He was not, however, against farming or gardening when done with the aim of enabling a good life. He, himself, planted beans to sell for money to meet his (admittedly small) expenses.

8. See Wendell Berry, *The Art of the Commonplace*; Scott Chasky, *This Common Ground*; Barbara Kingsolver, *Animal, Vegetable, Miracle*; Helen Nearing and Scott Nearing, *The Good Life*; Michael Pollan, *Omnivore's Dilemma*.

9. Richard Louv, in his book *Last Child in the Woods*, addresses this issue when he ponders where the environmentalists of tomorrow are now. He targets the increasing separation of children from nature as contributing to a dearth of future environmentalists.

I would add that children not only need to experience nature, children need to experience how their relationship to the natural world and their relationships to other humans are interdependent. Not only does time in the natural world ease our state of mind, stir our creativity, and refresh our capacity for attention, as Louv documents, it also opens our sensory selves to ways of moving in relation to other humans that express love. *Family Planting* enacts how.

10. When I use the terms "parent," "partner," and "progeny," I do so as a shorthand intended to span the many variations on these relationships that occur across human experience. "Parents," or those who care for us when we are too young to care for ourselves, need not be biological; "partners," or those we choose as our closest companions in life, need not be married to

us or of specific sexes; "progeny," or those for whom we are responsible as caregivers, can include human and non-human, biological and not.

Further, my point is not that the dynamics I describe within each kind of relationship occur *only* in that relationship, but that that relationship is a primary locus where they develop and from there, inform our relationships with, for example, siblings, friends, neighbors, co-workers, and non-human others.

11. The idea that *our bodily movement is making us* is a primary tenet of the philosophy of bodily becoming, which I introduce in my book, *What a Body Knows*. In a nutshell, the philosophy of bodily becoming holds that: we are bodies; our bodies are movement, and the movements that we bodies are making are making us. These three simple tenets unfold into radical implications for philosophical questions about who we are, what we can know, and how we ought to live our lives. Where *What a Body Knows* discusses the implications of this philosophy for how we experience our desires for food, sex, and spirit, *Family Planting* explores the implications for how we learn to love in our relationships with parents, partners, and progeny.

This idea of ourselves as the movement that is making us is an idea that aligns with classical expressions of continental philosophy, G.W.F. Hegel in particular, as well as with recent developments in neuroscience.

For an account of Hegel's Spirit (*Geist*) as a threefold movement of development, see his *Phenomenology of Spirit*. For an account of the role of bodily movement in building our brains, our consciousness, and our sense of self, see Rodolfo R. Llinas in *I of the Vortex*. See also Sandra and Matthew Blakeslee's discussion of body maps in the *The Body Has a Mind of Its Own*. For an account of how the western sense of self as an individual evolved into its current formulations, see Charles Taylor, *Sources of the Self*.

12. This book is a work in philosophy. By making this claim, I

am aligning myself with an established canon of thought and its time-honored tradition of stretching and evolving the boundaries of what can and should count as "philosophy."

In our current mind-over-body environment, philosophy is increasingly trapped in abstractions. Traditional aspirations of philosophers to self-knowledge, better living, life-enabling values, and a love of wisdom have been eclipsed by discussions about texts, logic, and language. Alternately, attempts to engage ordinary speech, Hollywood film, literature, and jokes in philosophical conversations represent efforts to reconnect philosophical discussions with human living. However, in both cases, too often the bodily dimensions of human existence are treated as raw material for higher-order reflections.

While the situation has been accurately depicted and critiqued by Maurice Merleau-Ponty (*The Phenomenology of Perception*), among others, we still await a significant correction in the field that will allow us to engage what Merleau-Ponty called "the lived body" more effectively as both a resource and critique for philosophy.

How will this correction occur? Part of what must happen involves a shift in sensory experience that will allow us to appreciate the centrality of *bodily movement* to our thinking selves. The idea that *what we think expresses how we live* already appears in the work of many, including Talal Asad, Michel Foucault, and Pierre Bourdieu, as well as feminist philosopher, Luce Irigaray. These authors pay attention to how bodily practices give our beliefs and values meaning for us. *Family Planting* advances this discussion by using personal anecdotes to trace the importance of sensory education for how we respond to the bodily challenges that arise in the context of our primary relationships. It offers a philosophy that is local and living, embodied and enacted.

Here again, I take a cue from Thoreau: "To be a philosopher is not merely to have subtle thoughts, but so to love wisdom as to live according to its dictates, a life of simplicity, independence,

magnanimity, and trust. It is to solve some of the problems of life, not only theoretically, but practically" (*Walden*, chapter 1, 11).

13. While I too confine myself to the "narrowness of my experience," I do so with an attitude that Ellen Langer describes in *Counterclockwise* as the "psychology of possibility." She writes, "In the psychology of possibility... only one participant is needed to prove that something is possible" (17). The challenge, then, is to explore the conditions that enable that possibility—in this case, what love can be.

Chapter 1: Movement Matters

1. Søren Kierkergaard, *Fear and Trembling*, 121.

2. Henry David Thoreau, *Walden*, chapter 7, 137. For an account of the roots of patriarchy in the control of agricultural processes and fruits, see Gerda Lerner, *The Creation of Patriarchy*. See also Riane Eisler, *The Chalice and the Blade*, for a discussion of dominator and partnership models of human relationship.

3. In *What a Body Knows*, I reject the mind over body logic that governs the modern western experience of a human self. I trace: how people learn to think and feel and act as if we were minds living in and over our bodies; why this sense of ourselves is at the root of a range of psychological and social ills, and how we can shift our experience of ourselves in a way that allows us to appreciate ourselves as the movement that is making us. When we do, as I demonstrate, we find resources in the pulses and frustrations of our desires that are guiding us towards health and well-being.

4. This approach to human nature aligns with aspects of complexity theory that describe the "self" as an open, self-creating, relational system rather than as the rational, monadic agent we inherited from enlightenment thinkers such as René Descartes, Immanuel Kant, and John Locke. However, my approach goes further in embracing the *bodily* dimensions of this

open system. It is not just that we are brains networked to other brains. Our brains are *parts* of bodily selves that exist to serve the ongoing, self-creating movement of a bodily self in its endless absorbing and discarding, inhaling and exhaling.

For an account of our minds as internalized bodily movement, see Rodolfo Llinas, *I of the Vortex*.

5. Questions about the nature of love, while compelling to philosophers and theologians for millenia, now occupy the attention of evolutionary biologists and cultural anthropologists as well. The challenge for these scientists is to explain social and altruistic human behavior in terms of Darwin's theories of evolution and contemporary accounts of selfish genes.

I argue that when we affirm that a human person is fundamentally and irreducibly an impulse to connect, the perceived dichotomy between selfish and unselfish behavior is no longer relevant.

See E.O. Wilson, *On Human Nature,* and Sarah Blafer Hrdy, *Mothers and Others,* for two arguments about why human beings have evolved into cooperative, empathic creatures whose survival depends upon their ability to create relationships.

6. The relationship of children to their parents is a favorite topic for contemporary psychologists. The reason, at least in part, is historical. The shift from a farm economy to an industrial economy that began in the nineteenth century and continued into the twentieth effectively separated the work place from the home place. It removed working parents from their children, and distanced nuclear families from their extended relatives. As a result, the parent-child relationship shouldered the responsibility of providing both parents and children with a large quotient of their emotional needs. This configuration of public and private spheres has provided people in the twenty-first century with unique challenges in creating relationships with one another, and so too with a unique opportunity for learning what it means to live in love.

7. Alice Miller has published many books on the effects of child abuse on children's emotional, spiritual, and physical selves. She has mapped the ways in which violence repeats itself from generation to generation, and pays particular attention to the ways in which our bodies remember and repress the memories of pain and humiliation. She advocates interaction with helping witnesses (who teach us love) and enlightened witnesses (who provide us with an opportunity for voicing our pain). Simply acknowledging and exposing our hurts in a supportive context, she argues, can catalyze healing. I agree.

I also contend that it is nearly impossible in the contemporary world for a child to emerge from childhood without experiencing the *sting* of impossible desire, no matter how loving his or her parents are. Some pain is inevitable, and the question is how parents help their children understand, embrace, and make use of that inevitability.

By tracing that inevitable sting to *bodily* changes, I open a path to healing that goes beyond safe sharing. We heal, I argue, when we *recreate* our self-immuring patterns of sensing and responding. In this way, the sting of impossible desire is a catalyst for helping us discover our own capacity to create relationships with a range of people in our lives that do and will nurture our bodily becoming.

As the following chapters reveal, feeling the sting of impossible desire is as essential to learning how to live in love as falling is to learning how to walk. The sting of impossible desire gets us moving along the trajectories of our own awareness and desire, so that we can begin to participate consciously in the rhythms of our bodily becoming. What we experience with caregivers thus helps us learn to open to partners and our own children, as well as with human and non-human others.

Finally, with this notion of healing, the goal is neither forgiveness nor reconciliation. Not only are there cases in which such actions are impossible, but even in cases where they are

possible, they are never enough. The *goal* is rather for persons to find ways of moving in relation to themselves and their parents that allow them to acknowledge the incalculable debt they have to parents for their very lives, while finding freedom from parents' criticism, judgment, and/or abusive behaviors. The challenge is to find a mutually life-enabling distance.

For Miller's work, see especially *The Body Never Lies, For Your Own Good,* and *The Drama of the Gifted Child.*

8. What is often assumed in discussions about relationships between adult children and their parents is that the relationship lies in the past. In many cases, the relationship lives in the present, where the older dynamics, even if not active on the surface, continue to shape the landscape of interactions. My perspective finds opportunities for growth in the relationship *because* of the ongoing pain.

9. Two helpful books on relationships that combine scholarship with practical advice are those by Harville Hendrix, *Getting the Love You Want,* and David Schnarch, *Passionate Marriage.* While my work has been influenced by both, I go further than either in claiming that the emotional *interdependence* of partners is a *desirable* development whose fruits we ought to cultivate, rather than a problem whose rough patches we need to manage. In my view, an ongoing desire for more is what a successful relationship produces.

10. Daniel Siegel's work exemplifies a shift in how psychologists are thinking about the importance of relationships to individuals. He writes: "brains evolved to be profoundly relational" (*Parenting,* 76). As he avers, brains need interaction with other human beings in order to develop.

Siegel also talks about the "natural push of the mind towards health" (*Parenting,* 214), where "mind" is a flow of energy and information. "Mind" in this rendering is itself a movement that resists categorization as either "body" or "mind" are typically understood.

In my terms, mind is a matrix of mental movements that our bodily selves make that has evolved to help us connect with whatever will sustain our ongoing bodily becoming. Minds serve our bodily selves by noticing, attending, predicting, remembering, and using all of this information to imagine and execute new patterns of sensation and response.

11. In most books about parenting, authors set out to provide parents with the skills and understanding that they need in order to manage and control their children's behavior. Many approaches guide caregivers to act with the goal of building self-esteem, self-confidence, and autonomy in their children—the traditional resources of an *individual*. Children are discussed as entities apart from their relationship with caregivers, while caregivers are considered apart from their relationships to their own caregivers and partners. Caregivers are assumed to be rational individuals who can calmly carry out a plan, once its logic is clearly presented.

Daniel Siegel is an exception in this respect: he affirms that caregivers' "leftover baggage" from their own experience as children interferes with their ability to care for their own children (*Parenting*, 129). As a result, he affirms that parents need to work on themselves in order to be better parents.

What is still missing, however, is the sense that the work parents need to do is not just on themselves, but involves figuring out how to move in relationship with their own parents and partners so that those relationships, where possible, are most likely to evolve into mutually life-enabling connections.

Chapter 2: Healthy as a Horse

1. Wendell Berry, *The Art of the Commonplace*, 86.

2. In our approach to horse care, we have been influenced by many individuals and some books, including work in natural horsemanship by Monty Roberts (*Shy Boy*) and Joe Camp (*Soul of a Horse*), as well as more classical approaches practiced by Allison

King and Audrey Hicks at Birch Hill Farm in Granville, New York.

3. Henry David Thoreau, *Walden,* chapter 16, 238. Thoreau thought this thought because he walked. See also his essay "Walking" in *Great Short Works,* 294-326.

4. Daniel Siegel (*Developing Mind, Parenting*) develops a theory of childhood memory formation that explains an adult's sudden flooding of emotion as a sign of unresolved childhood pain. I agree, adding that the fact of the flooding is what creates in us a possibility for healing. For the flooding not only overwhelms our mental sense of self, it animates the forces in us that can and want to generate a new sense of self. The question, then, is not how to stop the flooding, but how to allow its powerful currents to open us to the impulse to connect at work in this emotion.

5. Friedrich Nietzsche, *Portable Nietzsche,* 471. Nietzsche, like Thoreau, walked in order to think the thoughts that he would later write. The question that neither Nietzsche nor Thoreau answers adequately, however, is how the act of walking helps us think life-affirming thoughts. I argue that walking has the potential to catalyze our sensory awareness of the movement that is making us. Walking can draw our attention not only to the patterns of sensing and responding that we have already made and become, but to our power to create new ones. In this chapter, I enact this double efficacy in finding ways to move through emotional knots experienced with my parents, partner, and progeny.

See also, *What a Body Knows,* chapter 1.

6. Henry David Thoreau, *Walden,* chapter 17, 265.

7. Friedrich Nietzsche, in *Genealogy of Morals,* identifies the phenomenon of *ressentiment* at the core of western morality. Those who were unable to discharge their desires turned against those same desires, and then affirmed that what they were doing, in denying their desires, was of higher moral value. In preaching these values of asceticism to the strong, these weaker persons, the so-called priests, exacted their revenge. Thus the paradox: the act

of denying oneself can express and even strengthen one's will to live. Nietzsche's image of a free spirit who is not bound by hate and revenge inspires this discussion. Such a spirit, for him, *dances*.

See my book, *Nietzsche's Dancers*, Chapter 3.

8. Total presence moves beyond mirroring or empathy as a path to and practice of intimacy. Mirroring and empathy privilege the individual as a unit of relationship. When we affirm the unit of the relationship as *movement*, however, new possibilities emerge for articulating and understanding the dynamics of being both two persons and one bond: the bond itself has a life of its own. The bond lives in each person. It grows through each person. It calls persons to acknowledge and live their relationship as an ongoing, never-ending process of becoming present to what their impulse to connect with one another is creating in each of them.

Chapter 3: Fair Enough

1. Henry David Thoreau, *Walden*, chapter 1, 7.

2. For information on cow care, we have relied on local farmers, the Cattle Rustlers branch of 4H, and two books: *Barnyard in Your Backyard* and *Keeping a Family Cow*.

3. For critiques of industrial farming practices and their implications for the health of humans, animals, soil, water, and air, see work by Wendell Berry. His collection of essays, *Art of the Commonplace*, has been especially important for us.

Michael Pollan, in *The Omnivore's Dilemma*, details the governmental and agricultural policies that have produced the mountain of corn we feed to animals and humans, to the detriment of both. He is not alone in voicing concern for the CAFO's (confined animal feeding operations), genetically modified grains, and use of chemical fertilizers and pesticides that dominate agribusiness.

Interest is growing across contemporary society in devel-

oping local, organic, earth-friendly, and even family-centered farming practices. Other authors are engaging in their own living experiments as a way to discover new realms for what is possible.

See for example, Barbara Kingsolver, in *Animal, Vegetable, Miracle,* for a recent, notable experiment in living, where she and her family set out to grow all of their own food for a year. For a leading proponent of grass farming as an alternative to industrial methods, see Joel Salatin's work, beginning with *You Can Farm.*

4. My practice of yoga dates to a couple of months I spent in 1985 at Kripalu Ashram in Lenox, Massachusetts. The attention that Kripalu yoga pays to movement appealed to my dancer self. The aim of Kripalu yoga is to use the postures to find and release an energy flow that will guide a practitioner from one posture to the next.

I have also been greatly influenced by B.K.S. Iyengar's *Light on Yoga,* as well as my studies of modern dance, the Graham technique in particular. Martha Graham recognized that her focus on the movements of breathing as the source for her dancing aligned with yogic principles. See chapter 7 of my book, *Nietzsche's Dancers,* for a discussion of what Graham called her "way of doing things."

5. The metaphors of separation and severing with an end to shoring up an individual self are often used to explain and justify as normal the kinds of rebellion that occur among teenage children. Kids, we learn, have to rebel for a time in order to develop a sense of their own autonomy. They need to test limits so they can learn to find and make their own. These models of individual development assume as their ground that humans *are* individuals, and that separating from the caregivers is how humans become who they are.

However, there is increasing evidence that human beings are not individuals, or are not merely individuals, but are who they are as a result of the relationships they create along the way with those who support them in becoming who they are. While

children do learn how to feed, clothe, warm, and govern themselves, this fact is not a sign of their independence as much as it is of their ability to create the relationships that enable them to develop these capacities.

One implication of this fact is that our relationships with our parents are never over, even though we might wish they were. We carry them with us always in everything we do. These relationships deeply structure our philosophies of how the world works, regardless of whether we are conscious of it or not. As such, it is vitally important for people to learn how to metabolize the painful moments of these relationships in ways that allow them to affirm themselves *as capable of creating the relationships* they need to survive.

There are situations in which adult children will find it impossible to cultivate a relationship with their parents, particularly in cases involving chronic mental, physical, or sexual abuse. Even and especially in these cases, however, adult children must learn how to make moves in relation to their parents that allow them to affirm themselves and their desires. Sometimes, the life-enabling distance a child seeks in relation to his or her parents will be one that is out of contact range.

6. In chapter 2 of *What a Body Knows*, I introduce the cycle of breaths as a practice for helping cultivate a sensory awareness of the movement that is making me. Here, I use that cycle consciously to open up a space inside myself where I can feel what I am feeling, and invite the impulses within those feelings to unfold and make themselves known. The cycle of breaths includes four breaths that correspond with the elements: earth, air, fire, and water. Each breath draws the person breathing to notice his or her relationship to that element—the earth that supports from below; the air that circulates through; the fire that warms from within, and the water that flows up, down, and around. As a result the breathing encourages a person to experience her or his bodily self as relational, and as the

movement of relating to that which sustains its life.

The conscious use of bodily movement as a path to (self) knowledge is a theme that runs throughout my work, connecting the ideas developed here with my scholarly books on religion and dance, and with the analyses of desire in *What a Body Knows*.

This approach shares with Buddhist-based practices of mindfulness an attention to bodily presence. Siegel, for example, a mindfulness practitioner, affirms that, "sensations are a rich, untapped source of insight and wisdom" (*Parenting*, 226). At the same time, however, my approach differs in its focus on bodily movement as a way to release the rhythms of our breathing from static patterns. The reason why we need such movement, as Nietzsche describes it, is that "much ignorance and error have become body within us" (*Portable Nietzsche*, 189). The wisdom of our bodily selves, then, is not simply present; we grow more and more able to discern it as we cultivate a sensory awareness of how our movements are making us.

7. Harville Hendrix (*Getting the Love You Want*) affirms the healing that can happen in partnerships. In fact, he suggests that we are attracted to our partners because we recognize in them the potential to help us heal from our childhood wounds. We heal, he teaches, when we learn how to love our partner as he or she needs and wants to be loved.

Hendrix's theories were very important to me as I worked through relationship issues I describe in *What a Body Knows*. *Family Planting* moves on in its description of how healing happens by linking the healing potential of our partnerships to the bodily changes they entail. Partners have the potential to help us heal by stirring to life an impulse to connect with them that overrides the self-protecting, self-isolating patterns of sensation and response we created and became in relation to our parents.

8. For a history of marriage and its evolution into an ideal of two-becoming-one, see Stephanie Coontz, *Marriage, a History: From Obedience to Intimacy or How Love Conquered Marriage*. My

contribution to this ongoing evolution is to offer a perspective on intimacy that does not presuppose a union of two individuals, but rather focuses on how a shared love expands and grows as two singular selves, open to one another as the cause of their being.

9. Friedrich Nietzsche, *Portable Nietzsche,* 125.

Chapter 4: Egg Hunt

1. Friedrich Nietzsche, *Ecce Homo,* 272.

2. For information on how to raise chickens, we have relied on local farmers as well as on relevant sections of *Barnyard in Your Backyard* and the book *Keep Chickens.*

3. The notion of self-overcoming is one that Nietzsche develops in a number of his books, most notably "Thus Spoke Zarathustra" (*Portable Nietzsche*). Zarathustra's mission is to teach humans why and how they must overcome themselves. His point is that humans *are* this movement of self-overcoming, that is, they are this movement of creating values and ideals, which they then make real through their practices. It is by participating consciously in this process of overcoming themselves that humans realize the potential of their humanity. My work develops this idea of self-overcoming in terms of a rhythm of bodily becoming, in which we create and become the patterns of sensation and response that relate us to those who enable us to become who we are.

4. Theories of dream interpretation are many. I don't find a need to explain why we dream. Nor do I privilege all dreams equally. I don't often have memorable dreams. This dream, however, was an exception. It immediately appeared to me as highly significant, and the process of reflecting upon it and writing about it proved that it was. That significance, then, is not a function of the dream itself, but of how the act of attending to it stimulated my thinking to move in new patterns of understanding.

5. Friedrich Nietzsche, *Portable Nietzsche,* 251. This notion of "willing backwards" is a challenging one that dovetails with Nietzsche's ideal of eternal recurrence. The key to understanding these terms is to read them as "ideals" that we humans create as we seek values that guide us in affirming our lives. To say "yes" to life in all its manifestations releases us to participate consciously in its ongoing creation. For Nietzsche, a person who can affirm life in this way is a *dancer.*

6. After having this experience, I read Tara Brach's Buddhist-inspired book, *Radical Acceptance.* I prefer the term "affirmation" over "acceptance" because of the connection to the writings of Nietzsche, Martha Graham, and Isadora Duncan. It also suggests more of a dynamic quality. By affirming who we are, we release ourselves into the *movement* that is always already happening in us.

Chapter 5: Too Many Tomatoes

1. Friedrich Nietzsche, *Portable Nietzsche,* 317.

2. For gardening resources, we rely heavily on the Rodale books, especially the *All New Encyclopedia of Organic Gardening,* and *Rodale's Illustrated Guide to Organic Gardening.* We also use Tanya Denckla's *The Gardener's A-Z Guide to Growing Organic Food.*

3. My fascination with the seed metaphor and its play of affirmation and negation, living and dying, owes much to the notion of Spirit as developed in the philosophy of G.W.F. Hegel. Hegel identifies Spirit as a three-step movement that comprises both the content and form of reality.

One of his metaphors for Spirit is the acorn that grows through the stages of sprout and sapling, branches out into a trunk with limbs, and eventually creates new "notions" of reality, or acorns, that begin the process all over again. Each new shape of the oak both "negates" and "subsumes" the previous shape in a never-ending process of becoming what it is.

See Hegel's *Phenomenology of Spirit* for an introduction to his system, and his *Lectures on the Philosophy of Religion* for an application to the study of religion.

4. Henry David Thoreau, *Walden*, chapter 1, 63.

5. It was Harville Hendrix's work that helped me first name and practice the art of "mirroring" another human. It is at the core of his model. Daniel Siegel argues that mirroring is not enough to establish connection, we must also empathize.

Now I find there is another move to make as well: we must learn to hear the other person's thoughts and feelings, *regardless* of content, *as a desire to connect with us*. When we do, we can learn to welcome the content as the information we need to succeed in doing what we most want to do: love them.

Once we can name and acknowledge a partner's impulse to connect, the moves of mirroring and empathy come more easily. We recognize that the fact of sharing is far more important than the content. We can also recognize our own impulse to connect at work in our resistance to another's seemingly aversive actions. In these ways, then, we can find our freedom to move with our impulses to connect with one another, rather than pushing each other away in the fear of disappointment or judgment.

6. This self-comfort that I am describing is different than that proposed by David Schnarch. He advocates "self-soothing" as a response to the disappointment of not getting what we want from or with our partners. The taking-care that I am advocating here has to do with staying in touch with a sensory awareness of our desire for the other, knowing that we will find wisdom in its expressions.

Whatever we feel in a relationship is something that the relationship has created in us as a result of our wanting that relationship. What the relationship generates, the relationship must heal. From this perspective, self-soothing can function to smooth over moments that might otherwise yield transformative insights.

7. Henry David Thoreau, *Walden*, chapter 1, 4.

Chapter 6: Falling Away

1. Frederick Rogers, ed., *Dance*, 180.

2. "Beyond right and wrong" is an allusion to Nietzsche's *Beyond Good and Evil*. Nietzsche's point is that human beings need to: recognize that they are creators of value, take responsibility for the values that they are creating, and *revalue* the anti-life values that he associates with the ascetic ideal, Christianity in particular. Nietzsche does not deny the importance of having values, nor does he insist that all values are equal (as some critics contend). His point is rather that humans cannot *not* create values, and that they should do so in ways that honor and support their bodily ability to keep doing so.

My point in this chapter is that the bodily process of sensing and responding to a given encounter is one that unfolds in time, such that the meaning of any interaction can and does change. On the path to total presence, acknowledging our responsibility in creating the meaning of any encounter is critical: we commit to finding a catalyst to deeper intimacy in every challenge the relationship produces.

3. In *What a Body Knows* I discuss a desire for sex as a desire to give and receive a life-enabling touch.

Chapter 7: Pumpkins in the Compost

1. Henry David Thoreau, *Walden*, chapter 1, 8.

2. This perspective on our children as *enabling* us to become who we are differs from ones claiming that our children have something to "teach" us. It is different as well from the perspective that we need to resolve our childhood issues in order to be better parents. My point is that our children provide us with a unique opportunity to learn to create relationships that require us to exercise our impulse to connect in making patterns of sensing and responding that replace those modeled on the idea

that we are individuals first. In this way, I reconceive the parent-child relationship itself so that the challenge is how to cultivate a connection that always already exists, rather than how to attach two individuals, one with power and one not, securely to one another.

3. For a history of the human relationship to milk, see Anne Mendelson, *Milk: The Surprising Story of Milk Through the Ages.* Some in the homesteading movement, following the Nearings' example, eschew dairy products and the animal care they require.

4. Debates over what parents should want for their children continue to evolve. For the past forty years, the best science and psychology has claimed that self-esteem is the most important variable in determining a child's future success. As a result, educational programs, school curricula, and disciplinary practices all evolved for the purposes of meeting this goal.

However, recent research is calling into question whether self-esteem is the most important factor and whether the agreed upon measures for developing it in children (such as reward systems, grades, and extensive praise) even work.

See arguments by Po Bronson and Ashley Merryman in *NurtureShock,* as well as Alfie Kohn's *Unconditional Parenting: Moving from Rewards and Punishments to Love and Reason.*

I contend that what children most need in order to become who they have the potential to be is the opportunity to discover and exercise their impulse to connect with their caregivers. A best practice for parents, then, is to help children learn to create relationships that will enable the children's lives by demonstrating how in relation to them.

5. These internal debates echo the vocabulary of "choice" that dominates discussions of women's lives. The idea that women must choose between having children and having a career, however, is one that has always struck me as akin to a choice between eating and breathing. There is no choice. There is only

an illusion of choice. Yet that illusion fuels the "Mommy Wars" in which women fight against each other for what both sides want: the freedom to make a choice. The fact is, neither have it.

To have the freedom to make a choice would mean having the power to set the terms of the choice, so that women could choose to have children and exercise their career potential. Our society is currently organized in ways that make it difficult for women to create the network of relationships they need to support them in becoming the women they want to be.

For entry into these extensive debates, see Ann Crittenden, *The Price of Motherhood: Why the Most Important Job in the World is Still the Least Valued* and Stephanie Coontz, *The Way We Never Were.*

Chapter 8: Genesis

1. Merle Armitage, ed., *Martha Graham,* 102-3.

2. The premier of *Genesis* took place at the Rieman Center, Harvard University, in May 2001, with support from the Radcliffe Institute for Advanced Study, where I was a Fellow, and the Harvard Dance Program, directed by Elizabeth Bergmann.

The title alludes to the first book of the Hebrew Bible, in whose first three chapters "God" creates all that is. My idea in making the piece was to tell the story of creation from the perspective of a pregnant woman through the medium of dance.

The project is significant for two reasons. First, the dance presents dance itself as a medium that has something distinctive to offer our understanding of religious experience and expression. I discuss this claim at length in my first book, *Between Dancing and Writing.*

Second, the dancing frames movement—the movement of our bodily selves—as the means by which we participate in the ongoing act of creating our lives and our worlds. I explore this idea in my second book, *Nietzsche's Dancers.* For Nietzsche, dancing is an effective symbol for the revaluation of the Christian

incarnation.

3. The opening position of this dance is in honor of Martha Graham, whose classes begin with it. Graham's technique is based on the movements of breathing, and this sitting position allows the dancers to cultivate a sensory awareness of the movements of inhaling and exhaling as the dynamic source and center for their dancing. Graham dancers practice making these breathing movements in order to make themselves into dancers.

See *Nietzsche's Dancers*, chapter 7.

4. My understanding of dance and its power as a medium of expression owes infinitely much to three leaders of American modern dance, Ruth St. Denis, Isadora Duncan, and Martha Graham. I am also indebted to the philosopher who inspired these women to flesh out philosophies concerning the significance of dance as a form of religious experience and expression, namely Friedrich Nietzsche. I document these legacies in *Nietzsche's Dancers.*

5. See chapter 3, footnote 6. The cycle of breaths is one example of the kind of practice that is helpful in cultivating a sensory awareness of the movement that is making us.

6. This idea of a performance as expressing and making real the relationships that enable it to happen is an idea I first picked up from anthropologist John Blacking (*How Musical is Man?*). It is an idea that plays a central role in my work, including my analysis of the human desire for spirit in *What a Body Knows.*

7. Birth as a metaphor for creation has received scant attention in western theology and philosophy. The feminist philosopher, Grace Jantzen, documents this lack in her insightful book, *Becoming Divine: Towards a Feminist Philosophy.* She demonstrates how a larger share of attention has fallen on death as the act that gives meaning to life. *Genesis* aligns with attempts by feminists and others to address this imbalance.

See also Catherine Keller, *Face of the Deep: A Theology of Becoming* and Gordon D. Kaufman, *In the Beginning... Creativity.*

8. For a discussion of Martha Graham's classic, *Acts of Light,* see *Nietzsche's Dancers,* 213-6.

9. The debate over homebirth in the contemporary United States has ardent proponents on either side. While the balance is tipped far in the favor of hospital births, there is increasing evidence that home births are as safe if not more so than hospital births for women and infants, at least in the case of low risk pregnancies. The discussion was recently brought to the fore by Rikki Lake's documentary, *The Business of Being Born,* and its accompanying book, *Your Best Birth.*

For arguments from the former director of Women and Children's Health for the World Health Organization, see *Born in the USA* by Marsden Wagner, MD, MS. For the perspectives of a founding member of the Midwives Alliance of North America who has assisted over 2,200 natural births, see *Ina May's Guide to Childbirth.* We still need a philosophical discussion of the values, assumptions, and ideals at work in these debates.

For an excellent critique of our willingness to accept medical advice without question and the impact of such acceptance on our health and well-being, see Ellen Langer's *Counterclockwise.*

10. Martha Graham was fond of quoting the poet, St. John Perse, as saying that we have so little time to be "born to the instant."

Bibliography

References and Resources

Abram, David. 1996. *The Spell of the Sensuous: Perception and Language in a More-Than-Human World.* New York: Vintage Books.

Armitage, Merle, ed. 1978. *Martha Graham: The Early Years.* New York: de Capo Press.

Asad, Talal. 1993. *Genealogies of Religion: Discipline and Reasons of Power in Christianity and Islam.* Baltimore, MD: Johns Hopkins Press.

Begley, Sharon. 2007. *Train Your Mind. Change Your Brain: How a New Science Reveals Our Extraordinary Potential To Transform Ourselves.* New York: Ballantine Books.

Berry, Wendell. 2002. *The Art of the Commonplace: Agrarian Essays.* Ed. Norman Wirzba. Emeryville, CA: Shoemaker & Hoard.

Blacking, John. 1973. *How Musical Is Man?* Seattle, WA: University of Washington Press.

Blakeslee, Sandra and Matthew Blakeslee. 2007. *The Body Has A Mind of Its Own: How Body Maps in Your Brain Help You Do (Almost) Everything Better.* New York: Random House.

Bourdieu, Pierre. 1977. *Outline of a Theory of Practice.* Tr. Richard Nice. New York: Cambridge University Press.

Brach, Tara. 2003. *Radical Acceptance: Embracing Your Life with the Heart of a Buddha.* New York: Bantam Books.

Bradley, Fern Marshall and Barbara Ellis, eds. 1992. *Rodale's All New Encyclopedia of Organic Gardening.* Emmaus, PA: Rodale Press.

Bronson, Po and Ashley Merryman. 2009. *NurtureSchock.* New York: Twelve/Hachette Book Group.

Buell, Lawrence. 1995. *The Environmental Imagination: Thoreau,*

Nature Writing, and the Formation of American Culture. Cambridge, MA: Harvard University Press.

Camp, Joe. 2008. *Soul of a Horse.* Easton, PA: Harmony.

Cavell, Stanley. 1981. *The Senses of Walden.* Chicago, IL: University of Chicago Press.

Chaskey, Scott. 2005. *This Common Ground: Seasons on an Organic Farm.* New York: Viking Adult.

Coontz, Stephanie. 2005. *Marriage, a History: from Obedience to Intimacy or How Love Conquered Marriage.* New York: Viking.

Coontz, Stephanie. 1998. *The Way We Never Were: Coming to Terms with America's Changing Families.* New York: Basic Books.

Cozolino, Louis. 2007. *The Neuroscience of Human Relationships: Attachment and the Developing Social Brain.* New York: W.W. Norton & Company.

Crittenden, Ann. 2002. *The Price of Motherhood: Why the Most Important Job in the World is Still the Least Valued.* New York: Holt Paperbacks.

Damasio, Antonio. 1999. *The Feeling of What Happens.* San Diego, CA: Harcourt, Inc.

Damerow, Gail, ed. 2002. *Barnyard in Your Backyard: A Beginner's Guide to Raising Chickens, Ducks, Geese, Rabbits, Goats, Sheep, and Cattle.* North Adams, MA: Storey Publishing.

Denckla, Tanya. 2003. *The Gardener's A-Z Guide to Growing Organic Food.* North Adams, MA: Storey Publishing.

Doidge, Norman. 2007. *The Brain that Changes Itself: Stories of Personal Triumph from the Frontiers of Brain Science.* New York: Penguin Press.

Duncan, Isadora. 1981. *Isadora Speaks.* Ed. Franklin Rosemont. San Francisco, CA: City Lights.

Duncan, Isadora. 1928a. *Art of the Dance.* New York: Theatre Arts Books.

Duncan, Isadora. 1928b. *My Life.* New York: Liveright.

Eisler, Riane. 1987. *The Chalice and the Blade: Our History, Our Future.* San Francisco, CA: HarperCollins.

Foucault, Michel. 1980. *Power/Knowledge: Selected Interviews and Other Writings 1972-1977*. Ed. & Tr. Colin Gordon. New York: Random House, Pantheon Books.

Foucault, Michel. 1977. *Discipline and Punish: The Birth of the Prison*. Tr. Alan Sheridan. New York: Vintage Books.

Gaskin, Ina May. 2003. *Ina May's Gide to Childbirth*. New York: Bantam Books.

Goleman, Daniel. 2006. *Social Intelligence: The Revolutionary New Science of Human Relationships*. New York: Bantam Books.

Gould, Rebecca Kneale. 2004. *At Home in Nature: Modern Homesteading and Spiritual Practice in America*. Berkley, CA: University of California Press.

Graham, Martha. 1991. *Blood Memory*. New York: Doubleday.

Grohman, Joann S. 2001. *Keeping a Family Cow*. Dixfield, ME: Coburn Press.

Hanna, Thomas. 1988. *Somatics*. New York: DeCapo Life Long.

Hartley, Linda. 1989. *Wisdom of the Body Moving: An Introduction to Body-Mind Centering*. Berkeley, CA: North Atlantic Books.

Hegel, G.W.F. 1988. *Lectures on the Philosophy of Religion*. Ed. & Tr. Peter Hodgson. Berkeley, CA: University of California Press.

Hegel, G.W.F. 1952. *Phenomenology of Spirit*. Tr. A.V. Miller. New York: Oxford University Press.

Heinrich, Bernd. 2001. *Why We Run: A Natural History*. New York: HarperCollins Publishers.

Hendrix, Harville. 1990. *Getting the Love You Want: A Guide for Couples*. New York: HarperPerennial.

Hrdy, Sarah Blafer. 2009. *Mothers and Others*. Cambridge, MA: Harvard University Press.

Hrdy, Sarah Blafer. 2000. *Mother Nature: Maternal Instincts and How They Shape the Human Species*. New York: Ballantine Books.

Irigaray, Luce. 1993. *Sexes and Genealogies*. Tr. Gillian Gill. New York: Columbia University Press.

Iyengar, BKS. 1995. *Light on Yoga*. New York: Schocken Books.

Jantzen, Grace. 1999. *Becoming Divine: Towards a Feminist Philosophy*. Bloomington, IN: Indiana University Press.

Johnson, Don Hanlon, ed. 1997. *Groundworks: Narratives of Embodiment*. Berkeley, CA: North Atlantic Books.

Johnson, Kenneth and Betty-Anne Daviss. 2005. *British Medical Journal*. "Outcomes of planned home births with certified professional midwives: large prospective study in North America," 330:1416 (18 June).

Kaufman, Gordon D. 2004. *In the Beginning... Creativity*. Minneapolis, MN: Fortress Press.

Keeney, Bradford. 2007. *Shaking Medicine: The Healing Power of Ecstatic Movement*. Rochester, VT: Destiny Books.

Keller, Catherine. 2003. *Face of the Deep: A Theology of Becoming*. New York: Routledge.

Kilarski, Barbara. 2003. *Keep Chickens! Tending Small Flocks in Cities, Suburbs, and Other Small Spaces*. North Adams, MA: Storey Publishing.

Kohn, Alfie. 2004. *Unconditional Parenting: Moving from Rewards and Punishments to Love and Reason*. New York: Atria Books.

Kohn, Alfie. 1999. *Punished by Rewards: The Trouble with Gold Stars, Incentive Plans, A's, Praise, and Other Bribes*. Boston, MA: Houghton Mifflin.

Kierkegaard, Søren. 1983. *Fear and Trembling and Repetition*. Ed. & Tr. Howard V. Hong & Edna H. Hong. Princeton, NJ: Princeton University Press.

Lake Ricki. 2009. *Your Best Birth: Know All Your Options, Discover the Natural Choices, and Take Back the Birth Experience*. Wellness Central.

Lakoff, George & Mark Johnson. 1999. *Philosophy in the Flesh: The Embodied Mind and Its Challenge to Western Thought*. New York: Basic Books.

LaMothe, Kimerer L. 2009. *What a Body Knows: Finding Wisdom in Desire*. UK: O Books.

LaMothe, Kimerer L. 2006. *Nietzsche's Dancers: Isadora Duncan,*

Martha Graham, and the Revaluation of Christian Values. New York: Palgrave MacMillan.

LaMothe, Kimerer L. 2004. *Between Dancing and Writing: The Practice of Religious Studies.* New York: Fordham University Press.

Langer, Ellen. 2009. *Counterclockwise: Mindful Health and the Power of Possibility.* New York: Ballantine Books.

Lerner, Gerda. 1986. *The Creation of Patriarchy.* New York: Oxford University Press.

Levine, Peter. 1996. *Waking the Tiger: Healing Trauma: The Innate Capacity to Transform Overwhelming Experiences.* Berkeley, CA: North Atlantic Books.

Llinas, Rodolfo R. 2001. *I of the Vortex: From Neurons to Self.* Cambridge, MA: MIT Press.

Louv, Richard. 2008. *Last Child in the Woods.* Chapel Hill, NC: Algonquin Books.

McKibben, Bill, ed. 2008. *American Earth: Environmental Writing Since Thoreau.* New York: Library of America.

Mendelson, Anne. 2008. *Milk: The Surprising Story of Milk Through the Ages.* New York: Alfred Knopf.

Merleau-Ponty, Maurice. 1964. *The Primacy of Perception.* Ed. James M. Edie. Chicago, IL: Northwestern University.

Miller, Alice. 2008. *The Drama of the Gifted Child: The Search for the True Self.* New York: Basic Books.

Miller, Alice. 2006. *The Body Never Lies: The Lingering Effects of Cruel Parenting.* New York: Norton.

Miller, Alice. 1990. *For Your Own Good: Hidden Cruelty in Child-Rearing and the Roots of Violence.* New York: Farrar, Strauss & Giroux.

Nearing, Scott and Helen Nearing. 1990. *The Good Life.* New York: Schocken Books.

Nietzsche, Friedrich. 1989. *On the Genealogy of Morals and Ecce Homo.* Ed. & Tr. Walter Kaufmann. New York: Vintage Press.

Nietzsche, Friedrich. 1984. *Human, All Too Human: A Book for Free*

Spirits. Tr. Marion Faber with Stephen Lehmann. Lincoln and London: University of Nebraska Press.

Nietzsche, Friedrich. 1967. *The Birth of Tragedy and The Case of Wagner*. Ed. & Tr. Walter Kaufmann. New York: Vintage Press.

Nietzsche, Friedrich. 1966. *Beyond Good and Evil*. Tr. Walter Kaufmann. New York: Random House.

Nietzsche, Friedrich. 1954. *The Portable Nietzsche*. Ed. & Tr. Walter Kaufmann. New York: Penguin.

Peto, James, ed. 2007. *The Heart*. New Haven: Yale University Press.

Pollan, Michael. 2006. *Omnivore's Dilemma*. New York: Penguin Press.

Ratey, John J., with Eric Hagerman. 2008. *Spark: the Revolutionary New Science of Exercise and the Brain*. New York: Little, Brown & Company.

Roberts, Monty. 2000. *Shy Boy: The Horse that Came in From the Wild*. New York: Harper Paperbacks.

Rodale, Maria. 2005. *Rodale's Illustrated Guide to Organic Gardening*. New York: DK Adult.

Rogers, Frederick R., ed. 1941. *Dance: A Basic Educational Technique*. New York: MacMillan.

Roszak, Theodore. 1992. *The Voice of the Earth: An Exploration in Ecopsychology*. Grand Rapids, MI: Phanes Press, Inc.

St. Denis, Ruth. 1978. "Credo," in *Dance News*. January.

St. Denis, Ruth. 1950-9. "Seeds of a New Order," Clippings file, Dance Collection, New York Public Library.

St. Denis, Ruth. 1939. *Ruth St. Denis, An Unfinished Life*. New York: Harper & Brothers Publishers.

Salatin, Joel. 1998. *You Can Farm*. Swoope, VA: Polyface Publishing.

Schnarch, David. 1997. *Passionate Marriage: Keeping Love & Intimacy Alive in Committed Relationships*. New York: Henry Holt, Owl Books.

Sheets-Johnstone, Maxine, ed. 1992. *Giving the Body Its Due*.

Albany, NY: State University of New York Press.

Siegel, Daniel J. & Mary Hartzell. 2004. *Parenting from the Inside Out: How a Deeper Self-Understanding Can Help You Raise Children Who Thrive.* New York: Tarcher/Penguin.

Siegel, Daniel J. 1999. *The Developing Mind: How Relationships and the Brain Interact to Shape Who We Are.* New York: Guilford Press.

Smith, Linda B. 2006. "Movement Matters: The Contributions of Esther Thelan," *Biological Theory* 1(1), 87-89. Konrad Lorenz Institute for Evolution and Cognition Research.

Taylor, Charles. 1989. *Sources of the Self: The Making of the Modern Identity.* Cambridge, MA: Harvard University Press.

Thoreau, Henry David. 1953. *Walden & On the Duty of Civil Disobedience.* New York: Rinehart & Co.

Thoreau, Henry David. 1982. *The Great Short Works of Henry David Thoreau.* New York: Harper & Row.

Topp, Ellie and Margaret Howard. 2001. *The Complete Book of Year Round Small-Batch Preserving.* Ontario, Canada: Firefly Books.

Van der Leeuw, Gerardus. 1963. *Sacred and Profane Beauty: The Holy in Art.* Tr. David Green. New York: Henry Holt.

Wagner, Marsden. 2008. *How a Broken Maternity System Must Be Fixed to Put Women and Children First.* Berkeley, CA: University of California Press.

Wilson, E.O. 2004. *On Human Nature.* Cambridge, MA: Harvard University Press.

Wigginton, Eliot, ed. 1972-2004. *FOXFIRE Series, Volumes 1 through 12.* Garden City, NY: Anchor Press.

Index